VIRTUAL REALITY, TRAINING'S FUTURE?

PERSPECTIVES ON VIRTUAL REALITY AND RELATED EMERGING TECHNOLOGIES

DEFENSE RESEARCH SERIES

Volume 1 Computer-Based Instruction in Military Environments
Edited by Robert J. Seidel and Peter D. Weddle

Volume 2 Applications of Human Performance Models to System Design
Edited by Grant R. McMillan, David Beevis, Eduardo Salas, Michael H. Strub, Robert Sutton, and Leo van Breda

Volume 3 Color in Electronic Displays
Edited by Heino Widdel and David L. Post

Volume 4 Advanced Technologies Applied to Training Design
Edited by Robert J. Seidel and Paul R. Chatelier

Volume 5 Learning without Boundaries: Technology to Support Distance/Distributed Learning
Edited by Robert J. Seidel and Paul R. Chatelier

Volume 6 Virtual Reality, Training's Future?: Perspectives on Virtual Reality and Related Emerging Technologies
Edited by Robert J. Seidel and Paul R. Chatelier

VIRTUAL REALITY, TRAINING'S FUTURE?

PERSPECTIVES ON VIRTUAL REALITY AND RELATED EMERGING TECHNOLOGIES

Edited by

Robert J. Seidel

United States Army Research Institute for the Behavioral and Social Sciences
Alexandria, Virginia

and

Paul R. Chatelier

Executive Office of the President
Office of Science and Technology Policy
Washington, D.C.

PLENUM PRESS • NEW YORK AND LONDON
Published in cooperation with NATO Defense Research Group

Library of Congress Cataloging in Publication Data

Virtual reality, training's future?: perspectives on virtual reality and related emerging technologies / edited by Robert J. Seidel and Paul R. Chatelier.
p. cm.—(Defense research series; v. 6)
"Published in cooperation with NATO Defense Research Group."
"Proceedings of a NATO Defense Research Group Panel 8, Research Study Group (RSG) 16 Workshop on Advanced Technologies Applied to Training Design, held at the HMS Nelson, March 7–9, 1995, in Portsmouth, England"—T.p. verso.
Includes bibliographical references and index.
ISBN 0-306-45486-6
1. Human-computer interaction—Congresses. 2. Computer-assisted instruction—Congresses. 3. Virtual reality—Congresses. I. Seidel, Robert J., 1931– . II. Chatelier, Paul R. III. NATO Defense Research Group. IV. Series.
QA76.9.H85V584 1997
371.33'46—dc21 96-53454
CIP

Proceedings of a NATO Defense Research Group Panel 8, Research Study Group (RSG) 16 Workshop on Advanced Technologies Applied to Training Design, held aboard the HMS Nelson, March 7 – 9, 1995, Portsmouth, England

ISBN 0-306-45486-6

A Division of Plenum Publishing Corporation
233 Spring Street, New York, N. Y. 10013

http://www.plenum.com

10 9 8 7 6 5 4 3 2 1

Printed in the United States of America

PREFACE

In 1988, the NATO panel governing human sciences (Panel 8 on Defence Applications of Human and Bio-Medical Sciences) established a Research Study Group to synthesize information relevant to Advanced Technologies Applied to Training Design. During its first phase, the RSG established an active exchange of information on advanced technologies applied to training design and stimulated much military application of these technologies. With the increased emphasis on training throughout the alliance, Panel 8, during its April 1991 meeting decided to continue with Phase II of this RSG focusing in the area of advanced training technologies that were emerging within the alliance. In order to accomplish its mission, the RSG held a series of workshops. Leaders in technology and training were brought together and exchanged information on the latest developments in technologies applicable to training and education. This volume represents the last in a series based on the NATO workshops. In Part One, it details findings from the last workshop, Virtual Reality for Training; and in Part Two, we provide a summary perspective on Virtual Reality and the other emerging technologies previously studied. These include computer-based training, expert systems, authoring systems, cost-effectiveness, and distance learning.

It is a natural extension to proceed from learning without boundaries to virtual environments. From the extended classroom to the individual or team immersion in a distributed, virtual, and collaborative environment is an easy conceptual step. On the technical side, however, we need to know the feasibility and the amount of added value in order to make cost-effective decisions for training or educational systems by incorporating virtual environments into our learning repertoire. At a workshop held in the United Kingdom in March 1995, it was determined we must ensure that those functions possible in the virtual environment can be operationalized. The chapters in Part One of this book have been based upon the presentations and discussions from that workshop.

Part Two of this volume is based on data provided and discussed at four topical workshops, discussions and presentations made at meetings of a NATO research study group on Advanced Technologies Applied to Training Design, and papers provided at a summary workshop. A collection of these papers is attached as Appendix A to Part Two. The current and projected advances in technologies that are and will be made available as tools to permit more efficient and effective training will skyrocket in the next decade.

Such changes will make the results of this volume significant historical data points awaiting revision and documentation.

Paul R. Chatelier
Executive Office of the President
Office of Science and Technology Policy
Washington, D.C.

Robert J. Seidel
U.S. Army Research Institute for the Behavioral and Social Sciences
Washington, D.C.

ACKNOWLEDGMENTS

We would like to thank the authors of the papers for providing an excellent coverage of this rapidly developing technology, the session chairpersons for providing excellent structure and management for each group of papers, and each session's discussants for their summary and personal views of their sessions papers.

Our special thanks go to Commander Anthony (Tony) Mizen, Royal Navy, the United Kingdom's Ministry of Defence's research study group member and the person responsible for our being able to have the VR workshop in Portsmouth. We are also grateful to Dr. Michael Strub, head of the U.S. Army Research Institute's field office in London for his technical and administrative assistance throughout the planning and conduct of the workshop.

CONTENTS

PART 2: LESSONS LEARNED OR LESSONS NOT YET LEARNED (BUT OFTEN REVISITED) ABOUT THE DESIGN, APPLICATION, AND MANAGEMENT OF LEARNING TECHNOLOGIES

Appendix A: Individual Papers from Lessons Learned Workshop

AN OVERVIEW OF VIRTUAL REALITY/VIRTUAL ENVIRONMENTS FOR EDUCATION AND TRAINING

Robert J. Seidel and Paul R. Chatelier

It is a natural extension to proceed from learning without boundaries to virtual environments. From the extended classroom to the individual or team immersion in a distributed, virtual and collaborative environment is an easy conceptual step. On the technical side, however, we need to know the feasibility and the amount of added value in order to make cost-effective decisions for training or educational systems by incorporating virtual environments into our learning repertoire. These topics and these issues were addressed at a workshop in the United Kingdom in March 1995. The chapters in Part One of this book have been based upon presentations at that workshop. It was determined that we must ensure those functions possible in the virtual environment can be operationalized. Therefore, the definition of virtual reality or virtual environment must be adequate to include the requisite learning functionalities. In that regard, it is useful to start out with an agreed upon definition of virtual reality; and this was accomplished by two of the NATO groups at one of our meetings.

Virtual Reality is "a multi-dimensional human experience which is totally or partially computer generated and can be accepted by those experiencing the environment as consistent" (NATO DRG Panel 8 - Exploratory Group O and Research Study Group 16).

An alternative definition which has been favored by some is that virtual reality may be defined as "human immersion in a synthetic environment". The latter definition we feel is rather restrictive while at the same time carries with it the implication that total presence within the simulation itself is what determines the virtual environment or virtual reality.

The latter definition would be more acceptable to those who consider helmet mounted displays (HMD) as the ultimate type of virtual reality immersion. On the other hand, if one considers the degree of immersion within the synthetic environment as relative to the tasks to be performed and the skill to be developed by the individual or the group then one is given a wider variety of environments which could be called virtual.

Let's examine this premise in detail. To begin with, we eliminate the need for physical proximity of colleagues, teammates, classmates, or instructors by creating a distance learning/training environment. This is clearly possible by the technology of networking,

Virtual Reality, Training's Future? edited by Seidel and Chatelier
Plenum Press, New York, 1997

simulations, and interactive software. Because we are able to communicate with others and perform required tasks without the physical pressure of either fellow performers or actual equipment, we have indeed created a work space environment which is virtual. Learning is thereby enabled without physical boundaries. The sense of identity within this environment by the performer is her or his reality; that is, a virtual reality. There's no question that this sense can be vastly heightened by immersion through the use of helmet mounted displays (HMD). With the HMD, we add a unique self-presence within an animated world. However, we ask the how much does this HMD experience add to the performance of the learner. Can there be degrees of immersion whereby we accomplish our purposes by adding sensory, cognitive and emotional dimensions without the HMD at a desktop workstation? What is the value added by HMD, and what purposes or what tasks does it serve best for learning purposes?

The initial chapter based on a keynote presentation by Dr. Bellman at the workshop describes examples of the value of incorporating the broader definition of virtual environment or virtual reality. Dr. Bellman describes the development of multi-user domains (MUDS), text-based virtual reality environments which are available on the internet. It is a case where the perceived presence within a virtual environment can readily be obtained for purposes of interaction within a domain, and yet not require any kind of HMD.

In this environment the MUDS "allow people the freedom of and richness of word picture, something that we can't imitate with our graphical environments...[the users] create rooms with rules about who and what enters those rooms and how and when they leave those rooms and what happens to them in these rooms...even with the simplest of construction languages, people experience a deep sense of being present within these virtual environments..." Dr. Bellman goes on to include some very interesting questions relating to VR and to MUDS as well, such things as: What are the rules for privacy guidelines in an virtual environment? How much should a VR environment be used for training or learning? Can there be too much time spent in VR? Can intelligent agents be added to the VR environment? There are other questions related to the ways to structure learning materials and create rich scenarios, all of which are a sign that the technology while having great potential is still not mature. That is to say we have many more questions than answers about the value of VR as training's future.

Having said that, it is important to note that there are some experiments that have been conducted. There are dimensions beginning to be examined as part of the VR environment. However, for most if not all of these dimensions we have yet to be able to cite their relative importance for alternative tasks to be performed, skills to be learned, and jobs to be accomplished as a result of exposure to virtual environment. Of course, the most important question is to identify the transfer value in cost-effective terms of training within the VR environment. Whether consistent adherence to reality is necessary or not is yet to be determined. Some levels of mismatch have deleterious effects such as simulator-sickness when the induced motion from a visual presentation is inconsistent with real world feedback as encountered in everyday life. The issues which need to be our focus as we conduct our research and attempt to apply VR to training are (RSG.16 Study Group Final Report, 1996; see Part 2, this volume):

1. *Location of the immersed operator's position.* In order to give the subject the illusion of being immersed in the world created through computers, we must provide the computer a series of real time data about instantaneous position of the body. This will provide the subject a virtual world, related to his own spatial and temporal references.

2. *Interfaces*. For each interface, various answers are appropriate in the military area depending on the application. Importance should be given to the cost/quality and performance trade off to choose the best solution for each specific application. Physiological constraints are essentially related to the technical possibilities of providing a sufficient visual field and a stereoscopic illusion.
3. *Visual Interfaces*. Digital representation progress permits very high quality numerical images. The remaining decision concerns the way to present these images to the operator in order that he get the sense of immersion without physical, physiological and psychological constraint. Current experiments are showing that sense of immersion is directly related to the size of the visual field. Effort should therefore concentrate on getting displays with the biggest possible field. Stereoscopic vision is important for tasks taking place in smaller than ten meters.
4. *Reality/Fidelity*. We must focus on providing information in terms of virtual space of activity rather than in terms of picture realism with the reality. From this perspective, techniques of image enrichment have a lot to offer. "Enhanced reality" is one important point to look at for applications regarding training teleoperation or remote battle. Cost/Effectiveness tradeoffs must be considered when deciding to use enhanced 3 D reality in VR vs. a 2D display, if training is for a task that provides the necessary correct operational feedback to the trainee. How to scope this out for a real situation is still under investigation.
5. *Auditory interfaces*, Actually there are two possibilities: stereo sound and 3D sound. In terms of practical application, 3D sound is interesting only when we want to improve the preformance by giving more information.
6. *Haptic interface*. Providing the operator with information on physical aspects of environment other than visual and auditory is an absolute necessity. The problem is then related to how: by stimulating the relevant organic sensor without simulating real surroundings or by simulating real surroundings or by simulating real surroundings without any specific interface (e.g., decisions should be made on a cost-effective basis but within the context of the operators task requirements).
7. *Psychological issues*. Virtual reality impact on the operatoris has to be considered seriously. As with each new technology, virtual reality will probably change our way of life. Some effects will be positive, teleworking will probably reduce the traffic as well as the stress. But there is also some risk of negative effects. Until further research is completed, expert opinion should be sought for each application in order to get a better grasp on the impact of VR immersion, cognitively and emotionally.
8. *The task*. Is it for training or for rehearsal? The demands of levels of detail need adjustment depending on the goals of the exercise. There is also the related problem of equipment and tethering of movement and its effect on performance. Related issues concern definition of the role of video and animation of what is observed, learned, retained and can be transferred to the real world.
9. *Appropriateness of the display and interactive capabilities for VR*. This implies that we have criteria for determining how to build and use these systems. This is leading edge research. Current investigations include development of new interaction techniques which give the user direct control in a natural way with an environment that includes some level of real reaction capability. In other words, when things fall, they fall at an expected speed and they go in the right direc-

tion. In addition, appropriate feedback to the participant mimics what they expect in the real world. An example of this includes the introduction of force feedback to data glove manipulation so that a virtual object does not get crushed on grasp.

10. *Evaluation methods to determine the effectiveness of VR.* The case in Virtual Environment is yet to be determined. To date most evaluation is introspective and anecdotal. Some non-immersive systems (IMAT) exist that are currently being evaluated as to their effectiveness but the results are not in yet (Ellis and Parchman, 1994).
11. *How to develop appropriate situations and scenarios to achieve adequate systems is the focus of authoring tool development.* It is critical that after one knows what level of granularity needs to be controlled for the real world transfer and has an idea how to assess performance in the VR environment, one needs to be able to make sure that critical task situations are encountered during exposure. The visual, auditory, haptic and other displays need to be manipulatable in prescribed, coordinated ways and capability to edit the 3-D images into coherent visual real world reactions in a dynamic way need to be developed.
12. *Authoring capabilities need to be developed to allow correct manageable control of what is being displayed to mimic the real world.* They should include ways that allow one to capture critical aspects of the task, to react to the system responses in real ways, and include means to follow alternative paths in the interactive environment task space.
13. *Virtual Reality requires interdisciplinary teams to adequately build and control the task environments.* While lip-service to interdisciplinary activities has existed from many years, this particular endeavor will need the integrated teams of researchers to be able to cover the complex situations which need to be controlled and manipulated to be effective. System design will need the integration of knowledgeable persons who know about software building and have expertise in human factors and in task modeling. In addition, to its effectiveness for the task at hand, this requires extensive evaluation within the psychological or human factors paradigm of study to know whether the system conveys what is intended.
14. *Cost of VR is a critical concern.* Anyone anticipating integration of VR for embedded training or for rehearsal needs to be aware of the up-front costs to get the problem unless fast machines with good graphics capabilities are available. This requires much more than an off-the-shelf PC or Mac platform provides. The granularity is significantly different for the cost.
15. *Speech understanding systems currently are trained for a specified domain and are not easy to modify.* In addition, they are noise cancelling microphones and have problems in variable noise environments. The microphones in speech understanding interface often are switch controlled because of ambient voice communications that are not intended for the device. This remains a problem.
16. *The role of non-speech auditory information is being studied.* It is unclear whether or not it can be used as additional channel for discrete information presentation.

The other chapters which follow can be characterized as relevant to one or more of the above issues. The domains of application cover a spectrum from ship piloting to parachute jumps, yet all have a common theme of simulating device manipulations. The chapter dealing with the use of virtual reality as a simulator for training ship handling skills

(Magee) provides the most advanced and practical, transfer of training example of the potential for VR. Dr. Magee collected data showing the feasibility and value of training ship pilots in a cost-effective VR environment. Here is the primary focus of immersion. Dr. Regian and his colleagues also studied transfer of training potential for VR spatial-navigational tasks and procedural-console based tasks. Dr. Regian showed that transfer performance was statistically equivalent after VR or CAI, even though the VR-based training systems were more expensive to develop, required more expensive delivery platforms, and maintained higher sensorimotor target-task fidelity than the CAI systems. He later presents a model for Instructional Engineering to aid decision making for instructional development and choice of media (VR and others).

In Chapter 4, Goldberg and Knerr describe their research on the use of virtual environments to train mechanized units using virtual environments. The research presented here represents some initial attempts to explore the behavioral requirements for simulating dismounted soldiers performance in virtual environments. Their research to date has resulted in two major conclusions. First, Affordable VE systems do not yet provide a natural multidimensional interface; second, VE can be a problem for training in VE, but does not seem to be an insurmountable one.

In Chapter 5, Canepa focuses on some of the possible applications of smell and touch to virtual reality training tools. He succinctly describes the characteristics and the problems of realizing the use artificial small and touch. In conclusion, he intoduces some studies related to the issues. While much remains to be done before Canepa's research will prove practicable for application, the ultimate key for the instructional designer will still be to relate the value of these dimensions in VR to the tasks required to be trained.

While Jones, in Chapter 6, describes how this concern can be readily translated into useful instruction in his discussion of telemedicine and its potential for future medical training.

In Chapter 7, Hue, et. al. describe a project that utilizes virtual reality training with a special force parachute simulator. They discuss the various tasks that are required and how this VR-type simulator helps prepare military for their parachute mission by incorporating environmental conditions such as day/night and wind.

In Chapter 8, Regan discusses some of the negative or unwanted side-effects of VR technology, such as nausea on the user. She nicely documents the frequency of occurrence and severity of severe nausea. Five percent of the subjects had to withdraw from the study due to the severity of their symptoms. Two possible causes of the side-effects documented are discussed. The first of these possible causes is that immersion in VR causes a conflict of the senses which results in the malaise. The second is that technological factors, such as the resolution of the displays, are responsible for some of the symptoms. Clearly, since these symptoms have been noted by Magee and Goldberg, et. al. as well, they will have to be taken into account when considering cost-effectiveness as a factor in each training application.

In Chapter 9 Morineau, et. al. using an input - process - output model discuss how learning earning deals with new inputs coming from environment. So, they want to assess the influence of virtual context on human input/output process via memory. They describe their research in which they examined the retention of words presented in a virtual environment and when environment changes from virtuality to reality and vice versa. No context-dependent effect is found, except a performance decrement of learning in virtual environment, but not on recall.

Lotens, et. al. in Chapter 11 discuss how VE technology can add functionality to training, compared to traditional technologies, including multimedia. Their chapter adds a much needed breadth to our discussion by suggesting that a training system using VE technology should consist of not only a presentation system, but also an instruction and evaluation system. As we noted the appropriate measure of success will be the transfer of training and not the realism of the presentation.

While not an experiment, the value of the applications of virtual reality/environments in training for space travel has been well illustrated in Loftin's report (Chapter 10) of training at the Johnson Space Center in Houston, Texas. In his report, Loftin describes the use of VR/VE for training astronauts procedures for replacement of parts of the Hubble telescope.

In Chapter 12, Gigley discusses the use of virtual environments (VE) for Navy operation and training. She points out that emphasis in the United States has been on developing several different virtual reality situation displays where different levels of immersion can be provided. These include CAVE environments, head-mounted displays integrated with other immersive interaction capability displays such as data gloves or the PHANToM device to study what is effective VR. She concludes that initial investigations have shown that VR is not a solution for all rehearsal and training problems. Sometimes the technology does not provide a suitable environment for the desired outcome. She concludes with some preliminary information on cost and why it should be raised as an important part of the approach. Her arguments are quite consistent with the points we raised regarding the simulator-sickness symptoms and whether it may be worth pursuing VR/VE training for some domains and not for others (see discussion of Magee, Goldberg, and Regan).

We conclude Part 1 with Chapter 13 by Penn, et. al. which develops some powerful insights into the architectural requirements for the future of VR/VE as the 21st century's most exciting education and training paradigm. They suggest that one of the most useful aspects of the program will be in training designers to become intuitive about the way the different domains interact. Penn and his associates describe how the Intelligent Architecture project aims to bring forward the use of computing to the earliest stages of design when the most critical strategic decisions are taken that affect the resolution of interdomain problems. The project provides simultaneous visualizations of the functional outcome of a proposed design from a range of points of view at once. Predictions can be made, of energy use, contraction cost and likely communications patterns between workers, and then presented to the designer in graphical or simple numeric form. This enables one to optimize the design from a number of points of view at once at the same time as getting a full, real time, interactive visualization of what the building will look like.

Each of the chapters of the various countries represents that nation's ideas regarding the relative importance of Virtual Reality for training. Therefore while the reader may see some overlap in interpretation, it is important to consider each chapter in its own right as an indication of a nation's perspective and priorities toward training.

PART 1

1

PLAYING IN THE MUD

Turning Virtual Reality into Real Education and Training

Kirstie L. Bellman

Defense Advanced Research Projects Agency
Washington, D.C.

Because I may sound critical of Virtual Reality (VR) research, let me start by saying how enthusiastic I am about this new computer-based technology. Computer-based technology in general has the potential to greatly impact the ways in which we educate and train all people. For military organizations, who expend great amounts of money, resources, and time on training and readiness, these capabilities can provide the key to meeting the requirements for increasingly sophisticated and adaptive military personnel systems during a time of decreasing budgets. For one, computer-based technologies are beginning to provide digital library and processing resources that are unimaginable right now to many isolated, understaffed, or severely restricted operational environments.

Furthermore, computer-based technologies have the great potential to customize and tailor training material to every individual need. This not only includes the formidable advantages of computer-based tutors that allow an individual a great deal of control over the pace and style of learning, but also the chance to access materials when and where they require the training (now called "just in time" training). Hence, it is now possible to plan strategies for continuous learning at home and on the job, with whatever depth an individual desires.

Lastly, and here is where VR comes strongly to the fore, computer-based technologies offer us the means of extending and enhancing every costly hour spent with live ammunition, weapons, vehicles, and operational environments in field exercises. Rather than reducing the value of the necessary field experiences, VR and other computer technologies can insure that the value of these hours are enhanced by both providing the much needed training prior to the field hours, and then again by providing new ways of examining and replaying the field experiences in the VR environments. With the new techniques we have for building, instrumenting, and collecting field data, the VR environments potentially can allow valuable personnel to replay their own or others' experiences and to experiment with different choices and outcomes. Along with this, troops can practice in a Virtual Reality environment events or scenarios that are rare or much too dangerous to do in normal training.

These then are the intriguing potentials of the technology, certainly justifying the attention and interest in VR research. The problem is that the field is in its first stage. There has been much too much hyperbole about it. Now we have to get beyond the initial proof of concept; we have to get beyond what I call "the demonstration mentality" that has occurred in this field. There are two things that are critical to the eventual success of this field and its ability to live up to its promise.

First of all, any mature technology—one that we are going to be dependent upon for adequate and realistic training—must be capable of being evaluated. Secondly, we have to carefully broaden our concept of Virtual Reality to include "functional realism"; or in other words, realistic in terms of what? In regards to what? Let me take each one of these points in turn:

EVALUATING VR ENVIRONMENTS

What data do we need to collect to see that VR lives up to its ideals?

In Figure 1, I have shown some of the expectations for VR on the left side and the pitfalls or potential traps on the other.

The first ideal is VR is the promise of situational realism. That is, somehow, and this goes back to my remarks in the beginning, VR will save time and money by allowing us to do virtual training instead of things that usually require field exercises or expert monitoring, or even things not possible in the field at all. The problem is that this situational realism is based on models—models of what we think is critical about the training for that environment. Just like any kind of modeling effort, we can have misleading distinctions; we can have ideas about what is effective and what is important in a situation that turn out not to be either necessary or sufficient. For example the VR field is dominated by marvelous, wonderful, stimulating, and intensive visualization. Is that the most important thing to a fighter pilot? If a fighter pilot is up in a plane, does it matter how realistic the scene outside the plane is? Or does it matter more how realistically their instrumentation responds to new types of maneuvers? Does it matter how much the various parts of the cockpit turn or jar him? What is it that has to be realistic in this situation to lead to effective training?

This leads directly into the second promise of VR, which is that Virtual Reality is more engaging and will greatly motivate users to participate in training, or indeed more broadly in education or other activities. The goal of VR environments is to be very engaging so that the learners will want to learn more and enjoy being part of it. This is a very important aspect of any kind of system that is trying to support training. We know that motivation matters. On the flip side, a great deal of the hyperbole that surrounds Virtual

The ideal	**The potential pitfall**
User engagement/motivation	Shallow glitz
Situational realism—saves money, time, practice rare events	Misleading distinctions; over emphasis on some skills; distracting
Active, constructive learner	Passive receiver in a fixed game
Tools and context adapts to user	User contorts self to fit rgid tecnology

Figure 1. Virtual reality evaluation.

Reality has to do with an overemphasis on "bells and whistles" with shallow or questionable underpinnings supporting the training goals for that environment.

Currently, there is a movement to bring in some of the very useful experience that so-called "edutainment" has to offer us in how one can use multimedia to better create a more realistic experience in a VR world. While welcoming this expertise, let me inject a note of caution. Simulation started out in military applications with rigorous requirements for accuracy and precision since it was primarily directed towards analysis. Over time, the military learned that it could take advantage of these simulations for training purposes and a happy marriage of purposes was made. However, recently I have noted a disturbing tendency to overemphasize the goals of the computer-based environments to be engaging and to de-emphasize the accuracy and precision that is also required in military training. We must not mistake the motivating appeal, appearance, or the sense of an experience that edutainment gives us for proof that the environment is sufficiently realistic for the required training. Let me give you an example. When someone making a movie wants to create gunfire, they can use people banging on sticks or corks popping out of bottles in the background with well-synchronized visual effects. In fact, as the famous movie producer Alfred Hitchcock showed, movie makers go out of their way to create the effects of experiences through illusions so as to not have to incur either the cost or the danger of the "real thing" for their actors. But what happens when we need to use that environment to teach about armaments? We must never lose sight of the key purpose of military training—the "actor" in the VR environment must be able to do the "real thing" after the training is over. Therefore, the VR must be realistic in regards to what we're training. If you're teaching that person to fire weapons, it better respond like a real weapon and that means it is not simply a matter of making the person "feel" like he was able to fire that gun.

The next point in Figure 1 is a critical one. At the moment, it is so hard to build these highly intensive visual environments, that users of VR environments basically have to accept the world as designed by the developers. Developers have worked very hard to create the best worlds for their users, and often they're impressive indeed. In fact, we have seen several examples in the field of really marvelous work in this area. However, the problem is this: one of the things we have learned in education and training is that the more the human is engaged in constructing how something works, in understanding the material and organizing it for themselves, and in working with that material, the more powerful the learning is. One of the hopes for Virtual Reality environments was that we would create an environment within which a human could learn, explore and practice their skills and knowledge. The problem is that the current VR environments are so hard to construct that you could end up with a situation such that instead of the active, constructive learner that we want, we get a passive, receptive, VR version of a "couch potato." We don't want a bystander in an environment dictated by someone else; rather we want to provide an environment that encourages and allows someone to structure the knowledge or the experience for themselves.

To have an environment that allows for active and creative participation requires highly flexible computer-based support. That is, do we have a set of models and computer capabilities that are realistic enough that a human being could really change the environment in many different, creative ways? If somebody is on a bivouac, they can build an igloo if they need to or they can pull down trees to do creative things like block a road for an enemy. Does the kind of VR environment we are creating allow any kind of creative, adaptive thinking by the user that hasn't been previously planned for and scripted by the developers? One could rightly argue here that there is a vast difference between the needs of an educational VR environment and a training VR environment. We certainly need debate in the VR and training community about how much active individual construction capabilities are needed by a training environment. However, I would like to highlight here three points to think about for whichever side of the argument you take: First, one of the advantages we are promoting in the use of VR is the ability to handle the unusual event—and unusual or rare could mean the need for unusual responses and individual creativity; second, some people will always argue for the need of field training because of the lack of realism in VR—the more we allow humans to do in the VR environment, the more they will favorably compare to field hours; third, there has been an increasing emphasis in training communities on the need for less rote training and training that emphasizes higher-order thinking skills—especially for leadership positions.

In all of these points on promises and pitfalls, I am not saying that any of these dangers are necessarily inherent in Virtual Reality environments. Rather, the point is to identify data that we need to collect as a community in order to be able to show whether or not we have fallen into these traps, or whether or not we have successfully accomplished any of the promises of Virtual Reality. That's what I meant when I said we have to get beyond the "demonstration mentality." It's no longer any good just to have someone approve the funding for a prototype project or to collect anecdotal evidence. Rather we need to know what aspects of our VR system are effective and where they are not, so that we can both further enhance and develop the appropriate technology and the appropriate uses of that technology. We need to develop the distinctions as a field that permit us to select what kinds of training situations benefit the most from VR, and indeed any technology. Furthermore, the decision-makers in charge of these projects need data not only about the efficacy of the new technology in achieving their training requirements, but they need to have data that helps them do trade-offs based on costs and benefits of the technology. Costs include not only the relative cost of the technology, but the impact on training all parts of their organization, the effect on operations and the cost of additional infrastructure, the costs of dropping other materials, and so forth.

Some of the most critical questions we have to ask ourselves are: when is VR inappropriately expensive for the training that we want to provide? Is it ever actually misleading or distracting from our training goals? People forget that, for example, in teaching, and I've had experience in teaching like many of you readers have, we often simplify on purpose or make diagrams in order to focus our students on a particular part of the problem. In an attempt to provide more realism, do we end up with a set of tools that are so expensive to develop that we have to overuse them for everything to justify the cost? Do we end up ignoring some of the things we know about training without VR?

EXPANDING OUR CONCEPT OF VR

The second major point of this address is to broaden our concept of what we mean by Virtual Reality. This, of course is closely tied to the most important evaluation question we ask, which is "given the task I'm training for, where does the VR environment have to be realistic?" If I'm teaching staff officers to be able to respond to new types of operations, then do I have enough social realism? If I'm in the cockpit, do I have enough haptic realism? Or auditory realism? For example one of the things that people found in some naval training exercises was that command and control personnel had trained in environments that were much too clean and orderly compared to the real situations, which got very noisy and confusing. Students not prepared for that realistically confusing and noisy environment, were sometimes thrown off. So these are some of the issues we need to be concerned about. In order to expand our concept of Virtual Reality, I am purposely going to talk about an area that many of you would not even consider as Virtual Reality—text-based MUDs.

What are Multi-User Domains or MUDs? MUDs [Bartle90], [O'Brien92], [Curtis92], [Curtis-Nichols93], Riner-Clodius94] are text-based virtual reality environments that are used largely for role-playing games on the Internet. Their history is an interesting moment in the history of science: at first, all their developers wanted to do was to create a form of adventure game that could be shared by others. For those not familiar with computer-based adventure games, as a user in such a game you are part of an interactive story that gives you choices about what to do and when, where, and how to play. So for example you might enter a castle dungeon and have to fight a dragon, complete with grabbing the treasure and running away with it to new adventures. All the developers of the MUDs (originally Multi-User Dungeons) wanted to do was to be able to have some other player join them in their playful adventures—to explore the castle or story environment together and plan together and see each other grab the treasure or slash the head off the evil gnome. But in the act of accomplishing this modest goal, they created some of the best examples of Virtual Spaces that I know [Landauer-Bellman94]. What I mean by Virtual Spaces is that you have a sense of a space, just like a conference room. A space where people can walk in and out; objects can be brought in and shared. I can show you slides up in the front of the room, or I can reach for a book over there. I don't see this sense of Virtual Space in groupware. Currently, in groupware you're able to view screens together, exchange e-mail or chat, move the cursors together on charts or maps, and in some recent tools, have additional supportive capabilities. These capabilities can be very useful for certain kinds of tasks. However, in my experience, when there are more than a few people engaged in these activities, the interactions become cumbersome and confusing.

On the other hand, in MUDs you can have large numbers of people—in different rooms, talking, working together on a large variety of objects. I call the MUD developers 'barnstormers' because it really is like watching the history of airplanes being developed: you have marvelous flying machines; you have some that are helicopter wings, bicycle wheels and they crash, and then you have others that are really taking off. And consistent with this analogy of the early days of flying, there are now many home inventors developing similar and yet different MUDs. There are, in fact, thousands of MUDs [Leong], some of them having ten thousand active players [Curtis92, White], [Crane], where hundreds of them could be in the MUD at any given time, running around, creating objects in real-time, and interacting with each other. They are doing something right. You have hundreds of thousands of people who have been living in small communities, in cyberspace on these MUDs, some of them for as long as 8 years. They have elected town officials; they walk around their towns, build, and live there. They have roles and functions that they play within those communities. To us, as scientists, we have to say there's something seriously interesting there. What are they doing right that they are able to live, work and build together in these virtual communities, and what could we learn about them for the rest of the field? Four years ago, while I was working on developing large design environments for space systems, I became very excited about the potential of this work.

Over the years what I have done is to characterize some of the qualities that make these environments interesting, and some of these I've listed in Figure 2.

MUDs are computer programs that in their simplest form have a database with some associated communication and data base management services and the interpreter for the construction language [Landauer-Bellman96], [Applegate-et-al.]. The usual architecture is a client-server one with the server containing the database and, at the moment, all the in-

Characteristics of MUDs	Relevance to education/training
Virtual space	Collaborative work
User construction languages	Learning by doing; active participation
Simple client-server architecture; low budget access	Inexpensive delivery of mechanisms, materials
Spatial metaphor	Good scheme for organizing large amounts of information
State-dependent materials, e.g. quests	Structuring learning materials
Robots—embodied utilities and evaluation	Combine individual tutoring with collaborative environment

Figure 2

teresting core services. The client program acts as an interface helping to connect the user to the server and sending the users' commands to move, talk, or build within the environment.

Above, I discussed perhaps the most important feature of MUDs which is their use as virtual spaces—spacious enough to allow a rich array of human interactions [Riner-Clodius94]. In Figure 2, I have added several others. One of the most important is the ability of a learner to become an author almost immediately. Text-based MUDs allow people the freedom of and richness of word pictures—something that we can't imitate with our graphical environments. MUDs have a number of programming languages associated with them, out of which comes the user construction languages. With those construction languages, users create objects ranging in complexity from mere description to small complex simulations. They create rooms with rules about who and what enters those rooms and how and when they leave those rooms, and what happens to them in these rooms. They create avatars or characters for themselves with descriptions. Even with the simplest of construction languages, people experience a deep sense of being present within these virtual environments partly because they have built those environments from their own imagination and they are present within those environments—moving, acting, creating, talking. This low cost of entry to MUDs has made these environments popular with a wide range of non-technical people. All people—not just what I call "technocrats"—can become builders in a very short amount of time. In fact, I've seen examples of eight and nine-year old children, who were raised in inner cities and were nearly illiterate, become, within a short amount of time, able to build up a whole environment. Their teachers, in several different projects have reported an enormous motivation to be part of these environments—having a noticeable impact on their efforts to read and to write well. One little girl comes to mind who built a thirty-room mansion with gardens and pools. Another, an equally little boy, showed me his gardens where when you looked at the flowers, they blossomed. As I just mentioned, MUDs are written in different languages. Often the variant of the word MUD reflects the underlying approach—so for example MOOs are MUDs written in an object-oriented language [Curtis-White], [White], [Hudson]. Others are called MUSHes, MUSEs, LPMuds, etc.. These different languages allow different behaviors of the objects created by the users. Some of these objects can be created and used in real-time. Pedagogically this can be very powerful. At one meeting of mathematicians on a MUD, some colleagues and I were joking about an "infinitely parallel quantum machine." While the others joked, I quickly created an object labeled thus with a few simple attributes, and threw it across the room to one of the others. Although this was done as a joke, think about the ability to, even at a primitive level, make a new idea visible—and something that others can pick up and walk out of the room with. One of the colleagues there that day still has my quantum machine. Aside from being able to become players quickly, another aspect of these environments is that they have very simple client-server architectures, which means that there are people on these environments who only have teletypes. These environments are world-wide. You don't have to have a sophisticated set-up to become a player or participant, which is one of the reasons they are enduringly popular.

Another interesting thing about these environments is that every object is a state machine. Therefore, and this again comes back to education and training, the objects that I am holding in my hand, the rooms I have walked through, the things I've accomplished in that environment will literally determine what I see and what objects do to me as I walk through this environment. These properties allow authors to set up "quests" or interactive stories that have game or logical features that must be accomplished to succeed. They are also easy ways of structuring learning material. One of my colleagues, a good amateur Egyptologist, set up a quest that requires one to learn some middle Egyptian—both vocabulary and grammar rules. If you don't tell the boatman to take you across the river in Egyptian, you can't cross—nor can you talk to the idols who give you other clues for finding the treasure and solving the puzzles.

Another interesting feature is that aside from the active behavior of the elements in the environment, you also have the ability for artificial intelligence programs, or computer programs that we call robots, to come into the same environment with the same client-server interaction that a human uses. They use the same commands that a human uses to move around the environment, speak in English or a natural language, and can be helpful companions to a person in the MUD. Some of the robots are so good that one cannot tell them from human players—they do indeed pass the Turing Test. I couldn't tell one was a robot until I saw it in a group situation where its responses became less fluent, presumably because its underlying parser couldn't keep track of multiple lines of conversation. The current robots give us many interesting ideas about the kinds of intelligent support that agents could do for people within virtual environments. They'll take notes for people, they'll tell them stories about the area, room, objects, and people in the MUD; they'll follow them around. They'll help them find things and do errands for them. In one of my education and training technology research programs, they are also becoming the avatars for computer-based tutors and evaluation agents.

Lastly, one of the attributes that both MUDs and other VR environments capitalize on is the spatial metaphor underlying these spaces. Human beings use spatial maps a lot; we are able to organize an enormous amount of data and information if we can spatially place it. So both in Virtual Reality and in our real world environment, the ability to place objects within a room (within a context) and walk into another room or context is very powerful.

LEARNING SPACES

I could literally talk for hours about MUDs; there's a lot of interesting work being done. There are psychologists, anthropologists, and sociologists who are doing Ph.D. research on MUDs, as well as computer scientists and engineers. In my Computer Aided Education and Training Initiative (CAETI), a large Defense Advanced Research Products Agency (DARPA) program, we have been combining MUDs and other Virtual Reality work to create powerful "learning spaces." The idea is to combine the qualities of MUDs and VR in general with other forms of computer-based training, particularly computer-based "tutors." Our goal is to take advantage of the best of both worlds—provide collaborative spaces within which there is also individualized tutoring and attention. Hence we have been experimenting with assigning robots to each individual in a collaborative environment. The goals for these "buddy" robots are to tutor, guide, and help evaluate the individual as they move through the training scenarios or educational activities in a MUD. The tutoring and feedback eventually will be directed towards any aspect of the environment—from the objects within it to the scenario under way to the interactions with other players. We want to take advantage of the qualities we are seeing in MUDs: low entry costs, constructive participation by the user; the growth and support of real community, the games that can structure learning materials and create rich scenarios within the virtual reality, and an environment in which artificial agents and humans can interact on an 'equal footing.' In addition to "souping up" these MUDs with additional tools and capabilities, we have been working with various educational and training communities to define what additionally we need beyond MUDs, VR, and computer-based educational tools to turn these environments into true learning spaces. Some of the things we are analyzing with these training and education experts have to do with traditional curriculum and content issues, but also there are new issues that deal with making the VR inhabitable by humans—a civilized place. For example, what are the rules for agents and privacy? How do we appropriately use evaluation agents? If we create "buddy" robots for each student, what should be our rules for what they "report" about the student's behavior? In these environments every comment and every action can easily be recorded. Do we have any privacy guidelines at all? Is everything that someone tries or plays with automatically public in these learning spaces? How much should any VR environment be used? When is a learner spending too much time in a virtual reality? This and many other serious issues about appropriate and aberrant behaviors associated with living with VR have been raised by an increasing number of psychologists and sociologists.

Let me leave us with a series of questions that can serve as a framework for interpreting education/training applications as the VR technology matures.

Many VR environments have focused on creating interesting spaces for the individual, sometimes in a strangely cut-off way from other individuals. The Advanced Distributed Simulation (ADS) community within the US Department of Defense has been working towards providing the right simulations and computer support for coordinated mutual training. There are many pockets of relevant research and development being done. VR, ADS, computer-based training, and now the MUDs which provide us with new ideas for good social learning spaces. We need to bring together these research communities to create the richest and most responsive environments for the individual, together with computer-based training that does individualized presentations, has good pedagogy, and good content. Then we will have the ability to combine the best of both worlds—powerful collaborative environments along with customized presentation, feedback, and attention to the individuals in the environment.

However, to realize this vision, we face several hard technical issues. One is the role and type of agents with which we want to have populate these worlds. There's nothing lonelier than being in a Virtual Reality environment alone. The semi-autonomous forces (SAFORs) and other agents that we are building need more sophisticated models of human behavior and interaction. We overall need better models and understanding of what we want from small or large group training exercises or group educational activities. Also, how do we handle these new powerful spatial metaphors? There are interesting hard issues about the distributedness of these Virtual Worlds. At a computer science level, it has to do with the underlying databases, where they are placed, and how you can jump with objects from one world into the other. From a user's point of view, it has to do with being able to put together multiple viewpoints. We can't see the whole battlefield all at once: How do we coordinate or script a large complicated set of activities? How do we decide how to partition these spaces and activities? Which part of the space and activities should be globally shared and which should purposely be local in view and perspective? It may be a useful pedagological device to show me the battlefield as if I were a Roman general or a bird hovering over the battlefield. However, I also need to train troops for the realistic scenarios where they can't see everything. In fact, learning to make reasonable decisions under that uncertainty—under the "fog of war" is part of the required realism for military training.

Another issue is how to form successful learning cultures? I talked about this a little bit when I asked what makes some MUDs, out of thousands, flourish and remain while other MUDs quickly blossom and die. What are the thriving MUDs doing right? Some of it includes clearly their strategies for dealing with privacy, security, and individual and group rights. These social decisions are reflected in all the standard computer science characteristics of these MUDs, e.g. simulation capabilities, database, communication, and libraries services.

Simulation capabilities will be a continuing haunting one for virtual reality because all of VR depends on models. Virtual reality requires complex models to be integrated with other models, and frankly, this is where some of the most difficult challenges lie for us. We've benefited enormously in all the fields that I'm associated with, from our modeling efforts, but we always have to remember that they are models. If there are models, there are assumptions. If there are models, there are fragile edges. We need to greatly increase our capabilities to integrate models in a way that allows to verify and validate our uses of them. This is true in any application, but especially in an area where we are claiming that a troop has sufficiently been trained to save his or others' lives. This is very much related to the continual theme of this address to broaden our concept of realism within VR. We need realistic capabilities for more than visual stimuli. Visual senses are clearly one of the dominant ones in a human being, but there are other senses to which we must attend. We are going to have to think about how important all the senses—from odors to tactile to auditory—are for any given tasks. For example, as a neurophysiologist, I've experienced how much odor matters. It matters more than what people want to say in polite company. Tactile stimuli also matters. You need to learn as a doctor how to reach in and touch; grab and pull in an appropriately determined way. These are things that have to be confronted. It isn't good enough to glibly say that we've handled most of the needed stimuli with visualization; that's not going to cut it.

Over and over again, I've stressed all of these things in terms of evaluation. The bottom line is how are we going to prove what we say is good or what we claim is good in VR or indeed any computer-based support? How are we going to improve our engineering discipline so that we can incorporate the results of good cognitive and social studies into the engineering of our technology? That's our critical challenge now.

REFERENCES

David Applegate, James Aspnes, Timothy Freeman, and Bennet Yee, TinyMUD, source code available via anonymous ftp from ftp.math.okstate.edu, in directory /pub/muds/servers/, in file tinymud-1.5.4.tar.Z

Richard Bartle, "Interactive Multi-User Computer Games", MUSE, Ltd. (December 1990), available via anonymous ftp from host "ftp.parc.xerox.com", in file "/pub/MOO/papers/mudreport.*", (availability last checked 16 October 1995)

John P. Crane, DragonMUD, accessible via telnet (or other MUD clients) at tinylondon.ucsd.edu 4201

Pavel Curtis, "Mudding: Social Phenomena in Text-Based Virtual Realities", in Proceedings 1992 Conf. on Directions and Implications of Advanced Computing, Berkeley, May 1992, also available as Xerox PARC technical report CSL-92–4, also available via anonymous ftp from parcftp.parc.xerox.com, in directory /pub/MOO/papers/, in files DIAC92.*

Pavel Curtis and David A. Nichols, ''MUDs Grow Up: Social Virtual Reality in the Real World", available via anonymous ftp from parcftp.parc.xerox.com, in directory /pub/MOO/papers/, in files MUDsGrowUP.*

Pavel Curtis, Stephen White, LambdaMOO, accessible via telnet or other clients at lambda.parc.xerox.com 8888, source code available via anonymous ftp from ftp.parc.xerox.com, in directory /pub/MOO/, in files LambdaMOO-1.7.7.tar.Z and others

Greg Hudson, ColdMUD, source code available via anonymous ftp from tiny.mcs.usu.edu, in directory /pub/brandon/VE/ColdMUD, in files coldmud- 0.10.3.tar.gz and coldmud-0.10.doc.ps.gz, or a slightly older version from ftp.math.okstate.edu, in directory /pub/muds/servers/, in file coldmud-0.10.2.tar.gz

Christopher Landauer, Kirstie L. Bellman, The MUDpage, http://tinylondon.ucsd.edu/~cal/MUDpage.html

Christopher Landauer, Kirstie L. Bellman, ''Integration Systems and Interaction Spaces", (to appear) in Proceedings of FroCoS'96: The First International Workshop on Frontiers of Combining Systems, 26–29 March 1995, Munich, Germany (March 1996)

Lydia Leong, MUD Resources Collection, http://www.cis.upenn.edu/~lwl/mudinfo.html

Mike O'Brien, "Playing in the MUD", Ask Mr. Protocol Column, SUN Expert, Volume 3, No. 5, pp. 19–20, 23, 25–27 (May 1992)

R. Riner and J. Clodius, "Simulating Future Histories", Anthropology and Education Quarterly (Fall 1994)

Stephen White, CoolMUD, source code available via anonymous ftp from ftp.math.okstate.edu, in directory /pub/muds/servers/, in file coolmud2.1.3.tar.gz

2

VIRTUAL REALITY SIMULATOR (VRS) FOR TRAINING SHIP HANDLING SKILLS

Lochlan E. Magee

Defence and Civil Institute of Environmental Medicine
North York, Ontario, Canada

INTRODUCTION

The Canadian Navy requires the use of training simulators to avoid the high costs and difficulties of training officers at sea. Other factors, such as fleet reductions and growing reliance upon the reserves, have amplified this requirement. The Chief of Maritime Doctrine and Operations (CMDO) requested the investigation of technologies that would enable the development of an inexpensive simulator for training ship-handling skills.

A prime requirement of the training system is the ability to simulate formation manoeuvres. These skills are now practiced at sea using old Bay Class training vessels that are expensive to operate and maintain. From their bridge, the student is taught skills of an Officer-of-the-Watch (OOW). He must learn to manoeuvre his ship, by itself and in company. He must do this in response to executive orders received by radio and in response to the actions and disposition of other vessels and objects in the environment which he observes from the flying bridge. Orders and reports are relayed to him verbally. He can see in all directions a view that is only partly occluded by structures on the deck such as funnels. He must learn to judge visually distance, turning rate, and relative velocity. He takes bearings using a peloris, and is able to monitor some aspects of the ship's performance by observing instruments on the bridge. He must learn to task, direct, and coordinate other members of the bridge team to guide the ship safely and efficiently.

Salient among the requirements for training ship manoeuvres is the need for a wide field-of-regard. A solution to this requirement dominates the design of most bridge simulators; the conventional solution is to provide a panoramic visual display using a large number of projection screens to surround the bridge. The designers of simulators for air traffic control (ATC) and air combat manoeuvres (ACM) training have also taken this approach because a wide field of regard is needed (Thomas, 1993). In ATC the simulated control tower is surrounded by projection screens. In some ACM simulators, an aircraft cockpit is placed at the centre of a large dome (e.g., 40 feet in diameter) whose inside is used as the projection surface.

Wide field-of-view technologies have also been sought by the film industry for entertainment because stimulation of the eye's periphery leads to a more compelling illusion of

Virtual Reality, Training's Future? edited by Seidel and Chatelier
Plenum Press, New York, 1997

presence, and self motion. While multiple screens can satisfy the requirement for a wide field-of-view and are technically straightforward to implement, their use has numerous disadvantages. Among these are the following: (1) High cost due to the need for a large number of image generators, projectors, and screens, (2) A large surface area requiring a large space for the display, (3) Bulky equipment that prohibits portability, (4) Projective visual distortions away from the design eye point, and (5) Inefficiency, because a large amount of detailed imagery needs to be generated at once while little of it is actually observed at any instant since the human observer has a relatively narrow cone of vision sensitive to detail.

Head-mounted displays attempt to avoid some of these disadvantages. The fibre optic head-mounted display (FOHMD) developed by CAE Electronics Ltd., for example, uses optical bundles to relay bright, high-resolution, high-contrast, large-angle images to each eye from remote image generators. Binocular imaging, and eye-slaved insets are also possible with this technology which suit applications where the detection of small, distant targets or stereoscopic perception are needed. However, the technology is expensive, and when matched to a helmet weighs several kilograms. Weight is an unwanted feature of head-mounted displays, especially for applications in which helmets are not normally used, since it will contribute to muscle fatigue, and may also help ,promote simulator-induced sickness. High resolution, binocular displays also do not seem to be a requirement for conning a ship in formation. Although beyond the range typical for stereoscopic perception, the other ships are fairly close (about 275 m), are large (about 50 m in length), and slow moving (about 18.5 kph).

These characteristics of the visual environment at sea suggest that less capable head-mounted displays will suffice for the training simulator. In the early 1980s, Michael McGreevy, at NASA Ames Research Center, used flat panels of the type used in small, portable televisions, in a head mount to display interactive images of Martian terrain. Fisher (1990) provides an historical account of the evolution of virtual interface technologies leading to the development of low-cost imaging systems reliant upon commercially available consumer products such as liquid crystal displays. Liquid crystal displays have limited resolution, brightness, and contrast. These deficiencies are most pronounced when the visual angles subtended by the display are large. Instantaneous fields-of-view greater than 60 degrees are often quoted as necessary for an immersive experience in the virtual environment. This immersive experience, "being there", is an important design objective because it is thought to impact positively upon learning and memory.

Other emerging technologies also provide inexpensive or alternative components that can be exploited in the development of a training system. These technologies include voice recognition, voice production, expert systems, precision tracking and local and long range computer networking. They permit portability, generic use, objective performance measurement and a reduction in the number of instructional support staff. However, few practical applications have attempted to reduce the technical uncertainty associated with their use in simulator training.

The following sections describe an exploratory development model of a ship-handling simulator designed to exploit the capabilities of commercial off-the-shelf technologies, including a low-cost, head-mounted display, and a field study designed to assess its useability and training effectiveness.

Exploratory Development Model (XDM)

A simulator, the Maritime Surface/Subsurface Virtual Reality Simulator (MARS VRS), was constructed to remove the technical uncertainty associated with the use of virtual reality technologies. An iterative design approach was used, involving subject matter experts from Venture, the Naval Officer Training Centre (NOTC) in Victoria, British Columbia. The simulator has three principal functional components: the OOW interface, the bridge team, and instructional facilities.

The interface to the trainee consists of an occluded, head-mounted display, an electromagnetic tracker, a microphone, a voice recognition system, and a speaker. An active matrix, colour LCD, head-mounted display is used (Liquid Image Corporation MRG 2). It provides a biocular, instantaneous field-of-view 65 degrees high and 84 degrees wide; pixel size is about 7 arc min (see Real Time Graphics, August 1992, 3(2), pg 10 for further characteristics and to compare this system with other commercially available head-mounted displays). A Polhemus Fastrack is used to sense head position and orientation (see Burdea and Coiffet (1994) for descriptive information, and for comparison with other 3 dimensional sensors). Visual imagery is provided by a Silicon Graphics Indigo [2] with Extreme graphics. The trainee is provided with uninterrupted observation of the ambient environment, including other ships in the formation. Each vessel is rendered using approximately 2000 polygons. Although the design approach is generic, allowing any ship in the Canadian Navy to be simulated, the application is presently focused on the Bay Class minor war vessel now used to train junior officers. The hydrodynamics of this vessel and its physical appearance are modelled. Instruments that the OOW needs to see on the bridge are computer generated. They appear on demand when the head looks up or down. In this way, the essential instruments can be represented larger than life, for readability, and positioned so that they do not block the trainee's view of the seascape. This technique, while attempting to overcome a limitation in resolution, provides a serendipitous benefit; it allows the instructor to know if the student checks his instruments.

Digital sound recordings are used for auditory signals such as fog horns and for the engine noise which is modulated with the throttle setting. These are presented by a single 35 watt speaker (Yamaha, model MS20S) positioned behind the student. An adjustable, directional microphone is attached to the head mount so that it can be suspended close to the lips. A Marconi MR8 speech recognizer is used to interpret the verbal queries and commands spoken by the student. It is housed in a PC, and is triggered when the student depresses a thumb switch held in his hand as he would hold a communications microphone aboard ship. A complementary voice production facility is used to link the OOW with a surrogate bridge team. The voice recognition system captures the OOW's spoken orders and encodes them into a format that the simulator can use to adjust helm or engine speed. In reply, the voice production system simulates unique voices for the yeoman, range man, helmsman and relative velocity man. For example, signals sent to the vessel are spoken aloud by the computer in their proper, decoded format as they would be by the yeoman aboard ship. The behaviour of the bridge team is simulated by software. The voice recognition system is also used to record commands for observation by the instructor, a Course Training Officer (CTO) or Officer Conducting Serial (OCS). The benefit of this approach is that it eliminates the need for instructional personnel to perform the bridge functions, facilitates scheduling, eliminates a source of uncertainty in the assessment of the trainee's performance, and provides an audit trail for later review and feedback. It also demands strict adherence to communication protocol. Keyboard entries can be made by the instructor to circumvent failure of the recognition system occasioned by poor communication practices, stress, or other factors that can limit the accuracy of the recognizer.

The instructional facilities of the MARS VRS address the needs of (i) lesson planning, (ii) monitoring and controlling the simulation during training, and (iii) reviewing and debriefing. A graphical user interface is used with multiple, successive or tiled windows, each having a specific purpose. A Silicon Graphics Indigo [2] with an XZ graphics subsystem hosts the interface. Lesson plans may be composed and edited in advance. They provide a script for the training exercise, listing the sequence of commands that will be issued by the instructor to the formation. During training, the lesson plan appears in one of four windows on the instructor's workstation. The instructor can schedule events as well as edit the lesson plan during its execution by selecting options from nested menus. A second window provides a time-stamped record of actions taken by the trainee for immediate or delayed feedback. To aid this process, a third window on the instructor's screen provides a visual representation of the ships in formation. It can show either a plan (overhead) view that displays the ships as icons, or a "virtual view" that displays the ships in a three-dimensional format. In the plan view, the relative position of each ship is represented by an icon located within a set of concentric range rings centered upon the guide. Alphanumeric information blocks display the ship type, call sign, speed, heading and rudder angle. In the three-dimensional view, the ships and their environment appear as a virtual world that can be explored interactively. This view shows the visual relationships among the ships from any perspective, including any bridge.

An important feature common to each view are trails left by the ships that visually record its path. Also common to each view is an option to display a standard solution. When selected, this option generates the path that would be followed if standard solutions were used to guide the ship's movement. The standard solutions are also used to automate the behaviour of ships that are not controlled by students. This allows the instructor to conduct exercises that involve several ships without requiring a full complement of staff or students.

A fourth window allows the instructor to take control of any ship. A graphical user interface provides the means for the instructor to start, pause and resume training and provides an event marker for flagging notable situations. The training exercise is recorded for re-animation. In this mode, the lesson plan, visual views and action logs are available. As well, there are utilities for controlling the review: stop, start, fast forward, rewind and skip-to-a-marked-event functions. These functions are also available for animating the performance of real ships at sea. This is done by replaying recordings of the ships' locations and orientations as they are obtained by differential global positioning systems and packet radio. The animation of real world events can be made interactive, and interleaved with the simulation, so that a student may retry in the simulator a manoeuvre that was conducted poorly at sea.

The instructor's interface also includes a second monitor that shows the changing visual scene presented to the student as he moves about. With this monitor, the instructor can tell whether the student looked toward an instrument, or checked clearance in advance of executing a turn.

METHODS AND PROCEDURES

Subjects

A total of 26 students (including two women) participated as subjects in this evaluation. They composed two successive classes, one class of sixteen reservists, the other a class of ten, regular force personnel. Half of the students in each class were randomly picked to receive simulator training. Unknown to the experimental team, the students in the first half-class were docked sea pay, approximately $50.00 each. The students were not reimbursed for this loss, and no compensation was arranged for the students in the second class after this fact was known.

Procedures

Two identical simulators were installed in nearby classrooms, at the Naval Officer Training Centre (NOTC) at Canadian Forces Base Esquimalt, near Victoria, British Columbia. One half of the 93.04 MARS (R) III class (Reserve class) was trained for a week with the simulators in September, 1993, and one half of the 66th MQC (Regular Force class) was trained with the simulators in January, 1994. Their classmates trained at sea, following the regular programme of instruction that made use of "Porte" class (Gate) vessels (about 38.3 m in length). An experienced CTO from NOTC conducted the training with each simulator. These were operated independently (i.e., they were not networked). On the first day, about 20 minutes was spent by each student to train the voice recognition system. Familiarization with the virtual environment and initial training were then provided for about 45 minutes. On following days each student received training sessions that consisted of a sequence of eight, basic (Level II) manoeuvres conducted in formation with two other ships whose behaviour was controlled by software that followed a standard solution. Students were provided feedback with use of the recording and animation features of the simulator. Each student was also assessed by the instructor each time using the assessment reports that would normally be used aboard ship to record the student's performance.

The instructors use the assessment sheets to evaluate performance on five components for each manoeuvre. The components include the student's ability to (1) plan and (2) execute a manoeuvre, (3) maintain station, (4) demonstrate bridgemanship (e.g., proper use of terminology) and (5) operate safely. Each component is scored out of ten. A final rating is provided for each component and a total score, out of 50, is determined that takes into account trends in the student's behaviour. In other words, some subjective weighting is given to the scores to reflect the instructor's overall assessment of the student's capabilities.

The first class received one training session each day. The second class received one session each day for the first three days, and two sessions each day on the fourth and fifth days of practice. These differences in the amount of practice, and its distribution, were occasioned by the difference in class size; as the smaller class gained proficiency it was possible to include additional training. These procedures are in accord with the way the training would have been managed if it had taken place at sea. Students normally have one turn daily aboard ship to practice manoeuvres, but with small class sizes, and as students become more proficient, additional opportunity for practice is made available to maximize the training value of time at sea.

Before each simulator session, each student was required to complete a questionnaire to record his well being. The questionnaire consisted of a check list that identified symptoms of simulator-induced sickness and their severity. Immediately prior to the training session each student performed a test of static balance. The students were expected to maintain the Romberg posture (i.e., feet together) with eyes open for one minute while standing upon a Kistler force platform (type 9284). Immediately after training, they repeated this test and later completed a second simulator-sickness questionnaire. They were also given a questionnaire to take with them, that was to be returned the next day, so that they could record the duration of persistent symptoms, their severity, and the occurrence of symptoms with delayed onset.

At the end of the week, the students completed a questionnaire that assesses the extent to which they were immersed in the virtual environment (Singer & Witmer, 1994). As well each student was requested to supply written thoughts and comments about the simulator.

All students were assessed at sea four weeks after the simulator training period. During the intervening time, they spent time in the classroom and aboard the training vessels learning other skills and adjusting to life aboard the Bay Class vessel. Three vessels were used in the assessment of transfer-of-training. One vessel contained all students who practiced with the simulator. Another vessel contained students who did not train with the simulator. The third vessel acted as the guide. The guide ship was manned by experienced crew. It manoeuvred little during the formation exercise. The purpose of the guide was to provide a reliable reference about which the other two ships adjusted their position.

The study was designed to compare the performance of the two groups of students using a common set of manoeuvres, balanced to account for differences in difficulty attributable to position within the formation. Each student performed the set of Level II manoeuvres practiced in the simulator, but not at sea. Two Course Training Officers aboard each student vessel independently evaluated each student as they took turns performing the manoeuvre set for the first time at sea. The officers used the assessment sheets that they would normally use to record student performance. The two course training officers who had instructed the students with the simulator were assigned arbitrarily to different vessels. In advance, they had spent time reviewing simulated manoeuvres to make their scoring methods consistent. The other course training officers were appointed from the pool of available instructional staff. The evaluations took place in Juan de Fuca Str., between Vancouver Island, British Columbia, and the State of Washington.

A differential global positioning system (DGPS) was also used to record the manoeuvres. Computers were installed aboard each vessel to record its position every second, with accuracy dependent upon satellite and ground station reception (approximately 5m). Students, instructors, and ship's company were aware that the training range had been instrumented in this way.

Although the study was originally designed to assess the students in the conduct of Level II manoeuvres, smaller than anticipated class sizes caused by military reductions, and favourable weather conditions, permitted assessment data to be gathered during the performance of Level III and Level IV manoeuvres within the same week. These manoeuvres represent progressive levels of difficulty, were untrained in the simulator, and were not controlled as tightly as the Level II test set. At the end of the week of testing the simulator-trained students were requested to provide written comments expressing their opinions about the value of the simulator.

RESULTS

The results reported in the following sections are partial observations. More comprehensive analyses of the data are awaiting a further publication, in preparation, that will attempt to make use of objective performance measures and control theory to model student behaviours. The paths followed by each ship, recorded by the simulation system during training ashore, and recorded by the differential global positioning system at sea, will be used to model the control strategies used by each student. The following sections provide results based primarily upon subjective reports by the students and instructors.

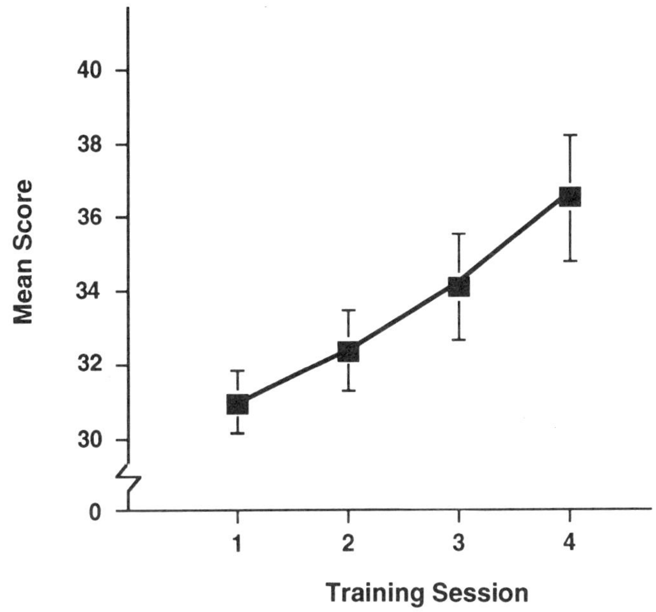

Figure 1. Mean scores (+/- SEM) for first four training sessions.

Learning

The mean scores obtained during the first four training sessions, following familiarization, are plotted in Figure 1, for both regular and reserve classes. The plot shows a large increase in performance from the second to the fifth training session providing evidence of learning. The gain in performance is meaningful since scores less than 29 are failures and scores greater than 40 are rare for novices.

Simulator-Induced Sickness

The presence of a symptom after simulator training, or an increase in the severity of a symptom reported beforehand, are the criteria used for determining its incidence. The most commonly reported symptoms include sweating, desire for cool air, eye strain, blurred vision, mental and physical fatigue, and after-sensations of motion. Some reports of loss of balance were made, mostly following the first and second training sessions. Most symptoms were rated mild, some moderate. One case of severe nausea was observed. The frequency and severity of these symptoms are similar to reports in the literature accompanying investigations of conventional simulators that do not use head-mounted displays.

Figure 2 provides a plot of the total number of symptoms reported by the reserves immediately following each of their four training sessions, and by the regular force members immediately following each of their six training sessions. The plot indicates that the incidence of symptoms is reduced to one half following the second session and suggests little decline in symptom frequency thereafter.

Few of the symptoms persisted. Headache was the most common, often lasting several hours. The largest number of students reporting headache was five, following the sec-

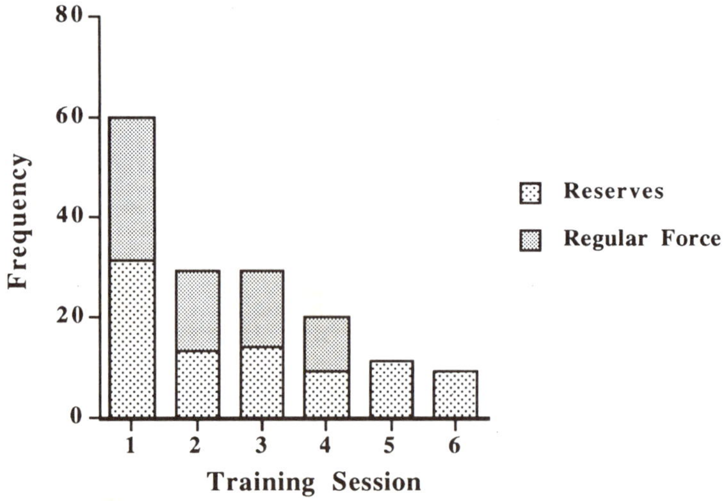

Figure 2. Total number of symptoms of simulator-induced sickness for each training session.

ond day of training. Mental and physical fatigue, drowsiness and energy drain were the other symptoms occasionally mentioned.

Balance

Fluctuations of the centre of pressure upon the force platform were determined separately for both fore/aft (x axis) and side-to-side (z axis) directions. Measures of standard deviation were determined for each balance test, including those surrounding the familiarization session. The analytic software (BioWare™ version 1.1) supplied by the manufac-

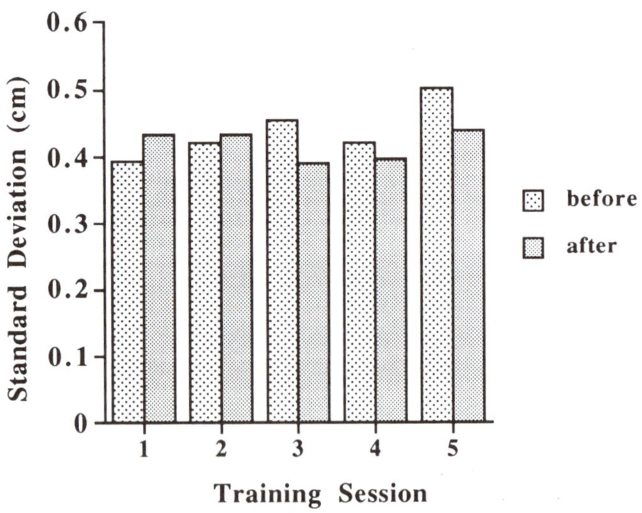

Figure 3. Fore/aft body sway before and after the first five training sessions.

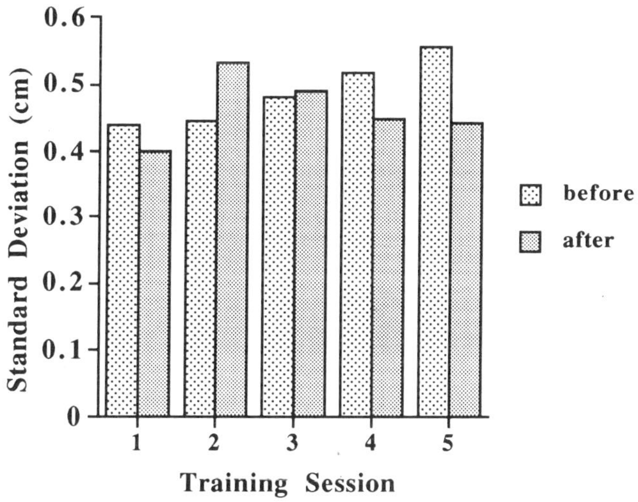

Figure 4. Left/right body sway before and after the first five training sessions.

turer of the force plate was used to calculate the standard deviations. Figures 3 and 4 provide plots of the results for fore/aft and left/right sway respectively.

The results were subjected to a one-way, repeated measures analysis of variance, using StatView™ 512+. Despite some reports of balance loss and some reports of other aftereffects related to postural instability, post-hoc comparisons revealed no reliable decrement in performance following training in the virtual environment, nor did multiple comparisons reveal practice effects that could mask postural disequilibrium.

Transfer-of-Training

The scores given by the two Course Training Officers (instructors) aboard each vessel were usually within one point of each other. The Level II scores assigned by each instructor for each student were correlated to determine inter-instructor reliability. One pair of observations was incomplete. The remaining pairs were assessed using the Spearman rank correlation coefficient in accord with the scale properties of the scores; Rho = .98, $p < .005$. This result indicates that the scores of **one instructor** when ranked predict extremely well the ranks obtained from the scores of the other instructor. On this basis, and because only the instructors who taught the students at sea were always available to further assess the Level III and Level IV manoeuvres, their evaluations alone are used in the following analyses.

The last score obtained during training with the simulator ashore partially predicts the score obtained during the first set (Level II) of manoeuvres at sea; Rho (11), corrected for ties, = .52, $p < .05$. The strength of this prediction can be compared to the values provided in Table 1 which contains the correlation coefficients for pair-wise relationships between scores for each level of manoeuvres. While as much as 62% of the variability in the performance of Level IV manoeuvres is accounted for by knowing the performances obtained in the conduct of Level III manoeuvres, only 38% of the variability is accounted for by knowing the performances obtained in the conduct of Level II manoeuvres. These results suggests a rapid drop in predictability with growing gaps in time or difference in manoeuvre level. In this context, the relationship between the final assessments obtained with

Table 1. Spearman Rho correlations, corrected for ties, between scores for Level II, III and IV manoeuvres

Level	II	III	IV
II	.73	.62	
III		.79	

the simulator, and the initial assessments sea, is encouraging because 27% of the variability in the assessments at sea is predictable, despite the fact that the simulator assessments occurred weeks in advance.

Figure 5 compares the average scores obtained by students trained with the simulator to the average scores obtained by students who were not trained with the simulator. The results suggest that simulator training facilitated performance at sea; Mann-Whitney U tests were conducted to determine whether the advantage is reliable for each manoeuvre set. A reliable difference between training methods was found for Level II manoeuvres; $U = 50.5$, $p < .05$, but not for Level III ($U = 61$) or Level IV ($U = 58.5$) manoeuvres.

DISCUSSION

On the basis of the evidence provided by the subjective assessments of student performance, it seems clear that learning occurred when students practiced with the simulator and that the skills they acquired during simulator training facilitated the performance of identical manoeuvres at sea.

The results also indicate that the training received ashore with the simulator was at least as good in preparing the students for Level III and Level IV formation manoeuvres as the training received afloat by the students who instead made use of the Porte Class vessels.

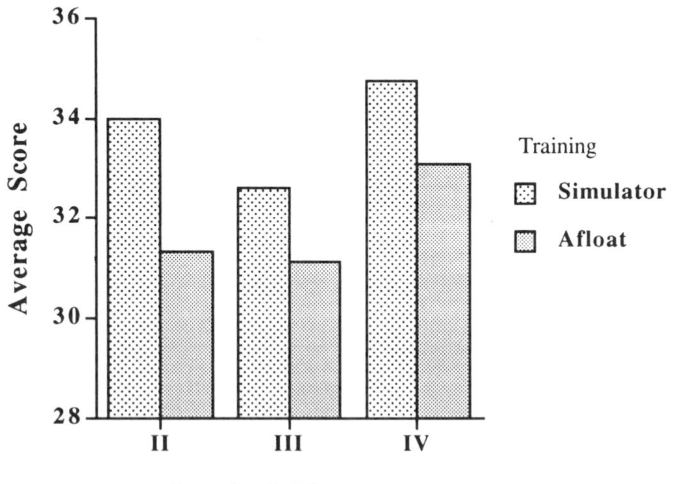

Figure 5. Mean scores for both methods of training for all manoeuvre levels.

Despite the presence of simulator-induced sickness, it did not seriously affect the useability of the MARS VRS training system. Although subjective reports sometimes indicated postural disequilibrium, objective measures of stability with the force platform failed to detect ataxia. It therefore seems reasonable to conclude that the MARS VRS provides an inexpensive alternative to training at sea, without serious concerns for useability. This means that the commercially available, low-resolution, head-mounted display used in this exploratory development is sufficient to convey the visual information needed to perform formation manoeuvres. The implication is that a virtual environment observed with a low-resolution, biocular visual display may be good enough for use in other applications where similar visual information needs to be conveyed. Voice recognition and production systems are also viable interface technologies that afford personnel reductions in support of training. The potential advantages of these components in simulator training are many, including low-cost, portability, generic use, deployability and low maintenance.

REFERENCES

Burdea, G., and Coiffet, P. (1994). *Virtual reality technology.* Toronto: John Wiley & Sons.

Fisher, S.S. (1990). Virtual interface environments. In B. Laurel and S.J. Mountford (Eds.), *The art of human-computer interface design.* Reading MA: Addison- Wesley.

Thomas, M., and Geltmacher, H. (1993). Combat simulator display development. *Information Display*, 4&5, 23–26.

Singer, M.J., and Witmer, B.G., (In review). Presence measures for virtual environments: Background & scoring instructions.

3

VIRTUAL REALITY FOR TRAINING: EVALUATING TRANSFER

J. Wesley Regian

Armstrong Laboratory (AL/HRTI)
Brooks Air Force Base
San Antonio, Texas 78235-5352
E Mail: regian@alhrt.brooks.af.mil

INTRODUCTION

Virtual Reality (VR) continues to excite the instructional technology community. In this chapter I define VR as a package of computer hardware, software, and interface technologies that allow a user to experience certain aspects of a simulated 3-dimensional environment. The simulated aspects of the environment, or "world," typically include a stereoscopic, low-to-medium fidelity visual representation displayed on a head-mounted display system. Head tracking technologies often allow the display to be updated in accordance with head and body motions of the user. This, along with the stereo-binocular disparity of the images on the two screens (one for each eye), support the illusion of moving around in a 3-dimensional world. Most VR systems offer some means of interacting more intimately with the simulated world (beyond just looking around from a single location) by providing interface devices that allow the user to grasp and move objects, change the state of virtual switches, knobs and dials, and move themselves within the world.

I am particularly interested in the potential of VR for instructional purposes. High-performance VR systems are relatively expensive today, as compared to other platforms for computer-based instruction. However, there is no doubt that ongoing investment by the entertainment industry—coupled with continuing increases in microcomputer power per dollar—will steadily reduce the price difference between VR-capable and traditional computer systems. Nevertheless it will always be more expensive to develop and deploy VR-based instruction as compared to traditional computer-based instruction. Even when the cost difference is relatively small per hour of instruction and per delivery station, the total cost difference when summed across many hours of instruction and many delivery stations will be an important factor in selecting between the two. Thus it is important to know what types of tasks benefit from VR as an instructional technology, and which tasks are just as well taught in other ways.

Data are sparse with regard to the task-specific utility of VR as an instructional medium. Regian, Shebilske and Monk (1992) demonstrated that subjects can learn and then

Virtual Reality, Training's Future? edited by Seidel and Chatelier
Plenum Press, New York, 1997

perform two kinds of tasks in a VR. The tasks studied were a) navigation in virtual-spatial environments, and b) procedural console operations tasks on virtual consoles. Navigational tasks require individuals to learn and then navigate through a large-scale spatial environment. Because configurational knowledge of spatial layout is so important to navigational skill acquisition (Regian, 1986; Regian & Yadrick, 1994), and because VR supports simulated immersion in a spatial environment, we suggested that VR may be an excellent interface for teaching large-scale spatial navigation skills (Regian et al., 1992). Procedural tasks (e.g., Holmes, 1991) require the learning of a series of steps, often contextualized in a small-scale spatial environment. Because practice is so important to procedural skill acquisition (Anderson, 1982), it has been suggested that VR may provide an excellent interface for training procedural skills (Kreuger, 1991). The Regian et al. (1992) data suggest that it will be possible to design virtual work environments and that employees will learn to perform tasks in these environments. The data do not address the issues of 1) whether skills acquired in a VR will transfer to corresponding skill in the real world, and 2) whether VR is more effective than other, less expensive, training approaches.

It has been assumed that transfer from VR to real-world performance will occur (Kreuger, 1991; Rheingold, 1991). To the contrary, Kozak, Hancock, Arthur and Chrysler (1993) found no evidence for transfer from VR training to real world performance. In a simple pick-and-place task, a VR-trained group performed the real-world transfer task no better than a group that had received no training on the task. Although the VR group had shown a learning curve for training trials performed in the VR, that learning did not transfer to the real-world task. Only real-world training produced measurable improvements in real-world performance. Kozak et al. questioned the utility of current-generation VR for training real-world tasks. In a recent experiment we evaluated the transfer of training from VR to the real world for two tasks which are more complex than the one studied by Kozak et al. These included a procedural console operations task and a large-scale navigational task. In addition, we implemented simple Computer-Assisted Instruction (CAI) systems for the two tasks, using traditional two-dimensional screen representations, and we evaluated the transfer of training from 2D-CAI to the real world.

AN EXPERIMENT ON TRANSFER

Sixty subjects, from 18 to 35 years of age, were each paid for four hours of participation in an experiment to compare transfer of two types of skills from two types of computer-based instructional systems. Seventy five percent of the subjects were male, and all were high school graduates.

Two criterion tasks were created for the experiment. The procedural console task required subjects to perform a 39 step procedure to fire a missile, using a contrived task console. The building navigation task required subjects to navigate within a real office building. For each of the two tasks, a VR instructional system was developed, and then a corresponding CAI system was developed. Thus two instructional systems, differing primarily on interface technology, were designed to provide training for each of the two tasks.

The fictitious procedural console (Figure 1) was divided into an operational portion (the bottom half) and a decorative portion (the top half). The decorative portion consisted of two radar screens, a missile launch mechanism, and a missile exit window. The subject could not interact directly with the decorative portion, but if the procedure was carried out correctly on the operational portion, the subject would see the missile launch mechanism

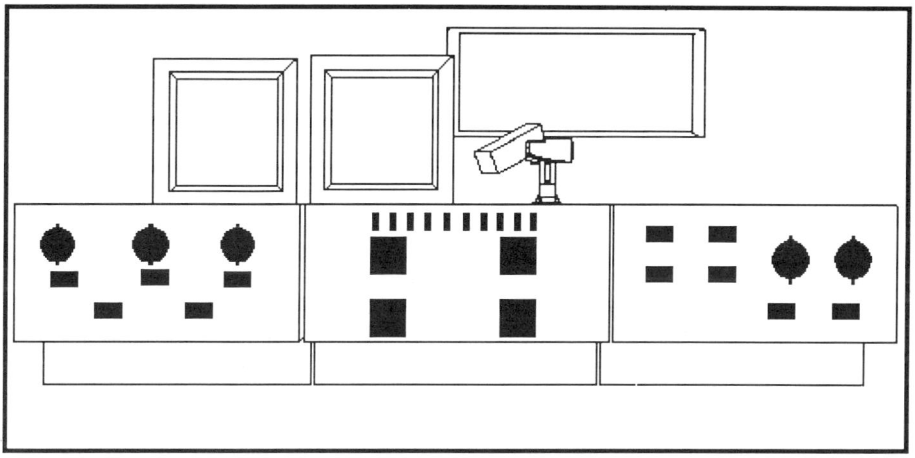

Figure 1. The procedural console task interface.

eject a missile that would then proceed out the missile exit window. The operational portion of the virtual console was divided into three rectangular panels arranged along a vertical plane. The panel on the far left consisted of three knobs and five buttons. The center panel consisted of four buttons, and the far right panel consisted of two knobs and six buttons. There was only a single correct sequence for operating the console. During training, the button or knob to be activated next in the correct sequence was highlighted. Also during training, each button or knob turned yellow when activated in the correct sequence. None of the buttons or knobs could be activated out of turn.

For both interfaces, the console was (by design) too large to fit into the subject's field of view. For the VR interface, approximately one-third of the console could be viewed at any time. Thus, subjects were required to turn their heads to the right or left to see adjacent portions of the console. VR subjects activated buttons and knobs by touching or turning them with their hand. For the CAI interface, exactly one-third of the console was on the screen at any time, and subjects were required to mouse-button on an arrow near the bottom of the screen to view adjacent portions of the console. CAI subjects activated buttons and knobs by clicking on them with the mouse.

In the transfer phase of the console task, subjects operated a physical, wooden facsimile of the console that measured 6 feet across by 2.5 feet high. The facsimile, in scale and color, was identical to the virtual training console except that it was limited to the operational portion of the console and had no decorative portion (radar screens, launch mechanism, and exit window). During testing, no prompt was provided as to which button or knob should be activated next (analogous to the training prompt). If subjects activated an incorrect button or knob, they were so advised, and an error was recorded. The console operations transfer test was administered three times.

The building navigation task was based on the first and second floors of the western half of building 578, Brooks Air Force Base, Texas. Building 578 is the Armstrong Laboratory Human Resources Directorate headquarters, and is a typical professional office building. Twenty rooms dispersed over the first and second floors were chosen at random to contain a site label (a unique letter, from "A" to "T") to identify the room. The training representations were built with the aid of original blueprints and maintained a high degree of spatial accuracy. The VR interface represented the building from the immersed per-

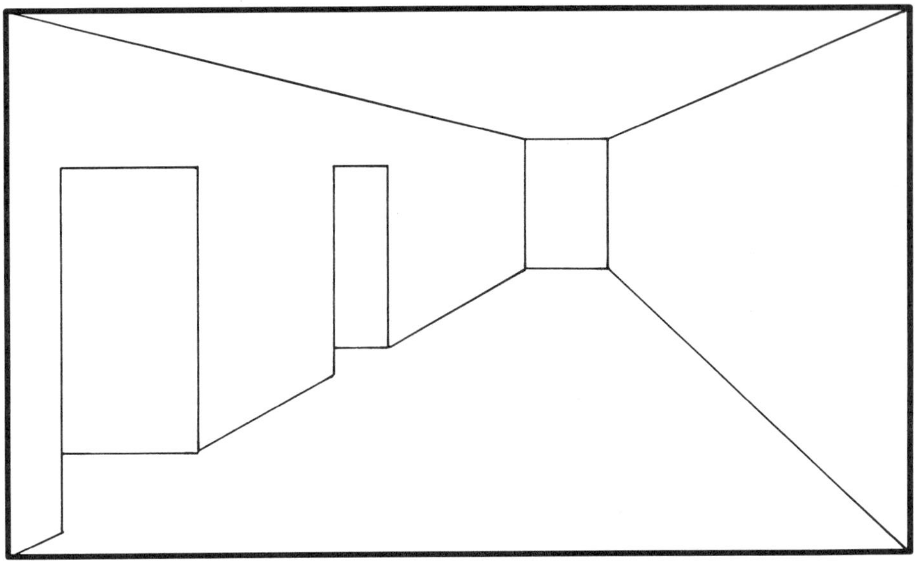

Figure 2. Notional depiction of the VR representation of a hall in building 578.

spective (Figure 2), and subjects moved through the world by pointing in the direction they wished to move. Although Figure 2 depicts the immersed perspective as an impoverished line drawing, the actual virtual world was presented to the subject as a detailed, full color, stereo-binocular image preserving depth (binocular disparity, size and parallax cues), color, and texture characteristics of the actual building.

The CAI interface (Figure 3) represented the building from the bird's-eye perspective, and subjects moved through the world by mouse-clicking on any door through which they wished to exit. While the floor layout was spatially accurate (to scale), the depiction

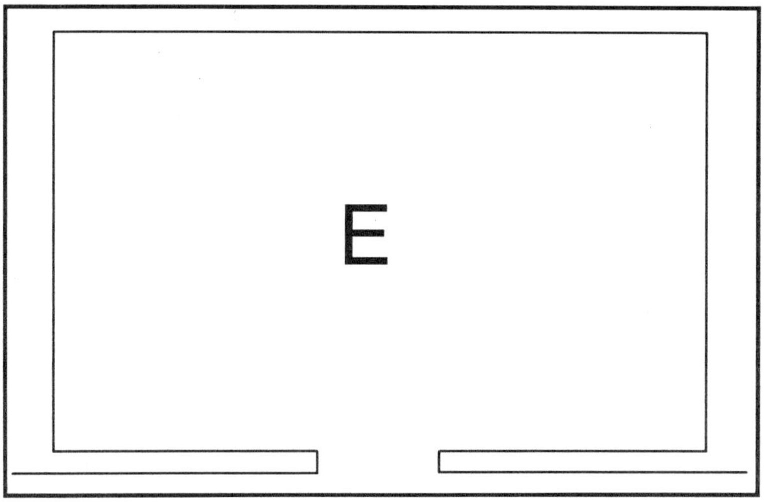

Figure 3. CAI representation of a room in building 578.

was devoid of depth, color, and texture information. Figure 3 accurately depicts the view of one room in the CAI interface.

Prior to the transfer phase of the building navigation task, subjects were prohibited from entering the areas in Building 578 that are modeled in the task. In fact, they only had access to one room in the building, the training room, which has a direct access doorway to the parking lot. During the transfer phase, subjects were placed in a room of Building 578 and were asked to walk, as efficiently as possible, to a specified destination room. During testing, no prompt was provided as to which route should be taken. The building navigation transfer test consisted of five such subtasks.

Experimental apparatus included a Silicon Graphics 4D 210/VGX, a Silicon Graphics 4D 310/VGX, an Apple Macintosh IIfx, and a Compaq 486c portable computer. Proprietary hardware and software supplied by VPL Research Inc. consisted of VPL LX eyephones, the eyephone control unit, standard VPL data gloves, data glove control unit, VID/IO video signal splitters, and POLHEMUS Isotrack 3-space tracking devices. The software used to create the static virtual worlds was RB2 Swivel. The software that controlled the virtual reality operation was VPL's Body Electric and the real time rendering software used on the Silicon Graphics computers was VPL's Isaac. The Compaq 486c portable computer was used to conduct the CAI portion of the experiment, using courseware authored with Asymetrix Toolbook.

Each task was trained using a computer environment and then tested in the real world. Half of the subjects learned the two tasks from VR-based instructional systems, and the other half learned from CAI systems. All subjects performed both of the real-world criterion (transfer) tasks. The procedural console operations task required performance of a motor sequence within a small-scale space (the virtual console). The navigational task required three-dimensional configurational knowledge of large-scale space (building 578).

For the console operations training phase, subjects saw visual prompts (green highlighting of the button or knob, in both VR and CAI conditions) indicating which button or knob to activate next. In addition, subjects were given either verbal (VR) or text-based (CAI) prompts describing what each of the button or knob operations accomplished. For example, they were told that the first button turned on the console, the second button activated the missile platform, etc. In addition, VR subjects were instructed by the proctor on how to successfully push buttons and turn knobs using a data glove. Subjects received ten training trials.

The console operations testing phase was the same for both groups. Three minutes were given to each subject to accomplish the same procedure that was taught during training, but on a full-scale wooden facsimile of the console. Subjects performed the procedure three times on the physical mockup. There was a two minute rest period between performances. If the subject deviated from the correct procedure, the proctor said to the subject "WRONG," recorded the step number, and recorded the latency. Other than this negative feedback, no help was given in the form of visual prompting, verbal prompting, or any other proctor assistance.

The training phase of both the VR and CAI building navigation task involved moving around in the respective environments, first under guided conditions and then under free exploration conditions. Each subject was first given three different guided tours of the building 578 representation. The three tours were identical across subjects. The tours were guided by way of textual and verbal commands given by the computer or the test administrator for the CAI and VR conditions, respectively . For example, one instruction was: "You are now facing room R. Proceed down the hallway on the right to the first doorway to the south. This will be room Q." Upon the completion of these tours, all relevant rooms and hallways in the building had been visited at least one time. Each tour had different initial and final rooms. Next, each subject was told they would soon be tested on their

Table 1. Errors in building navigation performance after VR-based training or CAI

	VR	CAI
Tour 1	2.1	1.3
Tour 2	1.2	1.2
Tour 3	2.1	1.8
Tour 4	0.5	0.4
Tour 5	1.4	0.8
Average errors	1.5	1.1

knowledge of the building and was given an hour to explore and become familiar with the building layout.

The testing phase of the building navigation task included five different tour assignments. Each tour had specific starting and goal rooms. The testing tours were not the same as the training tours. Subjects were asked to proceed on the shortest path between the starting and ending rooms and were told that their goal was to get from the starting room to the goal room while minimizing the number of intervening rooms and halls visited. The test tours were designed to be long enough that the probability of randomly traversing the shortest path between initial and final rooms was very small. The number of rooms visited in error was recorded for each tour.

For both of these tasks, VR-based and CAI-based training produced excellent transfer to real-world task performance. Subjects were able to perform the console transfer task, and navigate in the real building, with accuracy that was nearly perfect. Table 1 shows errors in building navigation transfer performance after VR- or CAI-based training. An error was recorded when subjects stepped into a room that was not on the ideal path they should have been following.

Table 2 shows errors and latencies (in seconds) in console transfer performance after VR- or CAI-based training. An error was recorded when subjects touched a button or knob out of sequence. For both building navigation and console operations, there were no reliable differences in transfer performance due to training condition.

CONSIDERING VR FOR TRAINING: A MEDIA SELECTION ISSUE

In the cases described above, transfer performance was equivalent after VR or CAI, and thus there would be no reason to select VR over CAI as an instructional medium for these tasks. To the contrary, for these tasks one arguably should select CAI because it is

Table 2. Errors and latencies in console performance after VR-based training or CAI

	Errors		Latency	
	VR	CAI	VR	CAI
Test 1	1.7	1.0	65.2	59.1
Test 2	1.1	0.6	48.0	37.5
Test 3	0.5	0.4	25.1	29.3
Average	1.1	0.7	46.1	42.0

cheaper to develop and deliver. It is important not to over-generalize from results such as these. These results are task-specific, and do not even remotely support the contention that CAI is generally superior to VR-based instruction.

Deciding whether to use VR as a feature of an instructional system should be treated as a media selection issue. This perspective has two important implications. The first implication is that VR is only one possible instructional medium among a variety of candidate media. Since VR is not likely to be the cheapest alternative, it is reasonable to ask if the added expense is justifiable. If convincing data are not available to support the assertion that VR is necessary or sufficient to achieve a desired transfer performance level on a given task, then the assertion should be considered suspect. Empirical evaluation of the assertion, using designs like the one described above, is required to resolve the question.

The second implication is that VR alone is merely a display medium for a simulation, which is not the same as an instructional system. The effectiveness of VR as a medium for instruction depends on the pedagogy that is applied in the context of the VR. For example, note in Table 1 the (non-significant) trend for the superiority of CAI over VR for transfer of building navigation skill. We conducted a follow-up experiment in which we modified the pedagogy for the VR condition, requiring subjects to move between bird's eye perspectives and immersed perspectives during training. This pedagogical change resulted in a reversal of the previous findings, producing a similar non-significant trend—but this time for the superiority of VR over CAI.

IMPLICATIONS FOR INSTRUCTIONAL ENGINEERING

Our research on VR as an instructional medium is part of a larger effort to develop a framework for Instructional Engineering. *Instructional Engineering* is the systematic development of principles for instruction—based on the empirical refinement of well-specified theories of learning and performance—and the application of these principles to the implementation of instructional materials. The TRAIN (Training Research for Automated Instruction - Regian, 1992) project at Armstrong Laboratory is developing a framework to support the principled implementation of instruction. TRAIN pursues Instructional Engineering through a systematic program of laboratory and field research using computerized tasks, VR, CAI, and Intelligent CAI as tools for the study of instruction and learning.

Figure 4 depicts the approach to Instructional Engineering that my colleagues and I are applying in the TRAIN project. Our primary goal is to derive principles for instruction of tasks performed by individuals. We began by postulating a broad, fully-specified, and well-supported theory of human learning. The theory includes a comprehensive taxonomy of the categories of knowledge and skill that support performance, and a complete theory of how these knowledge/skill types are acquired. Based very directly on that theory of learning, a general model of instruction was postulated. In an ongoing series of studies, components of the instructional model are systematically and rigorously tested, by evaluating their effectiveness in teaching diverse criterion tasks. The 14 synthetic tasks which make up the criterion task set were developed with the dual intentions to 1) systematically sample across the knowledge/skill taxonomy, and 2) provide representative laboratory models for important categories of real-world tasks. Converging evidence from this ongoing series of experiments, and from other published data on learning, is used to drive the iterative refinement of the learning theory, knowledge/skill taxonomy, instructional model, and criterion task set. This systematic approach to studying human learning and individually performed tasks has led to significantly enhanced instruction, more efficient

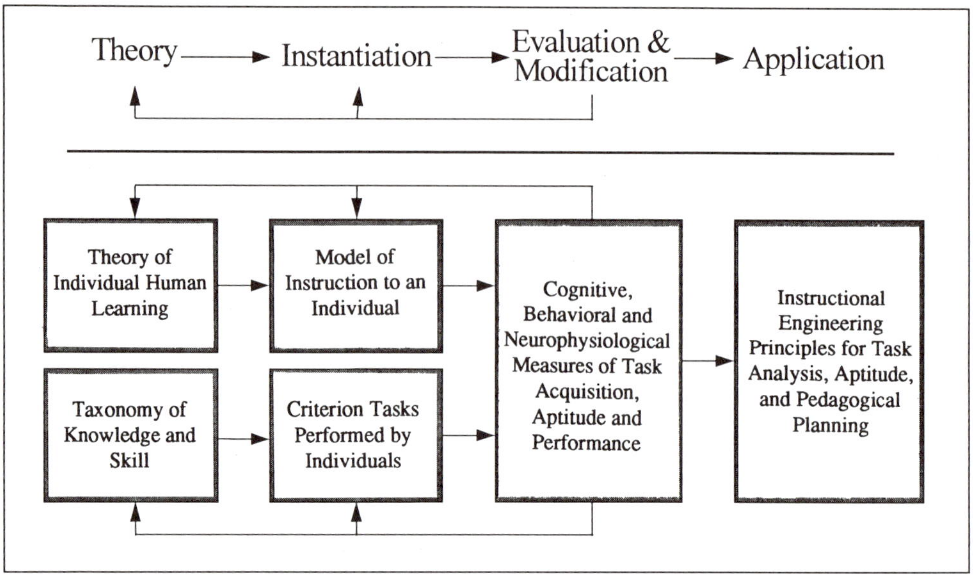

Figure 4. An approach to instructional engineering.

and reliable task analysis procedures, and better aptitude-based selection and prediction technologies.

The TRAIN approach to Instructional Engineering involves four inter-related components. These are 1) a Cognitive Taxonomy that allows decomposition of tasks in terms of requisite knowledge/skill types, 2) a General Learning Theory that specifies how those knowledge/skill types are acquired by humans, 3) a General Instructional Model that specifies how instruction of those knowledge/skill types can be optimized, and 4) a Criterion Task Set that provides domains in which to study instruction, learning, and performance. For purposes of this chapter, the Cognitive Taxonomy provides a framework for explaining why VR and CAI provided roughly equivalent instructional environments for the particular building navigation and console operations tasks described above.

The TRAIN Cognitive Taxonomy categorizes tasks in terms of representationally primitive knowledge and skill types that support human performance in task performance. The current taxonomy is limited to tasks performed by individuals and includes perceptual, cognitive, and motor task bases along one categorical dimension, and desired task performance levels along the other. Table 3 summarizes the current taxonomy, TRAIN Cognitive Taxonomy 2.0.

The purpose of this evolving taxonomy is to describe the performance bases of any individually-performed task at a level of analysis that supports 1) predictions about instructional approaches and media that will optimize task acquisition and transfer, and 2) generalizations about instructional approaches and media that will work across tasks. The approach reflects a generic information processing approach to psychology. All tasks involve one or more sequences of perception, cognition, and action. That is, the person must perceive the situation, decide what to do, and do it—with this sequence possibly repeating until the task is complete. At any stage in learning to perform the task, our focus is on those trainable factors which limit next-step performance improvements.

Table 3. Perceptual, cognitive, and motor bases of human task performance

	Perceptual basis	Cognitive basis		Motor basis
		Declarative	Procedural	
Basic Knowledge	Existing General Perceptual Skills	*Facts.* Propositions organized as Associations	*Rules:* Propositions organized as Productions	Existing General Motor Skills
Novice Performance	Emerging Task Specific Perceptual Skills	*Concepts:* Facts organized as Simple Abstractions	*Procedures:* Productions organized as Goal-Seeking Systems	Emerging Task Specific Motor Skills
Skilled Performance	Reliable Task Specific Perceptual Skills	*Schemata:* Facts/Concepts organized as Abstract Explanatory Systems	*Skills:* Production Systems sufficiently refined for Reliable Application	Reliable Task Specific Motor Skills
Expert Performance	Expert Task Specific Perceptual Skills	*Mental Models:* Facts/Concepts/Schemata organized as Autonomous Models	*Automatic Skills:* Production Systems fully refined for Autonomous Execution	Expert Task Specific Motor Skills

While nearly all tasks involve perceptual skills that must be available to reach expert performance, for training purposes we focus on special perceptual skills that are not acquired outside of training, or for any reason are not available to the individual. We conceptualize cognition as operations on an internal representation of task-relevant information. These representations may be first-order derivatives that maintain critical information about percepts, second-order representations that combine selected information from spatially or temporally distal percepts, or abstract representations with no perceptual basis. We focus on the type of representation that is developed in working memory and maintained over time, and the extent to which the operation draws on perceptually available information or information in long term memory. Every task requires some response, implying motor activity. We focus on those motor responses that are required to do the task but are not already available to the individual.

With regard to the tasks described in this chapter, building navigation and console operations, no task-specific perceptual or motor skills are required. That is, subjects come to the experiment already capable of creating cognitive maps from pictorial displays, walking through buildings, pushing buttons, and turning knobs. The two training approaches here applied are equivalent in the sense that they equivalently serve to create the new representations required for task performance. In the one case, that is the steps of a procedure and the layout of a console. In the other, it is the layout of a building. No special representations are required that are more readily created with one or the other of the two instructional approaches. While there are certainly other tasks for which the added expense of VR is worthwhile, the tasks described herein are not among them.

REFERENCES

Anderson, J.R. (1982). Acquisition of cognitive skill. *Psychological Review, 89*, 369–406.

Holmes, W.M. (1991). Intelligent tutoring systems for critical skills development in a real-time environment. *Proceedings 1991 Conference on Intelligent Computer-Aided Training.*

Kozak, J.J., Hancock, P.A., Arthur, E., and Chrysler, S. (1993). Transfer of training from virtual reality. *Ergonomics, 36*, 777–784.

Kreuger, M. (1991). *Artificial Reality II.* Reading, MA: Addison Wesley.

Regian, J.W. (1986). An assessment procedure for configurational knowledge of large-scale space. Unpublished doctoral dissertation, University of California, Santa Barbara.

Regian, J. W., Shebilske, W., and Monk, J. (1992). A preliminary empirical evaluation of virtual reality as an instructional medium for visual-spatial tasks. *Journal of Communication, 42* (4), 136–149.

Regian, J. W., & Yadrick, R. (1994). Assessment of configurational knowledge of naturally and artificially acquired large-scale space. *Journal of Environmental Psychology, 14*, 211–223.

Rheingold, H. (1991). *Virtual Reality.* New York: Summit Books.

4

COLLECTIVE TRAINING IN VIRTUAL ENVIRONMENTS

Exploring Performance Requirements for Dismounted Soldier Simulation

Stephen L. Goldberg and Bruce W. Knerr

U.S. Army Research Institute
Simulator Systems Research Unit
Orlando, Florida

Tactical training of combat units at battalion level and below has traditionally taken place primarily in the field. Field training exercises have allowed platoons, companies and battalions to use their equipment to practice maneuver and command and control skills. In the 1970's the limitations of field training were beginning to become apparent. As the range of weapons increased, land areas once capable of supporting exercises involving 20,000 soldiers could no longer support even battalion size units. Safety and environmental issues were restricting exercise realism, and local training areas lacked a way to evaluate exercise outcomes (Chapman, 1991). In addition, the costs associated with field training were increasing dramatically, while overall defense budgets were beginning to fall.

During the late 1970's and early 80's developments in training technology began to change the way the Army conducted collective training. Development of realistic engagement simulation technologies (Sulzen, 1987), such as the Multiple Integrated Laser Engagement System (MILES) and creation of a National Training Center (NTC) in the California desert resulted in a new model for collective training (Gorman, 1977). The MILES system could be appended to individual weapons, tanks and aircraft. It allowed for realistic weapons play that could be objectively scored. The NTC challenged units with a competent opposing force, under conditions which allowed for relatively unrestricted free play. The NTC's instrumentation system combined a vehicle tracking system with MILES weapons outcome data. It allowed performance on the NTC's simulated battlefield to be measured and accurate feedback provided to the soldiers and unit leaders. Collective tasks could now be trained and evaluated using objective process and outcome data. Rotations of battalion size units to the NTC provided them a capstone training event. The emphasis was no longer on simply spending time in the field but on training specific collective tasks, whose performance could be measured.

Virtual Reality, Training's Future? edited by Seidel and Chatelier
Plenum Press, New York, 1997

SIMULATION AND ARMY COLLECTIVE TRAINING

At the same time the NTC was starting to take shape, the Army was beginning to field simulators in significant numbers. The Unit Conduct of Fire Trainer (UCOFT) was fielded in 1985 as a means to train tank gunnery skills. The introduction of this device was significant in that Armor units had to trade off tank main gun ammunition from their yearly training allotment to pay for the UCOFT. The UCOFT started a trend toward focusing Army training on simulation as a primary training tool.

Simulation Networking (SIMNET)

The maturing of computer networking and graphics technology allowed simulator applications to expand from individual skills training to unit training. Simulation Networking (SIMNET) was a Defense Advanced Research Projects Agency (DARPA) program begun in 1983. It demonstrated the capability of networked computer systems to create a virtual battlefield on which meaningful collective training could be accomplished (Alluisi, 1991). The SIMNET network consists of manned simulators, emulators of combat functions (resupply or fire support), and semi-automated computer generated forces (SAF) used as opposing and adjacent friendly forces.

SIMNET introduced a number of new concepts that have become the defining characteristics of a new class of simulations known collectively as Distributed Interactive Simulations (DIS)(Thorpe, 1987). SIMNET has no central computer. Computing power is distributed across the network with each manned simulator and SAF station maintaining its own knowledge of the state of the virtual environment. Information is shipped around the network in data packets which are issued by entities on the network either periodically or when something happens to change the state of the simulated vehicle (entity) issuing the packet. Change of state packets are generated when vehicles begin to move or fire their weapons. Vehicle appearance packets describing how a vehicle should look are the type of packets that would be generated periodically whether or not anything else happens. Other simulators on the network receive the packets and use them to update their representation of the virtual world. The virtual environment on which the entities operate is a terrain data base which could either be non-geospecific or representative of any location in world. In SIMNET it is always high noon on a sunny day. As SIMNET matured the capability to collect network data for performance measurement and after action review purposes has also been developed (Meliza et. al., 1992). The result is a collective training experience that can have many of the same characteristics as training at the National Training Center.

SIMNET was developed by DARPA as a research instrument to demonstrate simulator networking technology. It did not go through the Army's normal procurement process. It was not designed to meet a recognized Army training requirement and it was not built with sufficient documentation or consideration for life cycle support issues. There were a number of areas in which the Army found SIMNET to be deficient.

Close Combat Tactical Trainer (CCTT)

The Close Combat Tactical Trainer (CCTT) is the Army's follow-on system to improve on SIMNET. CCTT has many of the same basic characteristics of SIMNET but its capabilities have been enhanced to overcome many of the problems identified in SIMNET (Goldberg et al., 1995). The manned simulators are higher fidelity than SIMNET simulators. The inside of a CCTT M1A1 tank simulator has more of the feel and look of a real tank. CCTT SAF are based on a thorough task analysis and are more capable than the SAF used in SIMNET. CCTT's graphics capabilities far surpass SIMNET's. CCTT's virtual battlefield looks much more realistic. CCTT has the capability to represent any time of day or night, and simulate a variety of weather, haze and smoke conditions. Initial reactions to CCTT during its developmental User Evaluations have been generally quite favorable (Schwab, 1995).

CCTT will begin to be fielded in early 1997. It will provide a relatively inexpensive means for mechanized units to conduct tactical collective training at the company and platoon level. CCTT still can be improved. For example, units training in CCTT cannot dig defensive positions or tank ditches in the terrain data base. Improvements are also needed in the design of CCTT's After Action Review System. Perhaps the largest single problem with both CCTT and SIMNET is their inability to effectively represent the performance of dismounted soldiers on the virtual battlefield. Both CCTT and SIMNET are vehicle dominated systems that at best do a poor job of representing the performance of dismounted infantry and other soldiers on foot.

Representing Dismounted Soldiers in Virtual Simulations

Networked combined arms simulators have been designed to train combined arms teams made up primarily of armored vehicles and helicopters. SIMNET has no fielded capability for representing dismounted soldiers. At least two attempts were made to integrate dismounted soldiers into SIMNET. Researchers at Bolt, Baranek and Newman created a dismounted infantry work station which proved clumsy to operate. An experimental version of a dismounted soldier SAF was developed by the Institute for Simulation and Training (Franceschini et al. 1993). Neither system was put into general use.

The less than adequate attempts at representing dismounted soldiers in virtual simulations have been undertaken to make the battlefield more realistic for the mounted combatants, not to train the dismounted combatants. In this regard they have been successful. Infantry serve to slow down armored vehicles by causing them to take care in not exposing themselves to dismounted anti-tank weapon systems. The introduction of IST's dismounted infantry SAF to SIMNET exercises at Ft. Benning, Georgia had the effect of slowing down the pace of the exercise dramatically (Francheschini and Petty, 1994).

CCTT relies on a dismounted infantry work station to allow fire team leaders to maneuver fire teams after they dismount from Bradley fighting vehicles. The leader sits before a bank of three monitors and controls his fire team through the use of a complicated joy stick that takes considerable training to operate. Infantry School proponent users have not been satisfied with this approach (Reiss, 1995) and other possibilities for controlling dismounted soldiers are being investigated.

THE NEED FOR A DISMOUNTED COMBATANT SIMULATION CAPABILITY

The need for a dismounted combatant simulation capability has been recognized for a number of years (TRADOC Training Technology Conference, 1989). General Paul Gorman has been an early and persistent proponent for development of this capability. In 1990 he wrote an influential paper which called for development of an individual portal or

I-Port into virtual environments. He felt that the I-Port would have use not only to help train Infantry soldiers and units, but to allow for virtual prototyping of new dismounted soldier equipment concepts (Gorman, 1990). As a result of Gorman's efforts DARPA sponsored a meeting at Snowbird, Utah in September, 1990 to address the topic of using virtual environments to evaluate individual protection concepts. The Snowbird meeting brought together representatives of the user communities and the scientists and engineers who could develop I-Port. Requirements for I-Port for training, mission rehearsal, concept development and virtual prototyping applications were discussed. Attendees felt that research funding and programs resulting in the development of I-Port would be an outcome of the meeting. Unfortunately, Desert Storm took precedence and a concerted effort toward development of I-Port did not occur in the early 1990's.

Dismounted Soldier Research Agenda

The U.S. Army Research Institute (ARI) for the Behavioral and Social Sciences had representatives at the Snowbird meeting. ARI, the Army's behavioral science laboratory, recognized that developing individual combatant simulations would require better understanding of a number of perceptual, human performance, and training issues. In 1991, ARI launched an individual combatant simulation research program with the following goals: identify requirements for individual soldier and leader accomplishments of collective tasks; determine the necessary characteristics of the simulation technology needed to produce a individual combatant simulation system; and evaluate the capability of such systems to train relevant tasks and have that training transfer to performance in the real world.

Just as tank crews in SIMNET and CCTT are operating in a crew station that is realistic and immersive, ARI researchers felt that dismounted soldiers also needed to be immersed in the virtual environment, not just to observe it from the windows of a workstation. This established the following simulation requirements: free motion of the soldier's eyepoint within the space; three-dimensional, real-time interactive graphics, with stereopsis if needed; multiple senses beyond visual (e.g., audition, touch); direct manipulation of objects; and multiple interacting, mutually visible, humans. Virtual Reality (VR) technology can provide those capabilities. Characteristics of VR technology include: visual and auditory displays, sensing head and body position and orientation, speech recognition, tactile and force feedback displays, representation of whole body movement, and biomechanical articulation of dismounted soldier models (Levison and Pew, 1993).

Development of VR technologies is outside the scope of ARI's mission. The ARI research program has rather focused on evaluating the capabilities of off-the-shelf hardware and software to produce effective immersive environments that are capable of simulating dismounted combatant tasks. Research has been aimed at addressing questions such as:

- Are some types of visual displays and controls better suited for training and task performance than others?
- Does visual immersion improve learning of configuration, locations of objects, and routes through the environment?
- Which scene details are most important for task performance and transfer of training?
- Does immersion in VE cause disorienting side-effects? If so, how can they be reduced?

THE VIRTUAL ENVIRONMENTS RESEARCH LABORATORY

ARI established a Virtual Environment Research Laboratory in 1992 in order to investigate the above and related questions. The laboratory is located at the University of Central Florida, Institute for Simulation and Training (IST). ARI research psychologists work cooperatively with IST computer scientists and engineers. Research Psychologists are primarily responsible for design of experiments, specification of required environments, running research subjects, analyzing data and reporting results. IST's computer scientists and engineers have created the required environments, developed software needed to capture data, and configured hardware to meet the needs of the particular experiment.

The research has been approached in a sequential fashion beginning with a systematic review of dismounted soldier task requirements (Jacobs, et al., 1994) and an analysis of their supportability in VR. A review of previous research was conducted to identify work in the area training and performance in virtual environments. The initial review found only one previous article by Regian, Shebilske, & Monk (1992) which addressed the use of virtual environments for training. There was, of course, extensive literature in many of the perceptual and learning areas we wished to explore in a virtual environments context.

The Virtual Environments Performance Assessment Battery

ARI's experimental program began with development of a Virtual Environments Performance Assessment Battery (VEPAB) (Lampton, et al., 1994). The VEPAB consists of a set of simple tasks and performance measures developed to assess human performance and the effects of immersion in the virtual environment as a function of training and system characteristics. The battery serves several functions. First, the tasks provide a means to bring research participants to a basic level of proficiency in prerequisite virtual environment skill (e.g., locomotion, manipulating objects). Research participants can learn to walk through virtual environments using a VEPAB task prior to participating in an experiment that might use a more complex virtual environment. Second, the tasks can be used as "behavioral benchmarks" for interface hardware and software comparisons, to determine the effects of system changes (display resolution, update rate) on task performance. Third, task performance can provide statistical controls for future research. Finally, they provide a baseline for investigating side effects, such as simulator sickness.

The tasks were chosen because they are components of military tasks that dismounted soldiers would perform in virtual environments. The VEPAB tasks, however, require no military training or experience. This permitted ARI to use college students as research participants. Five task categories were derived from the simple concept that soldiers move, communicate, and employ weapons: vision, locomotion, manipulation, reaction time, and tracking. The VEPAB tasks are listed by category in Table 1.

Four experiments have used all or some of the VEPAB tasks. The first experiment examined the sensitivity of task performance to different control devices. A major objective was to determine the sensitivity of the tasks and measures to differing methods of interacting with virtual environments. The experiment compared research participants ability to move and manipulate objects with either a space-ball or joy stick after a limited amount of practice. The second experiment used a subset of the tasks to examine the effects of extended practice on performance. In order for the tasks to be useful they also had to show a learning effect with practice. A third experiment investigated the impact of stereoscope versus monoscopic visual displays on performance of VEPAB tasks. Stereoscope displays are a cost driver in that they require twice the compute power of monoscopic displays. Demonstrating equivalent performance with either display type

Table 1. Virtual environment assessment battery tasks

Vision	Manipulation	Tracking	Locomotion	Reaction Time
Acuity	Slide	Head Control, Stationary Target	Corridor	Simple
Color	Dial	Head Control, Moving Target	Back-up	Complex
Distance	Bins	Device Control, Stationary Target	Turns	
Search		Device Control, Moving Target	Figure 8	
			Doorways	
			Windows	
			Elevator	

would allow VR systems to be developed with lower end graphics capability. The fourth experiment compared performance on VEPAB tasks using a variety of visual display hardware (monitor, low-end helmet mounted display, and high resolution BOOM display). The purpose of this experiment was to baseline performance on various display devices for the tasks and to see if performance varied as a function of task type. All the experiments also permitted collection of data on the frequency and severity of simulator sickness experienced while in the virtual environment.

The results of the first three experiments have been documented in a variety of ARI reports, conference papers and journal articles: the initial assessments of the VEPAB and comparison of control devices in Lampton, Knerr, Goldberg, Bliss, Moshell, and Blau, (1994, 1995); the effects of extended practice in Knerr, Goldberg, Lampton, Witmer, & Bliss, (1994); and the comparison of monoscopic and stereoscopic HMDs in Singer, Ehrlich, Cinq-Mars, and Pappin (in preparation). The documentation of the fourth is still underway. In general, the results of these experiments indicate the following: with some exceptions, the VEPAB tasks have an adequate reliability and the appropriate level of difficulty for making the kinds of comparisons in which we are interested. For the types of systems, tasks, and participants we employ, most tasks are performed better with a joystick than with a spaceball. This better performance persists even after extensive practice. The use of stereopsis in HMDs does not enhance performance significantly when the object being viewed is farther than five feet away (see figure 1).

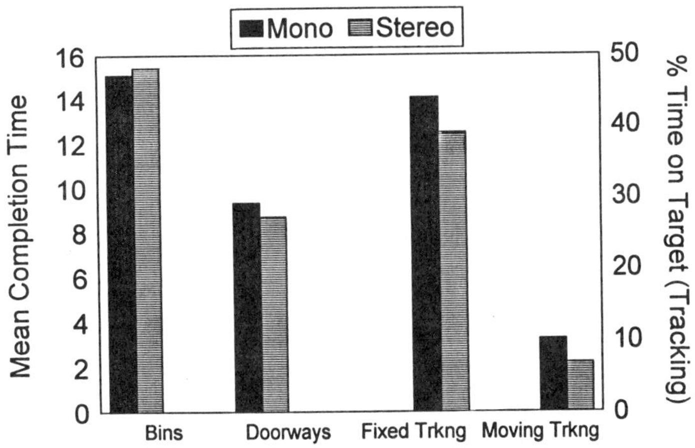

Figure 1. Performance with monoscopic and stereoscopic displays.

Spatial Knowledge Acquisition

An experiment was then conducted to test the relative effectiveness of VE for training and transfer of spatial knowledge as it relates to wayfinding in large buildings. Wayfinding or navigation in a complex building may be especially relevant to a hostage rescue situation or other missions performed by special operations forces.

For this experiment (Witmer, Bailey, & Knerr, 1995), a highly accurate computer model of a large office building was constructed. Sixty college students who had no previous exposure to the building first studied route directions and photographs of landmarks, either with or without a map, then were assigned to one of three rehearsal groups. These were: a VE group that rehearsed in the building model; a building rehearsal group that rehearsed in the actual building; and a symbolic rehearsal group that relied on verbal rehearsal of the route directions. The VE group viewed the building through a head-tracked boom-mounted stereoscopic display. Subjects were then tested for transfer of training in the actual building. Both time to complete the route and number of wrong turns during the transfer test were assessed. As shown in figure 2, students trained in the building made fewer wrong turns and travelled less distance than did students who were trained in the virtual environment (VE). VE students, in turn, made fewer wrong turns and took less time to traverse the route than did subjects who were trained symbolically.

The results suggest that individuals can learn how to navigate through real world places by training in a virtual environment. While those who rehearsed in the computer building model were significantly slower and made more errors than the group that rehearsed in the actual building the differences in their transfer performance where small enough that they may have no practical importance. In addition, the building model trained group did learn routes much better than those who verbally rehearsed route directions, even for subjects who had previously studied a map.

The effectiveness of the building model was probably limited by characteristics of the display device and by the interface that controlled movement. Research subjects in the

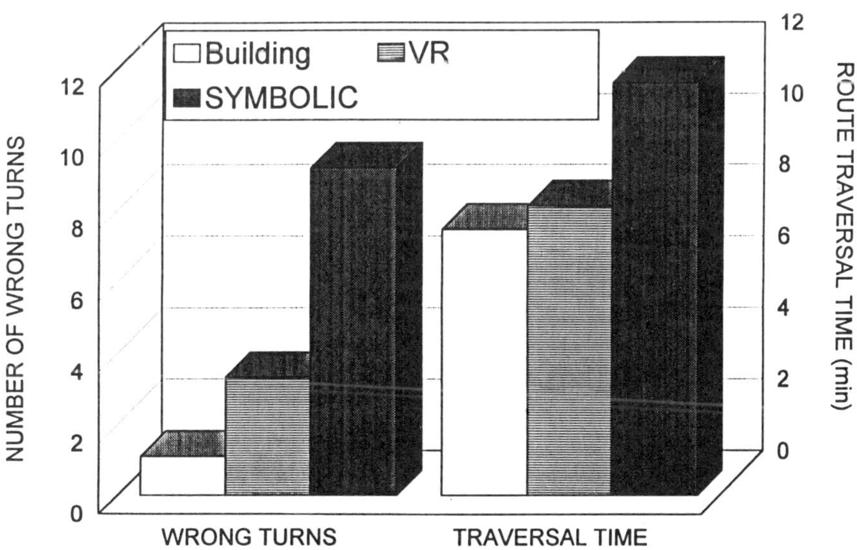

Figure 2. Performance in transfer test by training group.

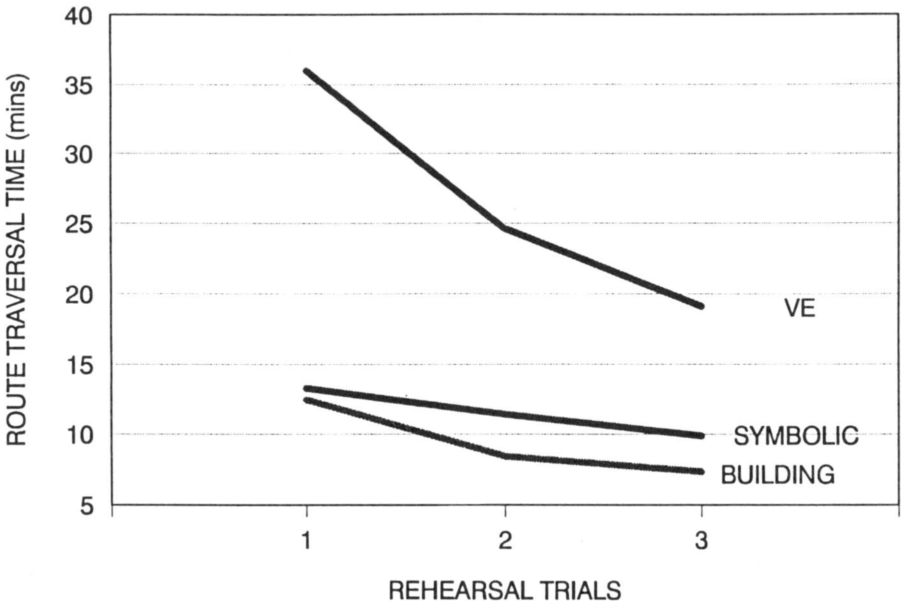

Figure 3. Rehearsal time by training method.

virtual building rehearsal group had to not only learn the route they also had to learn to use the virtual environment interface equipment. Figure 3 compares rehearsal times for the three rehearsal conditions over three trials. The virtual rehearsals took longer than the other rehearsal methods, but the rehearsal times improved dramatically over the three trials indicating that the subjects in this group were also improving their virtual environment maneuvering skills. As the quality of VE control and display devices improve and become more transparent to the user, the effectiveness of VE as a training medium could equal or surpass real world environments for training some real world tasks.

Acquiring Spatial Knowledge in Outdoor Environments

In our most recent experiment, we have attempted to extend the spatial knowledge acquisition research from the interiors of buildings to exterior terrain. Two terrain data bases were built to represent terrain like that in and around Fort Benning, Georgia. The experiment conducted using these environments was designed to investigate tasks which include searching for the enemy, identifying unit positions for defense and offense, and identifying safe or dangerous positions and routes. A common ability underlying all of these activities is the spatial knowledge of the operational terrain possessed by the soldier.

Subjects were required to orient, move through the environment, and perform cognitive soldier-like tasks, e.g. identify threat areas, while in one of two VE configurations (High-VE of Low-VE) or in a control (map) condition. In the High VE condition, subjects viewed the terrain through a head-tracked HMD and controlled their movement by walking on a treadmill. In the Low -VE condition, subjects used the same HMD but controlled both their direction of view and movement with a joystick. Subjects in the control condition performed the same tasks while using topographical maps.

Preliminary analyses of landmark identification show that the VE subjects were significantly better than the Map trained subjects, and that this difference lies primarily between the High-VE condition and the Map condition.

Simulator Sickness in Virtual Environments

A threat to the successful use of VE technology is that some users of VE systems suffer unwanted side effects and aftereffects similar to, but not limited to, symptoms of motion sickness. These effects may degrade training effectiveness and jeopardize user safety and well-being. We have noted the occurrence of these symptoms in all of the experiments we have conducted to date. During each experiment we were careful to record the incidence and severity of symptoms. We administered a 16 item questionnaire (Kennedy, et al., 1993) that addressed symptoms related to nausea, eye strain, and dizziness. Significant variation was observed across individuals. In each experiment some users, between 4 and 16%, experienced discomfort to the extent that we terminated their participation. Figure 4 shows the SSQ scores for the experiments conducted in the Virtual Environments Research Lab.

Most participants enjoyed the VE experiments but reported some level of discomfort. While most people do not experience serious symptoms, as reported above a number of individuals do become uncomfortable enough that they cannot continue. The causes of the problem (Kolasinski, 1995) are not simple and they may not be completely eradicated by improvements in equipment. Our findings indicate that sickness resulting from VE immersion is a potentially serious complication in using the technology for training.

CONCLUSIONS

To date the military has focused on the use of virtual environments to train mechanized units using virtual environments. This has been due to the relative ease of building

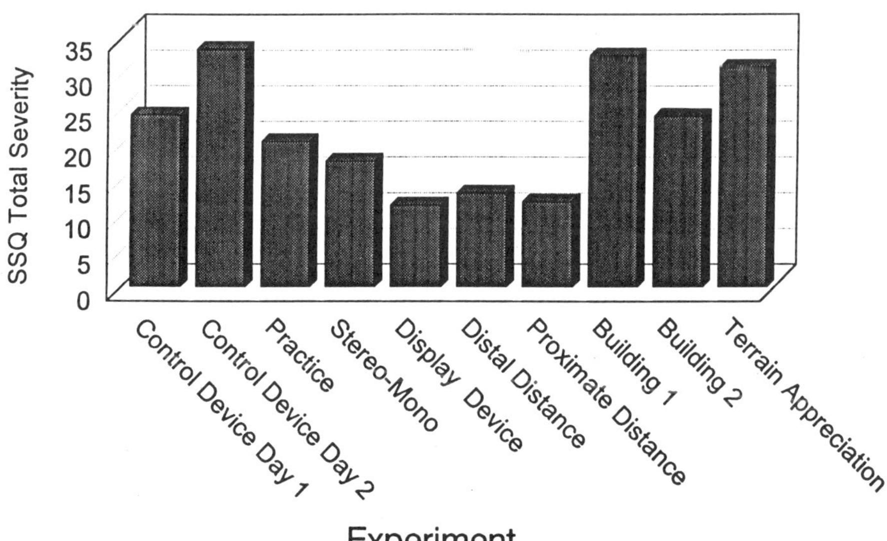

Figure 4. Stimulator sickness questionnaire total severity scores by experiment.

simulators and representing the performance of vehicles in virtual simulations. The need for a capability to include dismounted soldiers' performance has been recognized by leaders of the infantry and special operations forces. The research presented here represents some initial attempts to explore the behavioral requirements for simulating dismounted soldiers performance in virtual environments. In designing our research program we assumed that the purpose of training dismounted soldiers would be to teach them to react properly to situations and make leadership decisions that would lead to positive outcomes. We believed that training should not emphasize the actual physical performance of tasks. Our research to date has resulted in three major conclusions.

First, the characteristics of the student interface with the VE can make an important difference in performance and learning. Affordable VE systems do not yet provide a "natural" interface. The visual systems have low resolution, limited fields of view, or both. Locomotion is usually difficult, as evidenced by the frequency with which participants collide with walls and other objects. Our research has begun to suggest design tradeoff to overcome these limitations, such as using stereoscopic displays only when short distances must be perceived accurately, and high resolution monoscopic displays when recognition of distant objects is required. Designing a cost-effective VE training system requires a careful analysis of what is to be trained, and the resulting stimuli to and response from the trainee.

Second, VE can be an effective training medium. Even with simple training strategies, our subjects improved their performance both simple and complex tasks with practice in VE. Moreover, they were able to transfer what they had learned from the VE to the real world.

Third, simulator sickness can be a problem for training in VE, but does not seem to be an insurmountable one. Examination of our simulator sickness data across experiments suggests that long sessions in VE and frequent self motion are characteristic of research conditions that have caused the most discomfort. This is consistent with previous research (Kolasinski, 1995). Reasonable precautions, including careful monitoring of participants, and initial short training sessions having low nauseogenic characteristics, should preclude serious disturbances.

REFERENCES

Alluisi, E.A. (1991). The development of technology for Collective training: SIMNET, A case history. *HumanFactors*, 33(3), 343–362.

Chapman, Anne W. (1991). *The Army's Training Revolution, 1973–1990: An Overview* (Historical Study Series). Ft. Monroe, VA: U.S. Army Training and Doctrine Command.

Franceschini, R.W., Parra, F.R., Watkins, J.E., Nanda, S., & Petty, M.D. (1993). *SAFDI User's Guide* (IST Technical Report 92–23) Orlando, FL: University of Central Florida, Institute for Simulation and Training.

Franceschini, R.W. & Petty, M.D. (1994). *Dismounted infantry in DIS-style scenarios: A SAFDI project overview.* In proceedings fo the Fourth CGF&BR Conference, pp 155–167.

Goldberg, S.L., Mastaglio, T.W., and Johnson, W.R. (1995). Training in the Close Combat Tactical Trainer. *Learning without Boundries: Technology to Support Distance/Distributed Learning*, Edited by Seidel, R.J. and Chatelier, P.R., Plenum Press, New York, pp 119–133.

Gorman, P.F. (1977). *Toward National Training Centers for the U.S. Army* (TRADOC Concept Papers). Ft Monroe, VA: U.S. Army Training and Doctrine Command.

Gorman, P.F. (1990). *Supertroop via I-Port: Distributed Simulation Technology for Combat Development and Training Development* (IDA Paper P-2374). Alexandria, VA: Institute for Defense Analysis.

Jacobs, R.S., Crooks, W.H., Crooks, J.R., Colburn, E., Fraser, R.E., Gorman, P.F., Madden, J.L., Furness, T.A., & Tice, S.E. (1994). *Behavioral Requirements for Training and Rehearsal in Virtual Environments* (ARI

Technical Report 1011). Alexandria, VA: U.S. Army Research Institute for the Behavioral and Social Sciences.

Kennedy, R.S., Lane, N.E., Berbaum, K.S., & Lillienthal, M.G. (1993). A simulator sickness questionnaire (SSQ): A new method for quantifying simulator sickness. *International Journal of Aviation Psychology, 3*(3), 203–220.

Knerr, B. W., Goldberg, S. L., Lampton, D. R., Witmer, B. G., Bliss, J. P., Moshell, J. M., & Blau, B. S. (1994). Research in the use of virtual environment technology to train dismounted soldiers. *Journal of Interactive Instruction Development, 6*(4), 9–20.

Kolasinski, E.M. (1995). *Simulator sickness in virtual environments* (ARI Technical Report 1027). Alexandria, VA: U.S. Army Research Institute for the Behavioral and Social Sciences.

Lampton, D.R., Knerr, B.W., Goldberg, S.L., Bliss, J. P., Moshell, J.M., & Blau, B.S. (1994). The Virtual Environments Performance Assessment Battery (VEPAB):Development and Evaluation. *Presence, 3*, 2.

Lampton, D. R., Knerr, B. W., Goldberg, S. L.,

Bliss, J. P., Moshell, J. M., & Blau, B. S. (1995). *The virtual environment performance assessment battery (VEPAB): Development and evaluation* (ARI Technical Report 1029). Alexandria, VA: U.S. Army Research Institute for the Behavioral and Social Sciences.

Levison, W.H. & Pew, R.W. (1993). *Use of Virtual Environment Technology for Individual Combat Simulation* (ARI Technical Report 971). Alexandria, VA: U.S. Army Research Institute for the Behavioral and Social Sciences.

Meliza, L.L., Tan, S.C., White, S., Gross, W., & McMell, K. (1992). *SIMNET Unit Performance Assessment System (UPAS) User's Guide* (ARI Research Product 92–0 Alexandria, VA: U.S. Army Research Institute for the Behavioral and Social Sciences.

Regian, J.W., Shebilske, W.L., & Monk, J.M. (1992). Virtual Reality: An instructional medium for visual-spatial tasks. *Journal of Communication, 42*(4), 136–149.

Reiss, David (1995) Personal communication, August, 1995.

Singer, M.S., Ehrlich, J., Cinq-Mars, S., & Pappin, J. (in preparation). *Task Performance in Virual Environments: Stereoscopic vs. Monoscopic Displays and Head-Coupling* (ARI Technical Report). Alexandria, VA: U.S. Army Research Institute for the Behavioral and Social Sciences.

Schwab, J. (1995) Personal Communication.

Sulzen, R. (1987) Winning the Airland Battle with Tactical Engagement Simulation. *Military Review*, May, pp. 8–19.

Thorpe, J.A. (1987). *The New Technology of Large Scale Simulator Networking: Implications for Mastering theArt of Warfighting.* In the Proceedings of the 9th Interservice Insustry Training System Conference (pp 492–501). Washington, D.C.: American Defense Preparedness Association, November 1987.

U.S. Army Training and Doctrine Command (1989) Training Technology Conference. Ft. Monroe, VA.

Witmer, B.G., Bailey, J.H., & Knerr, B.W.(1995). *Training Dismounted Soldiers in Virtual Environments: Route Learning and Transfer* (ARI Technical Report). Alexandria, VA: U.S. Army Research Institute for the Behavioral and Social Sciences.

5

ENHANCING THE VIRTUAL TRAINING TOOL

Introducing Artificial Touch And Smell

Gaetano Canepa*

Centro "E. Piaggio", Università di Pisa
Via Diotisalvi n. 2, Pisa, Italy
e-mail gaetano@pimac2.iet.unipi.it

ABSTRACT

This paper focuses on some of the possible applications of smell and touch to virtual reality training tools. In the first part the author will specify the characteristics and the problems of realizing artificial smell and touch systems. After, he will introduce some studies where he or the research centers where he works are directly involved. Most of the studies are just at the beginning.

1.0 INTRODUCTION

Virtual reality (VR) and teleoperation need advanced sensors and sense-reflecting devices (SRD). Some already well established technologies are binocular camera and stereo microphones (the sensors), 3D head-mounted-display and stereo headphone (the SRD). An important number of research groups works in the field, producing and investigating advanced technologies and software tools dealing with vision and hearing senses only (see [11] for a good panorama of actual commercial products and on going research).

However, psychologists have demonstrated that human decisions and comportment are influenced by all five senses: touch, smell and taste are thus important conscious and uncon-

---

* The author worked in two laboratories specialized in sensing and sense-actuation. One is the Biorobotics Laboratory at McGill University (Canada), specialized in force reflection and teleoperation researches. The other, where he works now, is the Centro "E. Piaggio" at Università di Pisa (Italy), specialized in transduction principles and technologies, and in robotics. This laboratory is investigating about touch and smell since 15 years while studying robot locomotion and medical devices.

For a review about haptic interfaces problems, characteristics, and state of the art see [11]. The same reference point out the ideal specification of kinesthetic and tactile interfaces.

See [11] for more information.

scious factors determining human behavior. If during a skillful work an operator usually does not taste anything, he surely touches something and can be influenced and helped by odors of the environment. In spite of the importance of senses like smell and touch, there still are not many research efforts and funding consecrated to them. Explanation could be found in the complexity and, thus, the costs of smell and touch research: as a matter of fact, the study of touch and smell represents a big research challenge. Touch, unlike vision and hearing, is a distributed sensitive system: therefore the virtual sense needs a distributed sensor and actuator to be supplied. Problems regarding smell have a different nature because nose is a "concentrated" sense. However, both sensing and actuation of smell are hard to realize because we have to deal with the organic nature of odors. Another important fact concerning lack of funds allocated for touch and smell research is that they are still not deeply used in the entertainment sector which is an important investor in virtual reality field.

The most used words speaking about VR are transparent, immersion, real, augmented reality etc. A number of VR researchers is investigating about the creation or the replacing of a completely immersive (and very sofisticated) interfaces. As a matter of fact, it is important, for someone working on VR project, to decide if "the technology must adapt to the operator or the operator adapt to the technology" [31]. A first hurried answer, whose reasoning is very logical, is that the technology must adapt itself to the operator [31]. However, there are a quantity of examples where human beings demonstrated a good degree of adaptation to technology. Driving a car, sailing a sailboat, flying with an helicopter, playing Donkey-Kong, playing a piano are all system having interfaces, absolutely not transparent, that man can use in a relatively simple and efficient way: at least better than a computer or a robot can actually do! Because of this argument our philosophy, when we deal with VR, is that interfaces should get command in an intuitive way (if possible), be easy to use (as much as possible), give the more information is possible but ... only as much is possible and useful!

The approach to VR that derive from this philosophy focuses a part of the energy on training and training tools, necessary to adapt the interfaces to man. Such training tools should try to emulate the real tool or instrumentation in both tactile, visual, hearing, and smelling side to avoid excessive gap between training and working phases. In this connection, experiments in psychology find evidence about the effect of context in memory and learning process [32]. Smell and touch experience (together with sound and visual happenings) may act as important source of training support. Evidence in VR training (reported in this book also) shows the effectiveness of this training method: passing from VR environment to real task is followed by a tangible improvement in performances. Learning transfer is roughly the same between real and VR console. It is a little bit like when passing from driving a small car to a Ferrari: it will be different but the preceding training will avoid many of the eventual problems!

As we will see in the following, it is reasonable to think that many of these new generation training tools will run on a PC in a few year. Moreover, with the development of international networks, it is also conceivable the possibility of groups of students working together, contemporary, in a virtual environment while being in different place.

2.0 SENSING AND ACTUATING TOUCH

The perception of the object is fundamental for grasping and manipulating it in a synthetic environment (SE) or in a teleoperation station. Perception and manipulation of a synthetic material are important in some tasks like medical training (surgical and generic training), molecular modeling, etc. Moreover, as for smell, it may be very useful to enhance the impression of reality of any synthetic environment.

Touch sensibility may be divided into cutaneous and kinesthetic sensibility. Cutaneous sensibility is related with fine form, slippage, pain, and temperature detection while kinesthetic sensibility is related to the perception of body segment rigidity, position, and movements. The union of cutaneous and kinesthetic sensibility is referred to as haptic sensibility. In connection with the twofold nature of the sense of touch also haptic actuation can be divided into a cutaneous and kinesthetic part. From a technical point of view, the most important property of the sense of touch is its distributed characteristic: both cutaneous and kinesthetic sensibilities need distributed sensing and actuating and this pose important problem to the engineer.

Neural receptors pathways, that are responsible for touch sensibility, are yet not completely understood. Considering that electronic neural interfaces are still too young and invasive, conveying force and displacement sensation to the nervous system of the operator may be made only by means of a mechanical system.

There are some things to keep in mind about haptic interfaces. First, they cannot be performed without sensing [10]. Second, it is necessary to choose between a fixed haptic system, with high power but low workspace, and a portable one that make necessary to carry around the actuators, usually heavy and cumbersome. Finally, the design of haptic interface requires:

- a knowledge of the human operator model, with a particular concern about the human resolution of haptic "images", in term of perception of the viscoelastic properties of the manipulandum, and of the maximum accuracy obtainable from a human operator (see for example [14,19–21]);
- a knowledge of human kinematics (in particular hand and limb kinematics) [26] and an optimal mapping of body position into a virtual environment or into a robot configuration [27].

The human operator model may be useful to implement adequate control strategies for the interface [21].

Haptic interfaces still mainly fall into the category of ground based devices, such as joystick, working both as sensor for action command and as force feedback. This group of devices still not includes advanced tool-handle system: the development of such kind of interfaces is one of the main experimental thrust in the SE field due to the need of control tools for telerobotics and Virtual World navigation and interaction.

A number of sensorized gloves are actually sold to detect the operator hand configuration enhancing the ability of the operator to give orders. This kind of gloves still do not perceive any tactile information and are not able to apply any active force to the hand. Prototypes of master gloves (able to apply force feedback to the operator) are being studied by some scientists: Burdea [3] introduced a very simple 3 degrees of freedom active glove, based on pneumatic actuators, that did not undergo further and necessary improvements; Bergamasco et al. [1] proposed a more sophisticated portable arm and hand master (in conjunction with a portable arm master) that is assembled using light materials and is tendon-driven. At present, it is the most sophisticated haptic device under study.

As regards advanced force reflecting masters (along with the Bergamasco arm) some interfaces are actually under study or in commerce:

- a high performance hand controller, developed at UBC University by taking advantage of a magnetic-levitated wrist [28]. Because of its low inertia the master is able to perceive the texture of manipulated material

Figure 1. The Dexterous Teleoperation System Master and Slave (presently sold by Sarcos Inc.). On the picture the author is teleoperating the slave robot using the master arm.

- a Dexterous Teleoperation Master System actually sold by Sarcos Inc.: it is a ground based exoskeleton (see Figure 1) attachable to the human arm and able to perceive its position and to apply force, thanks to high performance hydraulic actuators
- a ground based system built by Hunter et al. (at McGill University) to meet two different requirements: high bandwidth (more than 1kHz) and high accuracy (some nanometers): they would like to apply this device to perform teleoperated eye surgery [16].

Nature's actuators and sensing systems demonstrated wonderful design properties. Muscles, the actuators, have high specific power, high efficiency, high inclination to be distributed and effective cooling system. Tactile and kinesthetic receptors and nervous pathways form a very efficient monitoring system with miniaturized distributed sensors and transmission cable.

Trying to mimic nature we are investigating (in parallel with other laboratories) about the possibilities of developing artificial muscles [7–9,34] to obtain actuators with characteristics similar to the natural muscles. Some contractile polymeric gels have already shown to respond to chemical [7] or temperature [34] command and some conducting polymer to electrical command [8,9], but they are still in the research phase. Meanwhile traditional actuators are still used in robotics and virtual reality (see Hollerbach [15] for a good review).

The need of an efficient distributed sensing system, able to give the necessary information to perform closed loop control, is connected with the distributed nature of tactile actuation. In this field it is very difficult to obtain results comparable with the ones obtained by nature too. One of the possible solution we are investigating is to use a net of small microprocessors to pre-elaborate the sensor signals and send the information to the

Central Processing Unit using fast communication. The peripheral microprocessors acquire signal from various haptic sensors or from other sense district areas served by different microprocessors. The complete system can work in parallel and can perform simple tasks or programs like "spinal reflexes" and simple manipulation programs. The problematic ring of the chain is the sensor design. Untill now, there is no usable skin-like tactile sensors, while force sensors are still very expensive and not accurate. For this reason, we are actually developing a full sensorized glove (the "Piaggio glove") that will have both joint position and cutaneous tactile sensors. We also designed and realised [2] a number of multi-axial force/torque sensor to be used as joint torque sensor. On the other side, some position sensing devices (optical position sensing devices, micromachined linear and angular encoder, Hall effect sensors and other magnetic and optical sensors) are now available as micro or small kinesthetic position sensors.

3.0 SENSING AND ACTUATING SMELL

This work is addressed to people involved in using and developing training tools: I am conscious that introducing smell sensors and actuators could be a bit provocative. The actual cost of artificial nose is high and the enterprises that are now producing some kind of noses have a negative balance for the activity. Anyway, the possibilities of using artificial noses in the control of quality of a number of products (food, beverages, perfumes etc.) and in security applications show the enormous potential utility of such an instrumentation.

The sense of smell, in opposition with the sense of touch, is a concentrated sensing. Olfactory cells (localized in the olfactory bulb) are directly connected with olfactory nerve which carry smell information directly to brain. Well known physiological studies demonstrated that human beings reconstruct color images using only four different kinds of receptors: rods, sensitive to the light intensity (black and white vision, night vision) and cones, selectively sensitive to one of the three fundamental colors. Researchers arrived to this conclusion analyzing the different types of color-blindness. Does smell work in a similar way? Studying different ways to be "blind to smell" (a disablement call anosmia) some researchers affirm that, like cones, olfactory bulb may recognize complex odors as a combination of about 32 "fundamental odors" [23]. Consequently, using a combination of 32 different sensors, it could be possible to realize an artificial nose. Until now, industries and laboratories have produced artificial noses with no more than 20 different polymers.

The most important problem related to robotic nose is the very low concentration to which each sensor must be sensible (sometimes only a part on one hundred of million parts). This is an important problem, especially if we consider that these noses are often used to substitute skilled staff (employed to control food flavor) which is particularly sensible to very small amount of particular flavor. Another problem is the fact that the response of smell receptors and sensor is time, temperature and humidity dependent. Finally, the neural mechanism that connects the fundamental odors with the different smells we can perceive is still almost unknown.

The development of a smell actuator is connected to these problems: it is possible to think about an array of 32 actuators supplying concentrated smells, but it is difficult, without a sensor, to control the intensity of the produced smell and know the connection between the desired effect and the patterns to give to actuators.

A smell sensor has its applications: recently the Wall Street Journal [24] has published an article that gives a number of informations about enterprises producing artificial noses: field of applications (fish freshness, medical application, food quality control and other), budgets, and future trends.

Centro Piaggio is working on an artificial nose since five years [22,23]; at this moment a sensor has been built with polymeric transducers of new conception and a complete report is in progress. The development of this sensor is essential for the realization of the further part of the project: the development of a smell actuator. Another project is destined for the enhancement of the capability of our sensor: the realization of a neural network able to recognize odors [12]. This project is intended to understand and replicate the neural mechanism driving the human capability to distinguish and classify different odors.

4.0 SOME APPLICATIONS

A Committee on Virtual Reality Research and Development pointed out that the four most promising application domains for SE are medicine and health care; hazardous operation; training; design, manufacturing and marketing [11]. In the domain of medical and health care two projects were judged of particular interest: modeling the human body and studying the transfer of knowledge and skill gained using virtual training. A recommendation of the Committee was to support research on visual display and haptic interfaces.

4.1 The Virtual Patient

One of the projects we are developing (in collaboration with a set of other Departments of Università di Pisa, of Università di Pavia, and Università di Genova), using our experience on haptic sense, is a virtual patient for surgeons or general practitioners. This instrumentation is intended to train the surgeon for two situations: unusual dangerous situation in regular surgical operation, and teleoperated operation. Generic surgeons need a great amount of practice on real patient to develop the amount of skill and knowledge that is necessary to afford an operation as first surgeon. Unfortunately there is a number of unusual events in which a surgeon needs to take a number of fast and critical decisions. Because of the scarcity of these events it would be very useful to have an instrumentation allowing a good training for critical situations. On the other hand, with an adequate software and hardware, it could be possible to train a surgeon to tele-operate on a virtual patient in a number of different cases: eye and brain surgery, laparoscopies, reconstruction of nerves etc.

The development of such an instrumentation needs important competencies regarding to:

- the realization of small high-dexterity robots, necessary to build an haptic interface acting on the surgeon hands. Some authors [11,13,16,18,30] have already made advanced robots for surgery, in particular for eye-surgery, automatic pointing of a camera for laparoscopy, battlefield remote surgeon and others
- the conception of the sensing apparatus; the characteristics of this apparatus must be designed keeping into account the knowledge of the human behavior during a skillful and stressful task [19–21,31]
- the design of an adequate real-time software in connection with a computing hardware. This task is probably the less analyzed and still has a number of problems to be solved. In particular the simulation of viscoelastic, non-linear and vis-

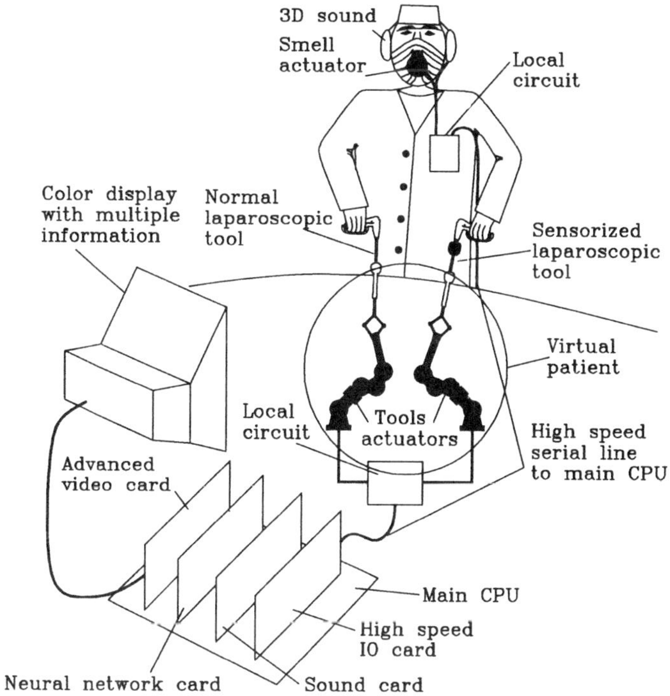

Figure 2. A schematic drawing showing the surgeon using the training tool.

ual properties of biologic material using a huge amount of information is still far to be realized in real-time. It has been estimated [17], that real-time simulations (using a typical finite-element model) of a mechanical interaction need a computational power of the order of 1 GFlops.

Our center and our collaborators have the necessary competencies and a project has just been started to realize a surgeon training tool (see Figure 2). We are actually working on all the three points, particularly on the last one using two techniques capable to work in real-time. We want to solve the non-linear time-dependent interaction problem between the surgical tools and the tissue using a distributed computing system (a neural network [4–6] rather than a finite-element software). During the manipulation the kind of contact and the behavior of the tissue can change: if the stress is too high a cut will occur, if a blood vessel is cut some blood will spill out etc. These events will be treated using an AI software developed to treat, in real-time, problems with not perfectly known information [25]. The same AI software, used to deal with exceptions during the simulated surgical operation, has been used to make autonomous diagnosis for some kind of sickness. It will be interesting to use this software in conjunction with the surgical tool to create a complete tool, able to simulate different situations during operation (and possibly give them a solution).

Our aim is to design the training tool using low-cost systems to allow a large diffusion of the instrumentation. The nowadays developments of low-cost fast CPU joined with image-processing board (or chip) and neural chips enable the development of this kind of cheap systems.

The virtual patient could be used to train the whole surgical team for difficult or unknown surgical operations. Two or more persons could collaborate using the same program and processing unit contemporary, in such a way to study the best position and strategy to deal, for example, with first-attempt or critic operations. If the training tool is able to perform virtual surgical operation by itself, it could train the first-surgeon's assistant or the nurse to be more effective (use the camera, move or keep the tissue, prepare the right tool, etc.). This kind of group training could be performed by means of a network, with obvious advantages (especially for small hospitals and schools). Moreover, with the impending possibility of a "telemedicine era", training tool for laparoscopy (and other surgical operations) could be used to train specialized surgeon to teleoperate: in particular it will be possible to introduce delay and inertia due to the transmission line and to the slave surgeon robot.

A simplified version of the training tool (with no expensive tactile feedback, for example) could be used to perform virtual travel inside the human body. The possibility of examining the inside of the human body before to see and practice a real operation is very interesting because at the first attempt students usually face some difficulties to recognize body parts (normal or sick) studied in an Atlas only: the scale, the point of view, the color etc., make the task harder. In the field of VR medical training tools Satava [29] produced a simulation tool with which it is possible to see the viscera of the human abdomen, interacting with them using a DatagloveTM (pushing or pulling them). He also developed an haptic interface for teleoperation. Anyway the last step, the association of a virtual viscoelasticity to the virtual viscera (touchable using the teleoperation interface), still lacks and the training tool cannot apply force to the operator.

With simple modifications, a surgeon training tool may be used to realize other training tools to be applied in other fields, for example the tele-manipulation and tele-maintenance of dangerous material and location.

4.2 Advanced Laparoscopy Tools

The virtual patient project just started: we were, till now, waiting to have the critic mass of knowledge necessary to produce a commercial instrumentation. One of the first step in this direction was the realization of a sensorized tool for laparoscopy. As it appears in Figure 3 this tool was very simple but such a project gave us the possibility to interact with surgeons "at work" and to establish important links with the university hospital.

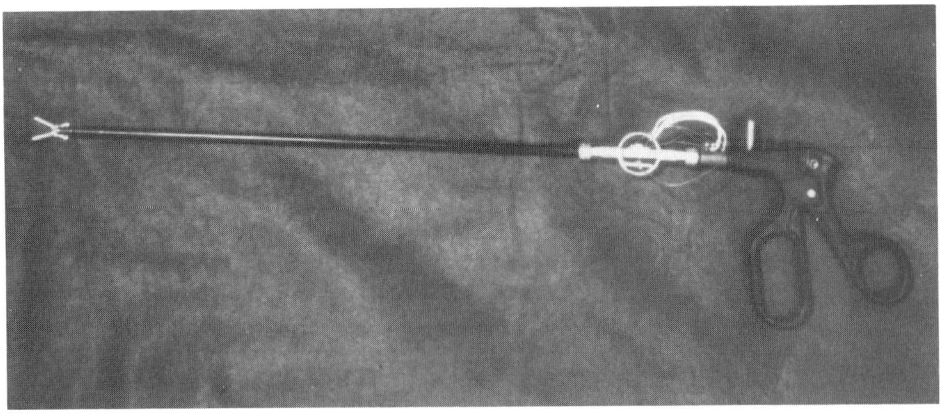

Figure 3. A picture of the first prototype of the advanced laparoscopy tool realized by Centro Piaggio. It shows the force and position sensors inserted in the long stylus near to the handling.

Together with the development of the sensor we developed a first prototype of force-reflecting device for medical application, based on a magnetoelectric actuator. We are now studying the application of electrorheologic materials (substances that change their rheological properties with the application of an electric field) to realize such devices. We are also realizing a de-coupling between the surgeon handle and the manipulator endpoint by means of a very simple couple of master and slave robots. This de-coupling should enhance the capability of the surgeon to feel the properties of the manipulated tissue and the applied force; these capabilities are at the moment compromised by the mechanical configuration of the tools.

Another trend of research we are just starting to explore is the study of different handlings for laparoscopy. We are interested by something that could replicate the usual way a human being manipulates soft thing, like during palpation. We think that such an approach could enhance the capability of a surgeon to manipulate viscera avoiding injury without loosing the grasp.

4.3 Visual Impaired Training Tool

Another project is going on in Centro Piaggio: the realization of advanced high-resolution-array tactile sensors. Sensors are made using two different technologies: piezoelectric and piezoresistive rubbers. A sensor made by a combination of the two materials is under study. This kind of sensors is intended as sophisticated tools for artificial finger of robots and arm prosthesis.

A different application of these sensors, studied at the Università di Pavia, is in the field of the training of visually-impaired persons. The sensor is used to read characters during training of the Braille code. This project is funded and regarded with interest by some associations of visually-impaired persons. One of the ideas that Pavia researchers are keeping in mind is the low cost of the devices and the serial communication of the device with any computer. The last characteristics allow the instrumentation to be plugged and played on most computers. The data produced by the sensors are analized by a neural network. This allows a very fast response of the system.

5.0 CONCLUSIONS

I introduced the idea that touch and smell senses are important for the quality of some training tools. An important concept I want to point out is that it is necessary to study sensing to realize a good actuation. I gave some examples of strategical applications of touch and smell to enhance advanced training tools.

Anyway, it is necessary to point out that actual funding in the field is not sufficient, in particular as regards hardware research [11]: a financial effort to support this activity is now necessary and will produce important advances.

6.0 REFERENCES

Bergamasco, B. Allotta, L. Bosio, L. Ferretti, G. Parrini, G. M. Prisco, F. Salsedo, and G. Sartini. An arm exoskeleton system for teleoperation and virtual environments applications. In Proc. IEEE Int. Conf. on Robotics and Automation, pages 1449–1454, San Diego, California, 1994.

Bicchi and P. Dario. Intrinsic tactile sensing for artificial hand. In R. Bolles and B. Roth, editors, Robotics Research, pages 83–90. MIT Press, Cambridge, MA, 1989.

Burdea, J. Zhuang, E. Roskos, D. Silver, and N. Langrana. A portable dextrous master with force feedback. Presence: Teleoperators and Virtual Environments, 1(1), 1992.

Caiti, G. Canepa, D. De Rossi, F. Germagnoli, G. Magenes, and T. Parisini. Towards the realization of an artificial tactile system: Fine-form discrimination by a tensorial tactile sensor array and neural inversion algorithms. in print.

Gaetano Canepa, Matteo Campanella, and Danilo De Rossi. Slip detection by a tactile neural network. In Proc. IEEE Int. Conf. on IROS, volume 1, pages 224–231, Munich, Germany, September 1994.

Gaetano Canepa, Maurizio Morabito, Danilo De Rossi, Andrea Caiti, and Thomas Parisini. Shape estimation with tactile sensor: a radial basis function approach. In Proc. IEEE Int. Conf. on Decision and Control, Tucson, Arizona, 1992.

Chiarelli and D. De Rossi. Modelling and mechanical characterization of thin fibers of contractile polymer hydrogels. J. of Intell. Mater. Syst. and Struct., 3:396–417, July 1992.

Chiarelli, D. De Rossi, A. Della Santa, and A. Mazzoldi. Doping induced volume change in a p-conjugated conducting polymer. Polymer Gels and Networks, 2:289–297, 1994.

Chiarelli, K. Umezawa, and D. De Rossi. A polymer composite showing electrocontractile response. In D. De Rossi, K. Kajiwara, Y. Osada, and A. Yamauchi, editors, Polymers Gels: Fundamentals and Biomedical Applications, pages 195–204. Plenium Press, New York, 1991.

Danilo De Rossi, Claudio Domenici, Piero Chiarelli, and Gaetano Canepa. Biomimetic approaches to the design of materials for artificial haptics and manipulation. In Proc. of MEDICON '92, pages 689–692, Capri, Italy, 1992.

Durlach and A. S. Mavor, editors. Virtual Reality: Scientific and Technological Challenges. National Academy Press, Washington, D.C., 1994.

Gestri and A. Starita. A neural network for odour recognition. In The Fifth Int. Meeting on Chemical Sensors, pages 1090–1093, Roma, Italy, July 1992.

Green, J. H. Hill, and R. M. Satava. Telepresence: Dextrous procedures in a virtual operating field. Surg. Endosc., 57:192, 1991.

Leon Harmon. Automated tactile sensing. The Int. J. of Robotic Research, 1(2), 1982.

Hollerbach, I. W. Hunter, and J. Ballantyne. A comparative analysis of actuator technologies for robotics. In O. Khatib, J. J. Craig, and T. Lozano Perez, editors, The Robotics Review 2, pages 299–342. MIT Press, Cambridge, Mass., 1992.

Hunter, T. D. Doukoglu, S. R. Lafontaine, P. G. Charrette, L. A. Jones, M. A. Sagar, G. D. Mallison, and P. J. Hunter. A teleoperated microsurgical robot and associated virtual environment for eye surgery. Presence, 2(4):265–280, 1994.

Hunter, S. Lafontaine, P. M. F. Nielsen, P. J. Hunter, and J. M. Hollerbach. Manipulation and dynamic mechanical testing of microscopic objects using a tele- micro-robot system. IEEE Control System Magazine, 10(2):3–9, 1990.

Hurteau, S. DeSanctis, E. Begin, and M. Gagner. Laparoscopic surgery assisted by a robotic cameraman: Concept and experimental results. In Proc. IEEE Int. Conf. on Robotics and Automation, pages 2286–2289, San Diego, California, 1994.

Jones and I. W. Hunter. Influence of the mechanical properties of a manipulandum on human operators dynamics: 1. elastic stiffness. Biological Cybernetics, 62:299- 307, 1990.

Jones and I. W. Hunter. Human operator perception of mechanical variables and their effects on tracking performance. Advances in Robotics, 42:49–53, 1992.

Kearney and I. W. Hunter. System identification of human joint dynamics. Critical Review in Biomedical Engineering, 18(1):55–87, 1987.

Nannini and G. Serra. Growth of polypyrrole in a pattern: a technological approach to conducting polymers. J. of Molecular Electronics, 6:124–128, 1990.

Persaud and P. Pelosi. Sensor arrays using conducting polymers for an artificial nose. In J. W. Gardner and P. N. Bartlett, editors, Sensor and Sensory System for an Electronic Nose, NATO ASI Series, Series E: Appl. Sciences, pages 212–237. 1992.

Pope. Smell of success is in the air in effort to emulate the nose. Wall Street Journal, March 2, 1992.

Ramoni. Ignorant influence diagrams. In M. Kaufmann, editor, Proc. of the Int. Joint Conf. on Artificial Intelligence, San Mateo, California, 1995.

Rohling and J. M. Hollerbach. Calibrating the human hand for haptic interfaces. Presence: Teleoperators and Virtual Environments, 2(4), 1993.

Rohling, J. M. Hollerbach, and S. C. Jacobsen. Optimized fingertip mapping: A general algorithm for robotic hand teleoperation. Presence: Teleoperators and Virtual Environments, 2(3), 1993.

Salcudean, N. M. Wong, and R. L. Hollis. A force-reflecting teleoperation system with magnetically levitated master and wrist. In Proc. of IEEE Int. Conf. on Robotics and Automation, pages 1420–1426, Nice, France, 1992.

Satava. Medicine 2001: the king is dead. In A. M. Digioia, T. Kanade, and R. Taylor, editors, First Int. Symp. on Medical Robotics and Computer Assisted Surgery, pages 2–5. Shadyside Hospital, 1992.

Satava. Robotics, telepresence and virtual reality: a critical analysis of the future. Minimally Invasive Therapy, 1:357–363, 1992.

Satava and S. R. Ellis. Human interface technology: an essential tool for the modern surgeon. Surgical Endoscopy, Submitted in 1993. In press.

Smith. Remembering in and out of context. J. of Exp. Psychology: Human Learning and Memory, 5(5):460–471, 1979.

Stussi, G. Serra, G. Stoppato Venier, D. De Rossi, M. Gallazzi, and G. Zerbi. Patterning of conducting polymers for sensors through chemical vapour deposition. In The Fifth Int. Meeting on Chemical Sensors, pages 1188–1191, Roma, Italy, July 1994.

Suzuki and O. Hirasa. An approach to artificial muscle using polymer gels formed by micro-phase separation. Advanced in Polymer Science, 110:242–261, 1993.

6

SURGERY 2001

Shaun B. Jones

Advanced Biomedical Technology Program
Defense Advanced Research Projects Agency
Washington, D.C.

There are exciting Information Age technologies being applied to medicine and surgery today. They include advanced diagnostics and imaging, remote medical and surgical intervention, informatics, virtual prototyping and simulation. In 1994, an informal estimate given during a National Science Foundation workshop suggested that 90% of the information desired by a physician to treat a patient can be acquired electronically. Examples included non-invasive imaging (X-ray, CT, MRI), vital signs, laboratory test results, patient records, treatment protocols, consultations and database searches. Physical examination, simple procedures and even basic surgery are being enabled by other sophisticated technologies allowing remote manipulation, palpation, and 3-D visualization using computer based anatomy and the new virtual reality surgical simulators. Thus anything a physician needs to know about a wounded soldier or patient can be acquired in electronic form and transmitted to a physician at a computer workstation. With the technologies of teleoperation, telemanipulation and telesurgery, the physician can bring expertise to the place where the soldier is wounded or the patient is sick. In addition, the same computer workstation used for surgery can provide a realistic wounded "virtual" patient for practicing life saving procedures on lethal injuries and, with a flip of the switch, be used for surgery on the real patient. This information revolution is the foundation of the fundamental change in medicine, and the cornerstone is the digital physician. It is Medicine's wake-up call to the information age.

The time could not be more perfect, for we now have the right type of physicians to take advantage of this new technology. The "Nintendo Surgeon" has evolved into the "Digital Physician". Younger physicians in the video/electronic generation have, in many ways, grown up "training" with these information age technologies. Not only are they embracing and comfortable with the new technology, now they are demanding it in both personal and professional settings. They enjoy sophisticated home video games, "surf" the World Wide Web and the "information super highway" and seek greater knowledge about the world using computer aided instruction, multi-media and virtual reality. To them, the future is Now, and it is all digital. Two of the most exciting future digital technologies on the surgical horizon are virtual reality and telepresence surgery.

Virtual Reality, Training's Future? edited by Seidel and Chatelier
Plenum Press, New York, 1997

Archetypal of telepresence surgery systems is the Green Telepresence Surgery System[1,2]. It exists today as a dexterity enhancing, remote surgical system that will permit a surgeon at a hospital to operate upon a patient at a site which is distant or dangerous, such as a rural hospital, the battlefield or space station. It consists of a surgical workstation which has 3-D stereoscopic monitor, stereophonic sound, and six degree-of-freedom instrument controllers (handles of actual surgical instruments) which have both the sense of touch and greatly enhanced dexterity. The system uses advanced force-feedback technology and is engineered in such a way the surgeon actually feels as if the surgery were being performed directly in front of him, when in reality the remote site (and patient) could be yards, miles, or even hundreds of miles away. This will permit a specialty surgeon in a distant medical center to provide assistance, mentoring, training and proctoring (or actually performing surgery), remotely in variety of unique environments. Because the system was designed to mimic open surgery, there will be a minimum of additional training required, thus permitting surgery with all the feeling, dexterity and 3-D vision of open surgery.

Another telepresence surgery system created by Hunter et al[3], focuses upon expanding the capabilities of human performance. In retinal surgery, the telepresence system scales the motion of the hand by up to a hundredfold, so 1 cm of the surgeon's hand motion moves the micro-scalpel 100 microns, and vision magnifies the retinal vessels to the size of a thumb. By applying sophisticated signal filtering techniques through the computer interface, the normal tremor of the human hand can be removed, thereby permitting accuracy and precision to 10 microns, a hundred times more accurate than the unaided hand.

Virtual reality surgical simulators, similar to flight simulators, are being designed to permit young physicians to "fly" inside of an imaginary body to learn anatomy or to practice surgery. Virtual reality uses 3-dimensional, computer generated graphic images to create a responsive environment, and by wearing a head mounted display (with a pair of television screens in front of the eyes), stereophonic earphones, and "smart" gloves, the surgeon or student can explore the 3-D anatomy and organs as if they actually existed. The addition of virtual surgical instruments permits the practice of surgical procedures[4]. The level of realism today is improving quickly beyond that of cartoon graphics. New datasets from the "Visible Human" integrate human data from CT and MRI scans with color photo-tomography. Using the "Visible Human", the level of realism will soon become near life-like. The addition of physical properties like organ deformation and muscle contraction, physiologic properties like bleeding or leaking of various fluids, and microscopic anatomy such as micro-glandular or neurovascular structures, will create a very powerful educational trainer. Virtual reality has also empowered patients to interact more effectively with health care providers, enhancing both evaluation and diagnosis as well as treatment and rehabilitation. Patients are using virtual environments to demonstrate precisely subtle sensory and motor deficits, overcome phobias and accelerate somatosensory rehabilitation. The challenge will be to understand how to take advantage of this technology to enhance the training of students and experienced physicians and better educate both our patients and ourselves.

Another application of VR is in medical planning, such as civilian disasters or mass casualty care. There is a new generation of individual simulators which, like a video game, can place the individual student or physician in an imaginary place, such as disaster or battlefield. The student, medic or surgeon can then practice triage or emergency first aid, and coordinate planning and training. This individual simulator, called I-Port, has an exercycle type base which based on the rate of pedaling allows the student to walk or run through the scene, and a head mounted display to see the scenery and other players, thereby being able to interact and practice in a collaborative, distributive simulated environment.

A third application is to use VR to prototype buildings, equipment and instruments. Today engineers build using a computer-aided-design (CAD) program, then test and validate before actual construction; we can now do this for medical equipment and instruments as well. There is currently an ambitious project, the "Operating Environment of the Future", which will build a complete operating room based upon advanced and modern materials, equipment and technology in order to totally rethink the way a surgical (or procedure) suite should be. This is based upon new requirements—"smart" materials, systems integration and information flow—for the future, not upon today's traditional architectural and engineering techniques. The room and equipment will then be "virtually" tested and evaluated (walking around, moving equipment, or adding and taking away the virtual objects) by all who will use or influence it, from physicians and nurses to administrators, materiel managers, clerks and janitors, in order to recruit the best ideas and optimal plan. Once everyone has had a chance to experience the room and provide a decided opinion, the iterative process will be complete and the room will be built.

This is the era of change to a new world order for medicine, one in which medicine has the opportunity to grasp these advanced technologies, accelerate knowledge acquisition, refine performance training, enhance capabilities beyond the frail limitations of the human body and dissolve time and space. The ultimate value of these technologies of robotics, telepresence and virtual reality is in the provision of better medical care for our patients.

REFERENCES

Green PS, Hill JH, and Satava RM. Telepresence: Dexterous procedures in a virtual operating field.(Abstr). *Surg Endosc* 57:192, 1991

Satava, RM. Robotics, telepresence and virtual reality: a critical analysis of the future of surgery. *Minimally Invasive Therapy* 1: 357–63, 1992

Hunter IW, Doukoglou TD, Lafontaine SR et al. A Teleoperated Microsurgical Robot and Associated Virtual Environment for Eye Surgery. *Presence* 4:265–80, 1993

Satava RM. Virtual Reality Surgical Simulator: The First Steps *Surg Endosc 7*: 203–05, 1993

7

VIRTUAL REALITY TRAINING SIMULATOR FOR LONG TIME FLIGHT

Pascal Hue,[1] Bruno Delannoy,[2] and Jean-Christophe Berland[2]

DGA/DSTI
[1]Etablissement Technique d'Angers
France
[2]Centre Aéroporté de Toulouse
France

ABSTRACT

This paper describes the project of realizing a virtual reality training simulator for long-time flights using a special force parachute.

The purpose of this simulator training is to be used by Airborne Division School to teach how to pilot and navigate with a parachute as well as to prepare new missions. The freefall phase and the opening sequence are not simulated because of their particularities in terms of environment and physical constraints. To reach this purpose, the environmental and training conditions have to be managed: night or day, wind, weight of the paratrooper and his equipment, instrument flight conditions, visual flight, use of night vision goggles. Some particular interfaces must be built to put the paratrooper in an immersive and particulary realistic situation.

INTRODUCTION

The first purpose of DSTI-ETAS (Direction des Systèmes Terrestres et d'Information, Etablissement Technique d'Angers) Human Factor team for this project was to verify the applicability of virtual environments in a context of advanced training and simulator. When we proposed the long-time flight using a parachute, the Airborne Division School and the DSTI-CAP (Centre Aéroporté de Toulouse) was interested too by the corresponding developments.

The Air Transport Centre (CAP) team has helped us to determine the characteristic components of parachute jumping which we are now going to study.

THE COMPONENT ELEMENTS OF PARACHUTING

The Parachute

Choice. The simulation of the act of falling beneath a parachute, including the handling of the controls, is based on a model of parachute which can be steered. Furthermore, the need to relate to the diverse missions of future parachutists requires that we work with a military parachute. Out of the two military models known at present, it has seemed appropriate to retain the G9 parachute of French design which has been tested at the CAP.

Such a parachute is made up of differents parts:

- The rectangular canopy, which is divided into several cells for aerodynamic control. This canopy has a leading edge and a trailing edge. The leading edge has an aerodynamic function and the trailing edge is designed for control.
- The rigging lines and elevators which link the parachutist to the canopy.
- A piece of tissue called a sleeve, or slider, which reduces the shock of opening of the main chute and can be retracted by the parachutist.

Glide Characteristics. The two main elements of a glide must be differentiated between, hence the difficulty in taking measurements needed for its modelling.

Straight Line (or Symmetrical) Glide. Pulling the toggles in straight line flight will vary the speed of the parachute to obtain a curve which represents the performance of the canopy in horizontal and vertical components of its velocity. This curve is called a polar profile.

The parameters which define a polar profile are:

- The horizontal velocity
- The vertical velocity

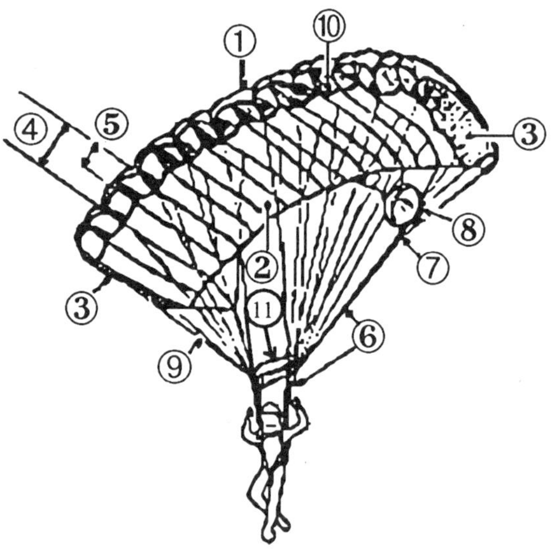

1. Top skin
2. Bottom skin
3. Stabilisers
4. Cells
5. Half cells
6. Left toggle
7. Braking/steering control
8. Extractor
9. Rigging lines
10. Air vents between cells
11. Sleeve/Slider
12. Leading edge
13. Trailing edge

Figure 1. Components of a parachute.

- The length of steering line pulled, which can be defined as a percentage:
  - 0 %: control not used
  - 100 %: maximum length pulled

A polar profile is valid for a given weight beneath canopy.

The polar profile corresponds to the glide characteristics of the parachute. One can place five significant points on the curve for the behaviour of the canopy.

1. *The point of maximum velocity—V Max:* This is one extremity of the polar profile under normal flight conditions. At this point, the parachutist achieves maximum horizontal and vertical speeds with the parachutist taking no action on the toggles. The evaluation of this point enables the maximum permissible wind speed to be determined, while retaining sufficient manoeuvrability for landing in safety.
2. *The point of minimum rate of fall—V min:* This point is the summit of the curve. Knowledge of this point enables the parachutist to deduce the percentage steering line to pull to make use of up-lifts (zones of ascendance, flight in tail winds).
3. *The point of stall—VD:* At this point, the horizontal speed is a minimum and the vertical speed is in general at its steepest on the polar profile. The visible consequences are a collapse of the profil of the canopy and deflation of certain of its parts.
4. *The point of best glide—VF:* This point corresponds with the maximum efficiency of the canopy. The course that enables the maximum possible distance to be achieved in still air. The best glide is the maximum balance between horizontal and vertical speeds.

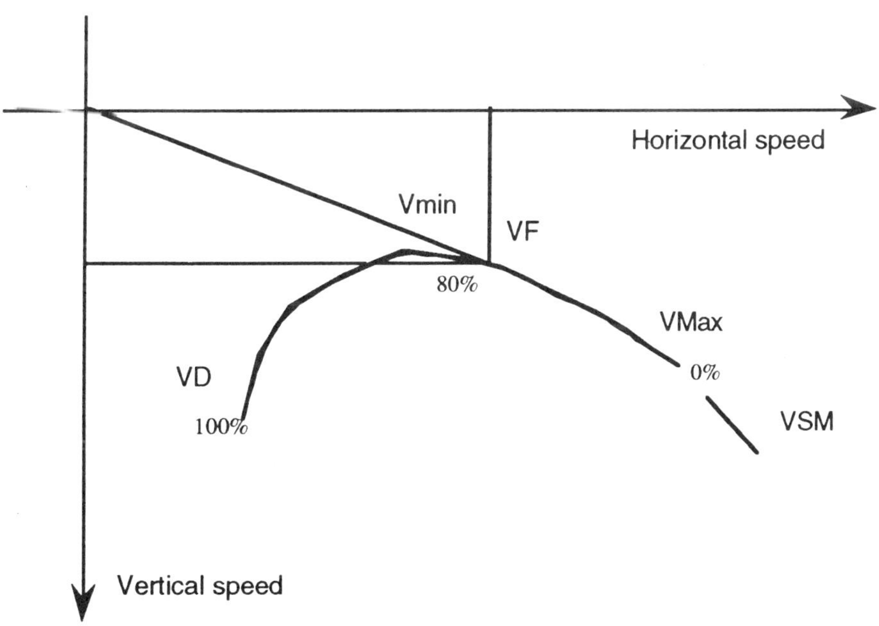

Figure 2. Example of a polar profile.

5. *The point of maximum overspeed—VSM:* The parachutist can put the canopy into overspeed by pulling on the front elevators. The trajectory plummets, the glide deteriorates but the horizontal speed is higher than the maximum horizontal speed obtained in a normal configuration. The visible consequence is a severe instability in pitch.

Control Principles. In order to obtain the mode of operation of the controls of a given parachute, one can measure the extension of the steering line and the effort needed.

Flight in Rotation (or Asymmetric flight). The kinematics of rotation include the time of rotation, the speed and the accelerations. The simulation of the accelerations is difficult.

Specific trials were needed in order to model the flignt characteristics of the G9 and to determmine the developments ot the flight performances of the parachute as a function of the actions on the controls.

Stable and Unstable flight. The parachutist differentiates between the two categories of flight:

- Stable flight
- Unstable flight

Stable flight is characterised by the absence of sudden changes of speed in the trajectory (at least in magnitude). From the point of view of the parachutist, this occurs without any control being given to the canopy or when controls are varied very slowly. This has the effect of noticeably diminishing the inertial forces to the point of rendering them negligible as far as the other forces present are concerned.

By contrast, a period of unstable flight following the violent execution of a command (sudden release of the toggles following a stall or a violent application of the controls ...) is in general a transitory phase.

The Parachutist's Environment

Introduction. One may consider that the parachutist's environment is defined by the position he occupies in space, that is to say by the configuration of the jump. This environment is also dimensioned by his field of vision as well as by the relevant elements for action within the environment. And above all on this point, there are the sources of turbulence for the flight.

Altitude of Opening. When they practice the High Altitude Low Opening (HALO) technique, Operational parachutists open at a height of about 1000 mètres. When the CRAP practice the High Altitude High Opening (HAHO), they open at about 9000 mètres.

<u>Distance of Opening—Target.</u> Operational parachutists: on sight, approximately 2 km. The drop takes place above the zone.

CRAP and HAHO technique: Long distances, depending on the mission (of the order of 20 km).

<u>Drop Zone.</u> Peacetime regulations stipulate a landing zone diameter equal to the height of opening (800 to 1000 mètres).

Definition of the Field of Vision. Degree of resolution of the visual image. According to parachutist's experience it seems that only the landing zone needs a high degree of resolution and representation in 3D.

Dimensions of the Visual Field. The glasses with the narrowest field of vision are those of the CRAP. Their field of vision is 40°. This field corresponds with the Virtual Reality helmet that will be used.

Sources of Turbulence (Gradients). The behaviour of the parachute can be upset by turbulent factors. the factors cause the chute to deviate from its forecast behaviour.

The sources of these gradients are the following:

1. Discontinuities in the air mass. (wind layers)
2. Passing behind another parachutist (20 mètres behind)
3. Disturbances on the ground
4. Atmospheric disorders around obstacles (to 1/3 of the height of the obstacle).

Activity Training

Instrument Navigation. This is a normal part of the activity of gliding under a canopy for the CRAP They must head towards a landing zone that is not visible due to distance. This requires equipment to provide direction. Because of the limited resolution of the Virtual Reality helmet, in this simulated mode, the parachutist will see the whole of his field of vision taken up by the instruments used for navigation.

On Sight Navigation. Following studies of videos of jumps, it seems that the notion of relief does not appear until very close to the ground, and then, as a funciton for the heights of elements ont the ground. By contrast, the shadows cast are noticed very quickly. All the geographical features: river beds, roads, the horizon, etc.., can serve as visual references.

The Steering of the Chute. With this type of canopy, the parachutist varies both the horizontal and the vertical speeds. As a function of the aspect ratio and the weight of the parachutist and his equipment, the chute will adopt a speed as defined by the characteristics of the polar profile for the given total weight. A simultaneous light pull on the two toggles will lower the trailing edge (the rear of the chute), causing a reduction in both the horizontal and the vertical speeds, and hence will increase the time of glide. By contrast, a substantial pull will cause an extreme lowering of the trailing edge and will provoke an aerodynamic stall, with deflation of the cells.

From the position of an average pull on the two toggles, a further tug on one causes a sensibly flat turn, with no great loss of height. From a zero extension, on the contrary, a tug on a single toggle provokes a turn with a strong incline and a major loss of height.

Furthermore, it is possible for a parachutist to execute turns with a simple displacement of his body without the use of the toggles.

These stratagems for flying form a part of the learning of the parachutist. They depend on the context of the mission and the objective to be reached.

Landing. In flight, the landing is made into the wind.

The stronger the wind, the more the presentation and approach to the point of landing must tend towards the vertical. When several mètres from the ground, a simultaneous pull on the two toggles brings the canopy into a position approaching a stall. For a second, it becomes stationery before slipping backwards: this is the rounding-out, as for the landing of an aeroplane, then comes the touch-down.

PRESENTATION OF THE SIMULATOR

Introduction

Controlling a parachute canopy could already be taught with a simulator developed by Systems Technology, Inc: the trainee pulls on two toggles with the force and feel of a parachute canopy. looking at a CRT display, he sees his feet and the ground below. As the jumper pulls on the toggles, he can see the effects of his maneuvering and the wind, and sense the approaching ground as objects grow larger.

This interactive scene motion provides the trainee with realistic, but non-fully immersive, perceptions.

Our objective is to go further into the realism of these perceptions in immersing the parachutist in experimentation, thanks to Virtual reality.

Functions Carried Out by the Equipment

Harnessing of the Operator. In order to make the simulation more realistic, the experimenter will be harnessed as in real life and hung under a gantry.

He will thus have available to him the usual controls for his canopy, which will give the responses to his actions as in real life and will teach the same behaviour in the handling of his chute, excepted for kinematic sensations. The changes in attitude of the canopy corresponding to changes in the actions of the parachutist will not be simulated in the images of the virtual world.

Immersion into the Virtual World. The parachutist will look into a Virtual Reality helmet with a field of view of 40°, wich is the same as that afforded by the glasses used in real life. The following of the movements of the head will take place with the help of magnetic technology sensors, habitually used in Virtual reality experiments.

The Handling of the Parachute. The handling ot the chute will be done using the same controls as in real life, with similar responses, both in the return of forces on the toggles and of the canopy being flown. The return of forces will be done by the software flying the appropriate device as a function of the parachutists weight and in accordance with the behaviour of the chute.

Functions Represented by the Software

Software Used. The Virtual Reality application will be developed around the Virtual Reality program CLOVIS of the firm MEDIALAB (France). The platform used will be an ONYX Machine from SILICON GRAPHICS, equipped with a Reality Engine2 board.

Mission Preparation. Before the start of a mission, the person responsible for the mission to be simulated must enter the information needed for its realisation:

- Type of simulation, on instruments or on sight
- Choice of the landing zone,
- Turbulences: wind profile, vertical gradients,
- Equipment used: normal vision, night vision,
- Parachutist's and his equipment weight.

These details will then be used as the simulation progresses.

Supervision. This functionality will allow:

- The visualisation of the simulation during its progress,
- The analysis of the mission after completion by rerunning the scene, as seen by the parachutist and in visualising the main parameters for the flight.

The Control of the Parachute. The behaviour of the chute will be calculated as a function of the percentage of pull on the toggles and the surrounding turbulences. As the results gained by experience enable the polar profile to be calculated only for the weights used during actual jumps, we will produce an extrapolation for the calculations in the simulated conditions rather than work with the results of a real time numerical model of the chute.

Immersion in the Virtual World. Instrument navigation simulation. From the start of the simulation down to an altitude of about 200 metres, the parachutist will have only an image of the navigational instruments in his field of vision which will give him the necessary indications for piloting the chute.

At an altitude of about 200 metres it will change to the simulation of the landing.

Simulation of the Jump on Sight. The parachutist will manoeuvre above the textured landscape of the zone over which he will be dropped. Account of the relief will be taken as a function of the parachutist's altitude and the heights of the components of the landscape.

At a height of about 200 mètres it will change to the simulation of the landing.

Simulation of the Landing. The landing zones will be entirely represented in 3D and the scene will be textured in order to increase the realism.

A windsock will be represented indicating the direction of the wind.

If the parachutist reaches an altitude from which he can no longer land int ther specified zone, we will stop the simulation.

The Virtual Environment. The elements deemed to be essential in the visual representation are:

- The rigging lines,
- The horizon,
- The overflight zone seen in altitude will depend on the use of a texture laid over a geometrically simple zone
- The touch-down zones will be modelled and textured in 3D with, in particular, the shadows;

- The chute itself, without taking account of its deformations
- The slider

CONCLUSION

The main difficulty concerns the use of the non-standard interfaces in the software and equipment environment used. The development of the virtual world in itself poses only the problems of the precision of the geometrical objects of the world.

Another difficulty is to know if the actual resolution available in the Virtual Reality helmets will be sufficient for every case to be simulated.

REFERENCES

Guy Sauvage, 1990, Parachutisme, Robert Laffont

Steve Aukstakalnis, David Blatner, 1992, The Art and Science of Virtual Reality: SILICON MIRAGE, Peachpit Press, Inc., Berkeley

Bruce D. Nordwall, 1992, Parachute simulator reduces risks of injury on first jump, Aviation Week and Space Technology

Dr G.J Jense, Jr, F. Kuijper, 1993, Virtual Environments for Advanced Trainers and Simulators, TNO-FEL, 49–57.

8

SOME EFFECTS OF USING VIRTUAL REALITY TECHNOLOGY

Data and Suggestions

Clare Regan

DRA
Ministry of Defence
Farnborough, Hants GU14 6TD, England

ABSTRACT

This paper discusses some of the effects on the user of immersive virtual reality technology. Effects in this context refers to negative or unwanted side-effects of the technology, such as nausea.

In a study that set out to document the frequency of occurrence and severity of side-effects of immersion in VR, 150 subjects were immersed in the VR system for 20 minutes. Subjects were required to provide ratings on a 1–6 malaise scale immediately prior to the immersion, at 5 minute intervals during the 20 minute immersion period, and at 5 and 10 minutes post-immersion. Subjects also completed a standard simulator sickness questionnaire both immediately before and immediately after the immersion. Sixty-one percent of the subjects reported some symptoms of malaise at some point during the 20 minute immersion period and 10 minute post immersion period. These ranged from symptoms such as headaches and eyestrain to severe nausea. Five percent of the subjects had to withdraw from the study due to the severity of their symptoms.

Two possible causes of the side-effects documented are discussed. The first of these possible causes is that immersion in VR causes a conflict of the senses which results in the malaise. The second is that technological factors, such as the resolution of the displays, are responsible for some of the symptoms. Clear experimental data is lacking on these issues, and hence a program of investigation is underway.

INTRODUCTION

This paper will discuss some of the effects on the user of immersive virtual reality (VR) technology. Effects in this context refers to negative or unwanted side-effects of the technology, such as nausea. Data will be presented which shows that such side-effects do

Virtual Reality, Training's Future? edited by Seidel and Chatelier
Plenum Press, New York, 1997

exist, and can be quite pervasive. Some suggestions will then be made about the causes of these side-effects and about variables that may have significant roles to play in dictating their severity.

DATA ON THE SIDE-EFFECTS OF USING IMMERSIVE VIRTUAL REALITY TECHNOLOGY

A study was carried out to document the frequency of occurrence and severity of side-effects of immersion in VR.

Hardware, Software, and Methodology

A PROVISION 200 VR system was used with a Virtual Research Flight Helmet and a Polhemus Fastrak tracking system. Subjects interacted with the system using a 3D hand device, known as a 3D mouse, which has buttons that the user can press to move forwards and backwards and to handle objects. The software used was the standard demonstration software provided by the manufacturers of the system. It consisted of a corridor off which there were several doors leading into rooms. The subjects were able to go into all of these rooms, and whilst in a room were able to interact with the objects in the room, for example by picking them up and moving them.

One hundred fifty subjects were immersed in the VR system for 20 minutes. Subjects were asked to provide ratings of malaise on a 1–6 malaise scale immediately prior to the immersion, at 5 minute intervals during the 20 minute immersion period, and at 5 and 10 minutes post-immersion (1=No symptoms; 2=Any symptoms, no nausea; 3=Mild nausea; 4=Moderate nausea; 5=Severe nausea; 6=Being sick). Subjects also completed a standard simulator sickness questionnaire both immediately before and immediately after immersion (Kennedy et al, 1993). This questionnaire invites subjects to report on the presence or absence, and sometimes severity, of a range of symptoms. It has been frequently used in simulator sickness research.

Results

8 subjects withdrew from the study. These subjects withdrew before the end of the 20 minute immersion period due to either nausea or dizziness that became so severe that they felt unable to continue.

Malaise Scale Results. The next figure illustrates the percentage of subjects reporting each of the ratings on the malaise scale as their highest across the full immersion and post-immersion period.

As can be seen from figure 1, 61% of the subjects reported ratings greater than 1 (no symptoms) at some point during the 20 minute immersion and 10 minute post-immersion period. Only 39% reported a rating of 1 throughout. Ratings of 2 were most commonly associated with dizziness, stomach awareness, headaches, eyestrain and lightheadedness.

The next figure illustrates the frequency of occurrence of ratings of 1 (no symptoms) and greater than 1 (all other symptoms) at each of the seven time periods at which ratings were assessed on the malaise scale.

Figure 2 illustrates the steady increase in the rate of reported symptoms throughout the immersion period with reported symptoms being greatest at the end of the 20 minute period when 45% of the subjects reported symptoms.

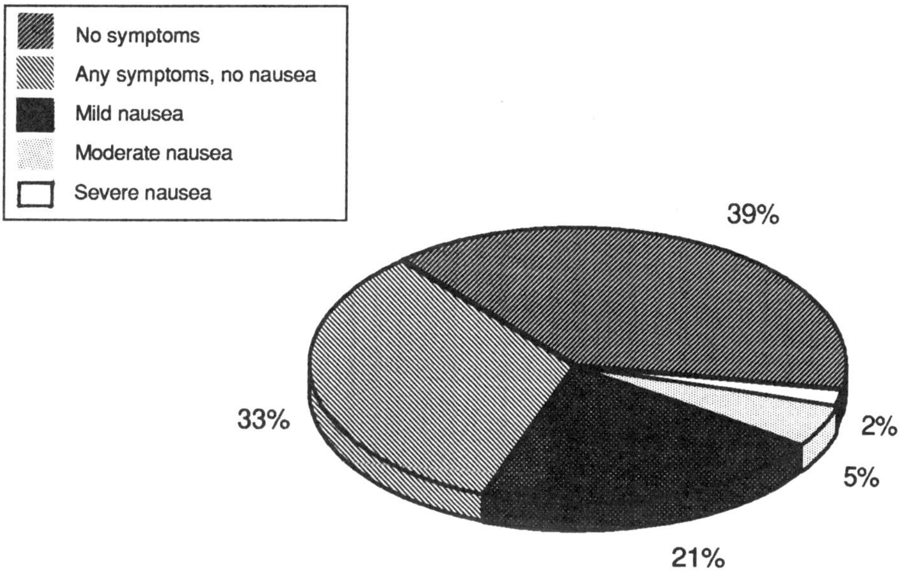

Figure 1. Percentage of subjects reporting each of the ratings on the malaise scale as their highest.

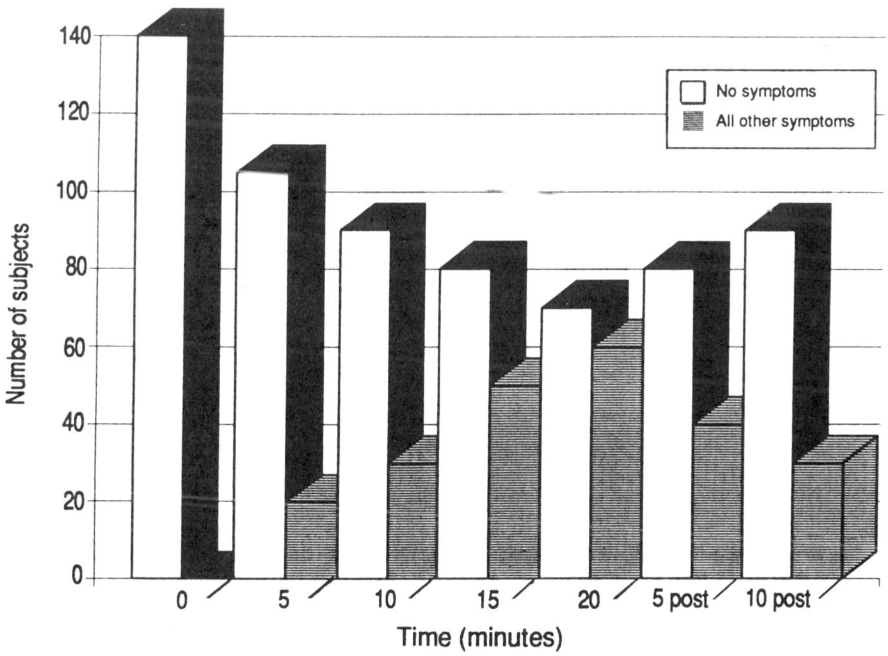

Figure 2. Frequency of occurrence of ratings of 1 (no symptoms) and greater than 1 (all other symptoms) on the malaise scale.

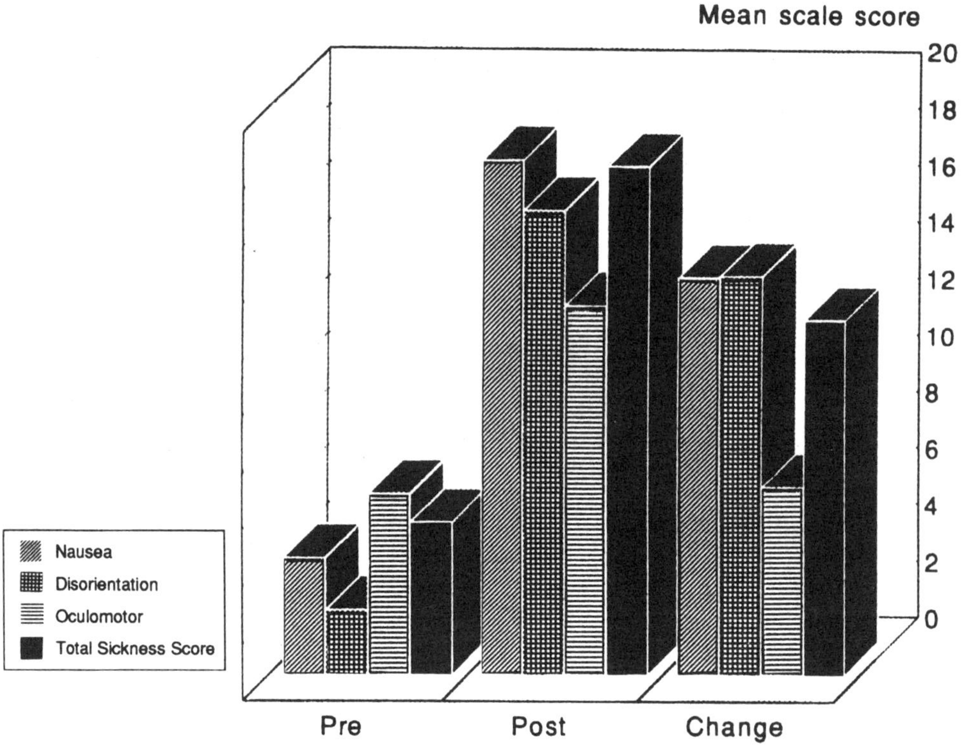

Figure 3. Symptom profiles on the Nausea, Disorientation and Oculomotor subscales.

Simulator Sickness Questionnaire Results. Kennedy et al (1993) specify a standard procedure for scoring this questionnaire. Adhering to this method yields three subscales—Nausea, Disorientation and Oculomotor—and a Total Severity measure. Scores on the Nausea subscale are based on the report of symptoms which relate to gastro-intestinal distress such as nausea, stomach awareness, salivation and burping. Scores on the Disorientation subscale are related to vestibular disarrangement such as dizziness and vertigo. Scores on the Oculomotor subscale are based on the report of symptoms such as eyestrain, difficulty focusing, blurred vision and headaches.

Figure 3 shows the pre, post and change score profiles that were derived from the questionnaire completed after immersion.

The data that was obtained with the PROVISION 200 system suggested that Nausea is the most significant problem, followed by Disorientation and Oculomotor problems, with the Disorientation problems being the more dominant of the latter two.

Conclusion

The results from this study suggested a high incidence of self-reported malaise resulting from the use of the immersive virtual reality system. 61% of the subjects reported some symptoms of malaise during the 20 minute immersion and 10 minute post-immersion period. These ranged from symptoms such as headaches and eyestrain to severe nausea. 5% of the subjects had to withdraw from the study due to the severity of their symptoms. The data suggested that adverse side-effects of immersive VR technology may be sufficiently common to threaten the suucess of further research using the VR system and of applications of the technology in its present state of development.

SOME POSSIBLE CAUSES OF THE SIDE-EFFECTS DOCUMENTED

This section will consider some of the possible causes of the side-effects documented above. Two main possible causes will be discussed.

The first of these is that immersion in VR causes a conflict of the senses which results in the malaise. The second is that technological factors, such as the resolution of the displays, are responsible for some of the symptoms.

A Sensory Conflict

Many of the side-effects which result from immersion in VR can be seen as similar to motion sickness symptoms. The fundamental signs and symptoms of motion sickness are nausea, pallor, flushing, cold sweating, abdominal discomfort, changes in gastric motility and changes in levels of circulating hormones. In addition, cardiovascular and respiratory changes have also been reported, along with a variety of other feelings and sensations.

The most commonly encountered forms of motion sickness are car sickness and sea sickness. However, another type of sickness which can be regarded as very similar to motion sickness is simulator sickness. Simulator sickness has been documented since 1957 when it was first reported in aircraft simulators (Havron & Butler, 1957). It now occurs with many current high performance simulators and reports are common. Kennedy et al (1989), for example, present data on simulator sickness in 10 US Navy flight simulators. Using data from 1,200 simulator flights they report symptoms ranging from drowsiness and eyestrain to severe nausea. Using the report of at least one characteristic motion sickness related symptom as the criterion for concern, incidences of symptoms for the different simulators ranged from 10% to 60%. Studies of Army and Air Force simulators have produced incidences of similar magnitude (eg. Chappelow, 1988; Gower et al, 1989).

Various theories of motion sickness have been proposed. Such theories are currently qualitative. None are yet capable of providing quantitative predictions of the degree of motion sickness that will occur in specific circumstances. They are useful, however, in providing a framework for the study of motion sickness.

The sensory conflict theory of motion sickness is currently one of the most popular theories. It offers explanations which can account for common forms of motion sickness such as car sickness and sea sickness, and it can also account for simulator sickness. The basis of the sensory conflict theory is that all situations which provoke motion sickness are characterized by a situation in which the signals transmitted from the visual system, the vestibular system and the non-vestibular position senses are in conflict with one another or with what we have come to expect on the basis of past experience. The conflict may be considered to fall into two main categories—either the information from the visual system and the information from the vestibular system are incompatible with one another, or the information from within the vestibular system is incompatible (ie. the canals and otoliths provide incompatible signals). Thus the explanation for motion sickness relies on the concept that a conflict of information received by the senses is a critical causal factor.

Immersive VR can be regarded as inducing sensory conflict when movement is controlled using some form of hand device as in the study reported earlier. It induces a conflict between the visual system and the vestibular system : the visual system suggests body movement but the vestibular system suggests a more static body position.

If this sensory conflict is responsible for at least some of the side-effects, such as nausea, that subjects experience during immersion in VR, then it would seem plausible that any intervention which would act to reduce the sensory conflict by bringing the visual and vestibular cues more into alignment would serve to reduce the side-effects. One possible way of reducing the sensory conflict would be to facilitate more natural methods of moving through virtual environments, in an attempt to provide more of the normal vestibular cues to movement. One possibility would be to couple subjects' movements on a treadmill to their movements through the virtual world. This would allow subjects to walk through a virtual environment. Another possibility would be to interface an exercise bike to the VR system so that subjects could cycle through a virtual environment. Thus method of movement may be a variable that has a significant role to play in dictating severity of side-effects in VR. We are currently carrying out some experimental work to investigate these alternative interaction paradigms.

Technological Factors

Sensory conflict may, or may not, offer a partial explanation for the side-effects of VR. It is unlikely, however, to be the full story. It is likely that some of the side-effects that individuals report during immersion are due to various technological factors or characteristics of current VR systems.

Three of the most significant of these factors are likely to be resolution, field of view and system lag.

Resolution

Low resolution head mounted displays (HMDs) are likely to cause greater visual system stress than higher resolution devices. However, the impact of improvements in resolution on nausea is unclear. There is some evidence that suggests that as technological advances have been incorporated into simulators there have been increasing reports of simulator discomfort. Kennedy, Lilienthal and Fowlkes (1991) report that "the problem is likely to be aggravated wtih advances in all forms of virtual environment technology and with trends for representing simulated environments in a more realistic fashion" (Biocca (1992)). The reasons for this are unclear, but perhaps suggest that visual enhancements may not entirely reduce malaise.

Field of View

It is not clear what the effect of variations in field of view are upon malaise during immersion in VR. Pausch et al (1992) conclude that the available findings with conventional non head-mounted simulator displays suggests that simulator sickness occurs more frequently and more intensely with wide field of view displays. However, it is not clear whether this finding will transfer to head-mounted displays. On the one hand, a wide field of view may create more compelling feelings of vection which may increase malaise; but on the other hand a narrow field of view may necessitate greater head movements by users which may also increase malaise.

System Lag

The literature on simulator sickness suggests that as system lag increases, subjects will become more likely to report symptoms of malaise. Anecdotal evidence also suggests that it is variations in lag, rather than lag per se, that subjects experience as particularly provocative. In the context of the previous discussion of sensory conflict, display update lags can also be seen as inducing a sensory conflict for the user. Such lags can induce a conflict when the time between an action (such as a head movement) and the result (the change in visual scene) become discernible. The visual-vestibular conflict here arises from discrepancies in time between the actual physical movement, which provides the vestibular cues, and the movement of the visual field.

However, there is currently little available data on minimum discernible lags or on acceptable levels of system lag.

Summary

These are all likely to be variables that have a significant role to play in dictating the severity of side-effects that subjects experience during immersion in VR. However, clear data on the importance of these factors is lacking. It is not sufficient simply to assume that there will be a short term technical solution and that technological developments will eliminate the problems. It is important that such factors are understood in order that an informed human factors input may be made to system development. We consequently currently have an experimental program underway to address these factors.

CONCLUSION

In conclusion, this paper has presented data on the adverse side-effects of using a current immersive virtual reality system. Although the data appertains to a particular combination of hardware and software, the results can be seen as representative of a general incidence of malaise likely to occur with the use of all current immersive VR systems.

The paper then proceeded to discuss two possible causes of the side-effects documented—sensory conflict and technological factors—and considered variables that may have significant roles to play in dictating the severity of the side-effects.

REFERENCES

Biocca, F (1992). Will simulation sickness slow down the diffusion of virtual environment technology? *Presence 1(3):334–343.*

Chappelow, J F (1988). Simulation sickness in the Royal Air Force : A survey. In *AGARD Conference Proceedings 433. Motion Cues in Flight Simulation and Simulator Induced Sickness.*

Gower, D W, Lilienthal, M G, Kennedy, R S & Fowlkes, J E (1988). Simulator sickness in US Army and Navy fixed- and rotary-wing flight simulators. In *AGARD Conference Proceedings 433. Motion Cues in Flight Simulation and Simulator Induced Sickness.*

Havron, M D & Butler, L F (1957). Evaluation of training effectiveness of the 2FH2 helicopter flight trainer research tool. *Naval Training Device Center, Port Washington, New York NAVTRADEVCEN 1915–00–1.*

Kennedy, R S, Lilienthal, M G, Berbaum, K S, Baltzley, D R & McCauley, M E (1989). Simulator sickness in U.S. Navy flight simulators. *Aviation, Space, and Environmental Medicine 60:10–6.*

Pausch, R, Crea, T & Conway, M (1992). A literature survey for virtual environments : Military flight simulator visual systems and simulator sickness. *Presence 1(3):344- 363.*

9

VIRTUAL ENVIRONMENT: FOR LEARNING OR FOR TRAINING?

A Cognitive Approach

Thierry Morineau, Paul Gorzerino, and Jean-Paul Papin

D G A / D S T I
Centre Facteurs Humains
Etablissement Technique d'Angers, France

ABSTRACT

Learning deals with new inputs coming from environment. Training involves mainly human outputs within environment. So, we want to assess the influence of virtual context on human input/output process via memory.

Experiments in Psychology found evidence of a context-dependent effect in memory process. Environment seems to play a role in acquisition and retrieval of informations and thus in learning and recall of informations.

In this experiment, we examine retention performance of words in a virtual environment and when environment changes from virtuality to reality and vice versa. No context-dependent effect is found, except a performance decrement of learning in virtual environment, but not on recall. Consequences are also discussed.

1. LEARNING AND TRAINING: INPUTS OF ENVIRONMENT AND HUMAN OUTPUTS

Learning is an acquisition of new information. And Virtual Reality has been considered as a potential tool for education. Bricken (1991) emphazises that "VR offers teachers and students unique experiences that are consistent with successful instructional strategies: hands-on learning, group projects and discussions, field trips, simulations,and concept vizualisation." (p.178). Concepts or unknown environments should become sensitive easily for everyone.

This point of view is not consistent with some evidence of Virtual Reality effects on learning. Wickens (1992) argues that a task performed with this kind of advanced user interfaces would produce a long term retention decrease in memory, despite an augmentation of performance level in situation. As Virtual Environment decreases cognitive effort, level of cognitive process required would not be satisfied to form mental links between representations of information to be learnt. Facilities in cognitive process introduced by more ecological interfaces means a reduction of mental activity and thus a degradation of learning.

Moreover, vizualisation of abstract concepts is not natural. A graphic computer model of ideas requires definition of representations. Features of representation are definied in accordance with rules. When you represent a molecule with forms and colors, this choice is driven by an analogical process and arbitrary rules (Colonna, 1993). With Virtual Reality, this representation may become the reality for the learner, who forgets arbitrary rules and who is a potential victim of visual distortions (Tversky, 1993).

Some experiments explored learning in virtual environment. Skill acquisition seems possible in virtual environment (Regian J. W. & Shebilske W.L., 1993) but transfer between virtual and real environments is not reliable (Kozak & al., 1993).

We suggest to differentiate between learning and training, even though they be two dependent notions. Learning consists in the acquisition of information provided by environment. Training involves mainly responses from human being on environment. The latter results from outputs (actions) of student on environment and the former from contextual inputs. For example, mission rehearsal is a training process. Virtual Reality can be used to simulate a mission. This application exists for astronaut crews, whose skills are tested before going into space (Null & Jenkins, 1993). But, simulators for instruction and conceptual visualization depend more on learning process.

2. EXPERIMENT

In this fundamental experiment, we test cognitive process in virtual or real environment during input acquisition and output restitution. Here, mental activity is represented by a simple memory task. Subjects must learn a list of words and remember it. This task can be described in sub-tasks, such as auditory encoding, mental organization facilitating storage, storage, retrieval in memory and verbal restitution.

In order to understand mental processes, many psychological researches concern memory. Some of them emphazise a singular phenomenon. Indeed, performance of recall seems to depend on environmental context. Subjects who learn and recall in the same environment have better memory for the information than those who change environment between learning and recall. Contextual changing decreases performance of recall significantly. This phenomenon is called "contextual dependent memory", which has been observed in 1921 by Smith & Guthrie (Farnsworth, 1934). This effect has been replicated (Godden & Baddeley, 1975; Metzger et al., 1979; Smith, 1979).

For explanation, we find that "presumably, memory is dependent on the environment because of contextual associations" (Dolinsky & Zabrucky, 1983). Connections between material to memorize and contextual cues presented in environment occur and produce the effect of dependency.

So, if Virtual reality constitutes a full environment, we can expect a performance decrement in recall when subjects change environment after learning, from virtual environment to real environment and vice versa.

2.1. Experimental Situation

Virtual and real environments used in this experiment are similar in their nature. Real environment corresponds to a room, where we find virtual reality system, personal

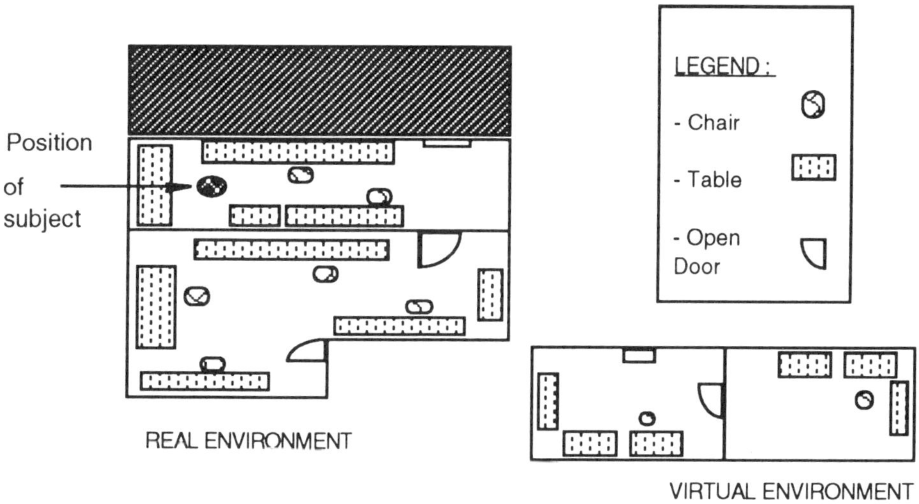

Figure 1. Maps of environments.

computers on tables and chairs. This room is near two other rooms. The first one is identical and the second one is in the dark.

Concerning virtual environment, its components are two rooms, where subjects will see computers, tables and chairs, like in real environment. They will interact with two telephones and discover a little aeroplane. No collision with objects, walls, ceiling and the ground are possible, except for the telephones.

2.2. Material

Virtual environment is fullfilled via a SILICON GRAPHICS Computer and a graphic card REALITY ENGINE2. V.R. equipment was composed of a Head Mounted Display EYEGEN3 from VIRTUAL RESEARCH, based on CRT technology, with a field of view of about 40° and an image resolution of 490X250 (NTSC).

Interaction was managed with Polhemus captors and a 3-D joystick, which was represented by a fixed hand in virtual environment. Software, called DVS, comes from DIVISION Corporation.

Note that after some problems, we had to change the Head Mounted Display. Last day of experimentation occured with a VPL RESEARCH Helmet, based on LCD technology with a field of view of 60° and an image resolution of 240X120 pixels.

Four lists composed of 25 words each were used. All the items were concrete and had high imagery values. Frequency was controlled. Each list was prepared to be homogeneous. Items were found in Paivio & al. (1968) and presented via tape.

2.3. Procedure

20 subjects, from 21 to 26 years old, coming from a Military School, Ecole d'Application du Génie, in Angers, took part in that experiment.

The experiment covered a period of 4 days. Each session included a 5 minute visit into the virtual environment and after that, a learning and recalling of the list. Each word

Table 1. Experimental conditions

Condition	Environment of learning	Environment of recall
N°1	Real	Real
N°2	Real	Virtual
N°3	Virtual	Real
N°4	Virtual	Virtual

was presented with a delay of 3 seconds. Instructions and items for each session were presented by auditory sensory channel. Learning and recall took place in virtual or in real environment.

An intra-subjects design was adopted. Each subject was tested in each experimental condition. Latin square techniques made it possible to control familarity effect with the task.

Note that 2 factors interfered with the procedure. Firstly, last session occured with a new Helmet Mounted Display, with an image resolution level lower than the first one. Secondly, 2 subjects were not available during 1 session. One of them was replaced by a new subject for the session. The other was replaced by a theoretical score, based on mean performance of subjects in the condition. So, 2 data on 80 were assessed. However, results keep their validity.

2.4. Results

We observe a main effect caused by the nature of learning environment. Performance of recall is lower when environment is virtual. An analysis of variance shows that virtual environment effect on learning stage is significant ($F=6.85$; $p=.017$).

But this effect disappears during phase of recall. Virtual environment during recall doesn't interfere with performance ($F=0.78$; $p=.39$). Thus, influence of virtual environment occurs only during learning phase, but not when subjects recall.

If we compare percentage of recall as a function of environment between our results and data found with divers, who must learn and recall words on the beach or underwater (Godden & Baddeley, 1975), scores are identical between "Real-Real" condition and "Dry-Dry" condition: respectively 38,4 % and 37,5 % of words recall. The same pattern appears for conditions in "special" environment: respectively 31,8 % of recall for "Virtual-Virtual" and 31.7 % for "Wet-Wet". So our data are reliable. And, except when conditions of environment change, people have the same performance under water and in virtual reality.

Another aspect of these results consists in the absence of context-dependent memory effect. No interaction is found between environments (virtual & real) and phases of the

Table 2. Mean percentages of words recall as function of learning and recall environment

Learning environment	Recall environment: Real	Virtual	Total
Real	38.4	38.6	38.5
Virtual	34.8	31.8	33.3
Total	36.6	35.2	35.9

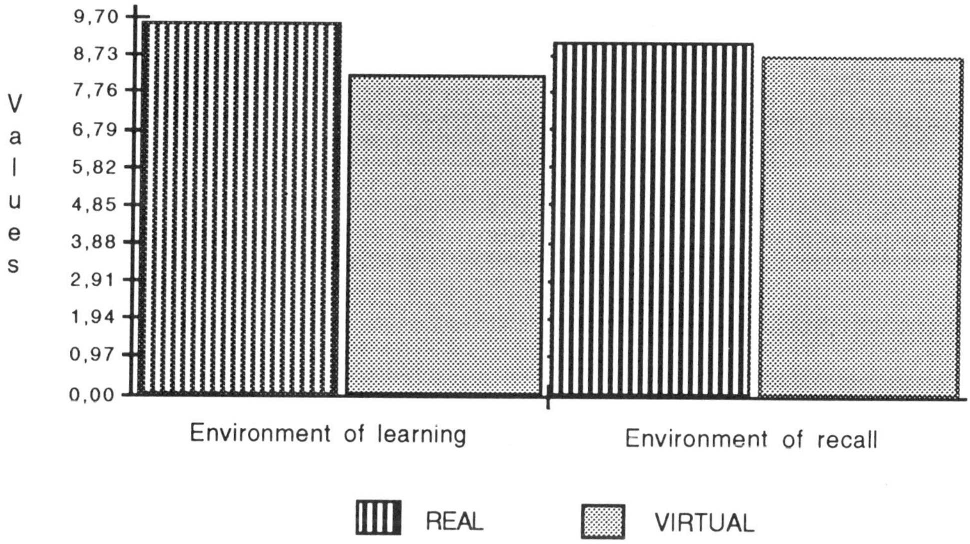

Figure 2. Items recalled.

task (learning & recall) (F=1.1; p=.31). When environment changes after learning, performance doesn't decrease. It is in contradiction with common issues in such experiments.

In order to improve our analysis, we focus on recall performance as function of serial position of words in list. So, we can divide a list in three parts. The first one corresponds to first list items (five first items). Generally, they are well recalled. This "primacy effect" is explained by availability of empty short-term memory to store new items.

The second part of the list are those for which recall is lower. The short-term memory has a limited capacity and central items overload memory. To improve remembering, subjects must organize information, in order to facilitate central items storage.

Finally, third part of the list deals with the last items encoded by subjects. Their recall takes advantage of their recency in short-term memory. During a couple of seconds, they are available in store and so have a good recall. It is the "recency effect". (see Lieury, 1986; Baddeley, 1993).

Observations allow to point out that central items are mainly affected by learning in virtual environment. Performances for primacy items and recency items are constant. Primacy effect appears clearly. But, recency effect is low. The reason is that delay between learning and restitution is quite long (30 seconds) and long enough to delete the phenomenon of recency (Baddeley, 1993).

Virtual environment effect during learning appears to be centered on central items of list. This is a strong effect. Statistical difference becomes very significant (F=15.6; p=.001).

What about evolution of the virtual environment influence on learning? If we look at scores of recall as function of the day, we find a regular decrease of virtual environment effect on learning. A practice or familiarization effect appears distinctly. This effect doesn't occur for phase of recall in virtual environment. Only learning phase is touched by it.

Note that a practice effect occurs even though each session were separed from the previous by 2 or 3 days.

Table 3. Mean number of words learned and recalled as function of environment, phase & serial position

	Primacy items (5 items)	Central items (15 items)	Recency items (5 items)
Environment of learning			
Real environment	3.1	4.78	1.75
Virtual environment	3.03	3.6	1.7
Environment of recall			
Real environment	3.03	4.3	1.83
Virtual environment	3.1	4.08	1.63

3. DISCUSSION

Virtual environment interferes with phase of learning, but not with phase of recall. It is quite surprising. This is likely to mean that only some particular stage of information processing in learning should be influenced by virtual environment. We have seen before that learning corresponds to the following sub-tasks: information encoding, organization, storage. Other stages can be connected to recall phase.

We think that virtual environment interferes with the organization stage. Indeed, encoding cannot be implied. This stage uses auditory sensory modality and this channel is constant in virtual and real conditions. A visual encoding could be victim of resolution quality or restricted field of view in virtual environment, but not an auditory encoding.

Storage cannot be implied because of the good storage of first items (primacy effect) in virtual environment. An influence of virtual environment on storage would likely reduce the primacy effect.

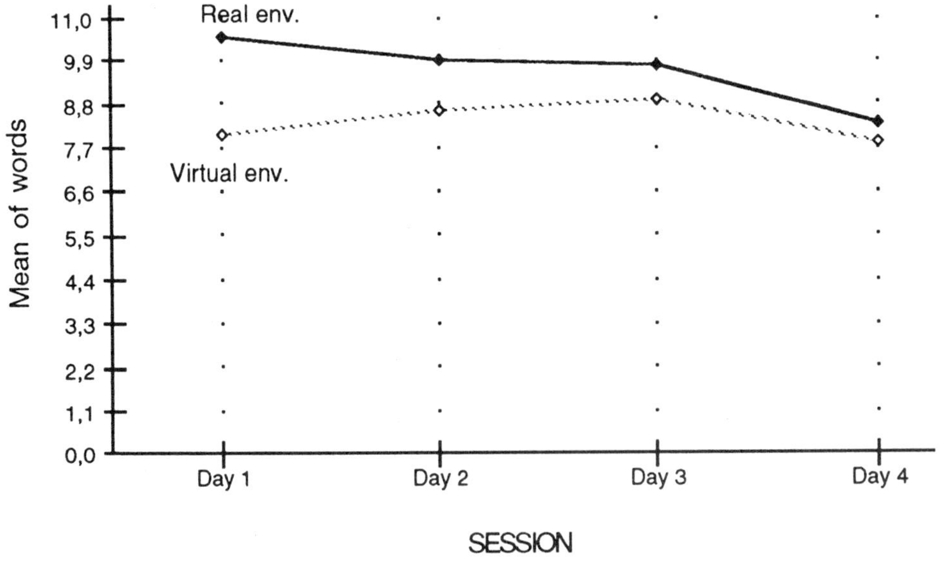

Figure 3. Evolution of recall as a function of learning environment.

Information organization seems to be the stage touched by virtual situation during learning. This influence is pointed out by the fact that central items are those which are more sensitive to process of organization. A deficit in level of organization causes a performance diminution in recall of central items.

But this degradation caused by virtual environment evolves towards a decrease of the phenomenon with time. A pratice effect occurs. This improvement of learning could mean that virtual environment causes a workload in memory. And the overload affects the process of information organization. But with pratice or familiarization of virtual environment immersion, subjects reduce the loading caused by virtual environment.

The present study shows an other phenomenon: an absence of context-dependent memory effect. Despite similarity between data found under water and our results concerning immersion in virtual environment, we don't find a performance decrement when subjects change environment. We interpret that by an assimilation process (Piaget, 1972) which conduces subjects to assimilate virtual offices to real offices. This issue is supported by spontaneous explanations of some subjects, who consider the presence of strong relations of similarity between virtual offices and real offices where they were during the experiment.

Subjects would retrieve the same cues in real and virtual environment. The consequence is a possibility to retrieve words in memory, despite environment changing.

4. CONSEQUENCES FOR LEARNING AND TRAINING

It seems that virtual environment causes a workload in memory, which interferes with high level process, such mental organization of information. As Wichens pointed out, virtual environment doesn't facilitate learning process. Two potential explanations are possible. The first one is in accordance with Wickens (op. cit.), a cognitive effort reduction in central processing system would cause a performance decrease in learning. The second possible reason consists in an augmentation of workload in central processing system, which interferes with normal learning process. Workload reductions for some sensory and motor ressources generated with advanced virtual interfaces could induce this augmentation of mental working in cognitive central system.

As we can see, a human adaptation seems to appear via our experiment. Virtual environment interference decreases with practice. That phenomenon contribute to explain the learning performance decrease in terms of workload interference in central processing system, rather than in terms of cognitive effort reduction. Familiarization with the special environment, where interactions are specific, improves the mental availability to process and organize items in memory.

Concerning training and more generally outputs production in virtual environment from human beings, any interference appears. A strong assimilation process can explain a retrieval of same cues between real and virtual similar but not identical environments.

At a cognitive level, Virtual Reality could be also a good tool for "outputs" activities, such as mission rehearsal, exercise and repetition.

5. CONCLUSION

With this preliminary experiment, we attempt to support an exploration of human behavior in virtual environment.

Virtual environment affects learning process, especially mental organization process. This phenomenon decreases with familiarization.

In phase of recall, we don't find any interference of virtual environment. But, a process of assimilation seems to facilitate retrieval of environmental cues, which support information restitution.

In one hand, these issues mean that Virtual Reality is a specific environment, where cognitive processes of environmental inputs are not easily activated. In another hand, human output processes seem to be facilitated.

These preliminary results show that a fundamental study on cognitive process is necessary to assess human behavior and to drive virtual reality application in learning and training.

6. REFERENCES

Baddeley A. (1993) "La mémoire humaine, théorie et pratique" Sciences et Technologies de la Connaissance, Presses Universitaires de Grenoble.

Burdea G. & Coiffet P. (1994) "La Réalité Virtuelle", Hermes, Paris.

Colonna J. F. (1993) "La visualisation scientifique" Revue scientifique et technique de la défense, 2, 117–124.

Dolinsky R. & Zabrucky K. (1983) "Effects of environmental context changes on memory" Bulletin of the Psychonomic Society, 21 (6), 423–426.

Ellis S.R. (1993) "Pictorial Communication in Virtual and Real Environments", second edition, Taylor & Francis.

Farnsworth P. R. (1934) "Examination in familiar and unfamiliar surroundings" Journal of Social Psychology, 128–129.

Godden D. R. & Baddeley A. D. (1975) "Context-dependent memory in two natural environments: on land and underwater" British Journal of Psychology, 66, 3, 325–331.

Kozak J.J. & al. (1993) "Transfer of training from virtual reality", Ergonomics, vol.36, N°7, 777–784.

Lieury A. (1986) "La Mémoire, résultats et théories", P. Mardaga Editeur, Bruxelles.

Metzger R. L. (1979) "The Classroom as Learning Context: Changing Rooms Affects Performance" Journal of Educational Psychology, vol. 71, n°4, 440–442.

Null C. H. & Jenkins J. P. (1993) "Nasa Virtual Environment research, Applications and Technology" A White Paper, Oct. 1993, NASA.

Paivio A. & al. (1968) "Concreteness, Imagery, and Meanignfulness Values for 925 Nouns" Journal of Experimental Psychology, Monograph Supplement, vol. 76, n°1, part 2, 1–25.

Piaget J. (1972) "Problèmes de psychologie génétique" Editions Denoël, Paris.

Regian J.W., Shebilske L.W. & Monk J.M. (1993) "Virtual reality: An Instructional Medium for Visual-Spatial Tasks", 29th International Applied Military Psychology Symposium, 26–30 July, Cambridge, U.K., 1–14.

Smith S. M. (1979) "Remenbering In and Out of Context" Journal of Experimental Psychology: human Learning and Memory, vol. 5, n°5, 460–471

Tversky B. (1993) "Distortions in memory for visual displays" in "Pictorial communication in virtual and real environments", Ed. Ellis S.R., second edition, Taylor & Francis, 61–75.

Wickens C.D. (1992) "Virtual Reality and education" IEEE International Conference on systems, man and cybernetics, 18–21 oct., Chicago, vol. 1, 842–847.

10

VIRTUAL ENVIRONMENT TECHNOLOGY IN TRAINING

Results from the Hubble Space Telescope Mission of 1993

R. Bowen Loftin,[1*] Robert T. Savely,[2] Robin Benedetti,[2] Chris Culbert,[2] Laura Pusch,[2] Robert Jones,[2] Paige Lucas,[2] John Muratore,[2] Mason Menninger,[2] Mark Engelberg,[3] Pat Kenney,[3] Lac Nguyen,[4] Tim Saito,[3] and Mark Voss[3]

[1]University of Houston-Downtown
[2]NASA/JSC
[3]LinCom
[4]I-Net

ABSTRACT

Virtual Environment (VE) technology has the potential to provide an intuitive human-computer interface of unprecedented power. Since 1990, the Software Technology Branch (STB) of NASA's Johnson Space Center, in cooperation with the University of Houston-Downtown, has been exploring the use of this technology for training, mission planning, and mission rehearsal as a adjunct to ongoing work in Advanced Training Technologies. Virtual Environments can "place" an individual into any scenario that can be copied or imagined. Thus, VEs have the potential to reduce cost and increase the availability of training that relies on expensive and often unique simulators. The STB's principal objective is the integration of VEs with its mature Intelligent Computer-Aided Training (ICAT) technology.

Simulations of elements of Space Station Freedom and Space Shuttle payloads (such as the IntellSat captured during STS-49) have been developed to test the technology's efficacy as a training tool and to identify specific research and development needs to improve training performance. During the latter half of 1993 a complete training environment for the Hubble Space Telescope (HST) repair and maintenance mission (STS-61) was built and integrated with a limited capability ICAT system. This VE was used to train over 100 members of the HST flight team—by far, the largest use of this emerging technology for a "real" application.

* Correspondence: Mail Code PT4 NASA/Johnson Space Center Houston, TX 77058 713-483-8070; 713-244-5698 (fax) bowen@gothamcity.jsc.nasa.gov

The results of this training activity have demonstrated that VE technology, especially when coupled with an ICAT system, can have a positive impact on task performance, while reducing training costs and increasing training availability. The STB has also demonstrated the ability to share Virtual Environments over long distances for collective training and concurrent engineering (with NASA/Marshall Space Flight Center and the U.S. Army). Additional activities include the creation of software tools that support the rapid development and maintenance of virtual environments by training personnel and the development of a Virtual Physics Laboratory as an educational "spinoff" of this NASA activity.

INTRODUCTION

A rapidly maturing technology first proposed in the 1960s [Hall, 1963; Sutherland, 1968; Vickers, 1970] is now being explored as a means of delivering training to NASA astronauts and ground-support personnel. Usually described as "virtual reality" (or virtual environments or synthetic environments or virtual worlds or artificial reality), this technology can provide multi-sensory data, enabling the observer to "suspend disbelief" and act as if he or she were actually somewhere else [Chung, 1989]. The technology also enables direct interaction with objects in the virtual environment, enabling the user to directly exercise control over the environment [Minsky, 1990].

Extensive research and development in virtual reality technology has been stimulated by its application in areas such as engineering design [Orr, 1989], architecture [Brooks, 1987], data visualization [Batter, 1972; Ouh-Young, 1988; Brooks, 1988; Fuchs, 1989], and teleoperation [McGreevy, 1991]. The work reported here joins a small group of efforts that have specifically examined the potential of virtual environments in training [Regian, 1992; Knerr, 1993; Kozak, 1993]. A closely-related project is also investigating the use of virtual environments in science education [Loftin, 1993; Dede, 1994].

NASA'S VIRTUAL ENVIRONMENT TECHNOLOGY FOR TRAINING PROGRAM

The NASA/JSC Software Technology Branch (STB) has been exploring the application of Virtual Environment Technology to training since 1990. Simulations of elements of the Space Station, Space Shuttle, and Space Shuttle payloads have been developed to test the technology's efficacy as a training tool and to identify specific research and development needs to improve training performance. In addition, the STB's activities include: (1) an evaluation of tactile, force, and temperature feedback mechanisms to enhance training transfer; (2) the integration of virtual environments with Intelligent Computer-Aided Training (ICAT) technology; (3) the sharing of Virtual Environments over long distances for collective training and concurrent engineering (with NASA/Marshall Space Flight Center), (4) the development of software tools that support the rapid creation, extension, and maintenance of virtual environments by training personnel; and (5) the development of virtual science laboratories for educational use at many levels.

A VIRTUAL ENVIRONMENT FOR HUBBLE SPACE TELESCOPE MISSION TRAINING

During 1993 a major project, replicating all relevant repair and maintenance scenarios for the Hubble Space Telescope mission (STS-61), was completed. Over one hundred members of the flight control team were trained, beginning in September, 1993, with this system, providing an opportunity to demonstrate the potential of virtual environment technology in training.

Six distinct training scenarios were created using two NASA-developed software tools, an ANSI C compiler, and a computer-based audio application. The Solid Surface Modeler (SSM) program was used to develop the individual environment models, or objects. This software tool was originally created at the NASA Johnson Space Center specifically for building detailed 3D objects for animations and conceptual simulations. Beginning with elementary shapes (i.*e.*, primitives), the complexity of objects was increased by combining these or altering them with geometric manipulations. Object surfaces were defined as flat or smooth with SSM, as were the color of objects using an 8-bit color palette.

The Tree Display Manager (TDM) is a real-time graphics visualization tool used to create a hierarchical representation (*i.e.*, a relationship tree) of the 3D models created with SSM. This tool was used to describe the organization of the HST elements in each scenario and to allow users to alter their view points. TDM was also used to encode the mobility and constraints of the virtual objects and to define characteristics such as light sources and objects' trajectories. The TDM tool was also developed at the NASA Johnson Space Center.

A proprietary software graphics library (Silicon Graphics, Inc.) and supporting software (developed by the STB) was used to render the virtual environments. In addition, limited Intelligent Computer-Aided Training [Loftin, 1992, 1994a] capability was integrated into the virtual environment to provide for object identification and to guide users through the complex procedures developed for the HST maintenance mission.

Figure 1. A view of the entire Hubble Space Telescope, docked to the space shuttle. The astronauts (one attached to the Shuttle's Remote Manipulator and the other working in the Shuttle's payload bay) are preparing to replace the telescope's Wide-Field Planetary Camera.

Figure 2. Astronauts trained extensively in the Weightless Environment Training Facility. Here an astronaut practices positioning a mock-up of the Wide-Field Planetary Camera. Note that many of the divers shown in this scene are employed in overcoming the viscous effects of the water when astronauts move objects. Such training was unavailable to most members of the Hubble Space Telescope Flight Team.

To accommodate the use of audio feedback in the training, the SoundTool utility provided on Sun Microsystems Sparcstations was used. This software has the capability of recording sound and storing the data as digital audio files, and playing these files over internal or external speaker systems. All of the sounds associated with the six HST scenarios (*i.e.*, object identification and status messages) were recorded with SoundTool.

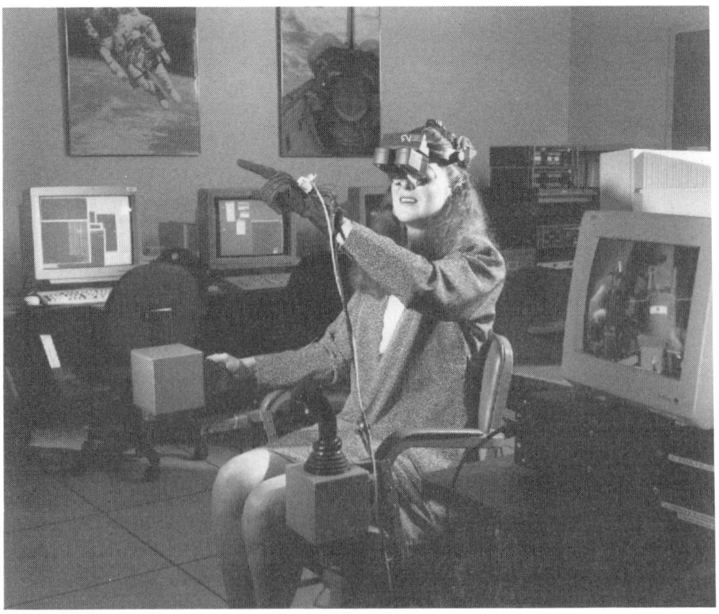

Figure 3. A flight controller uses the Hubble Space Telescope Virtual Environment for Training.

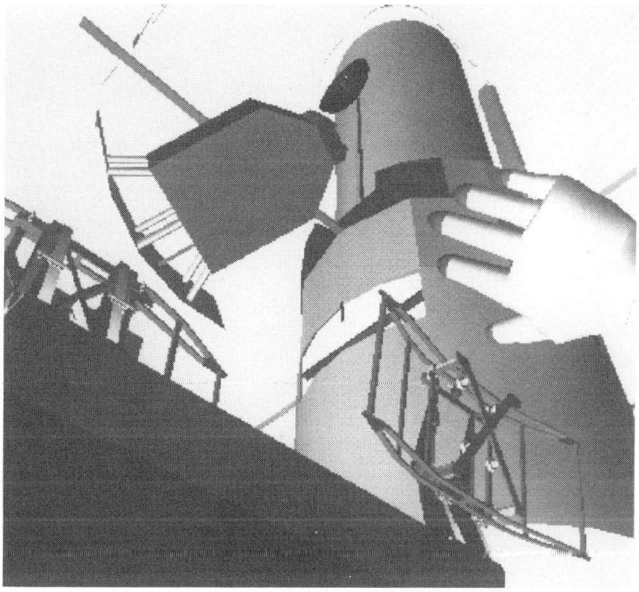

Figure 4. A typical scene within the Virtual Environment used for training for the Wide-Field Planetary Camera replacement task.

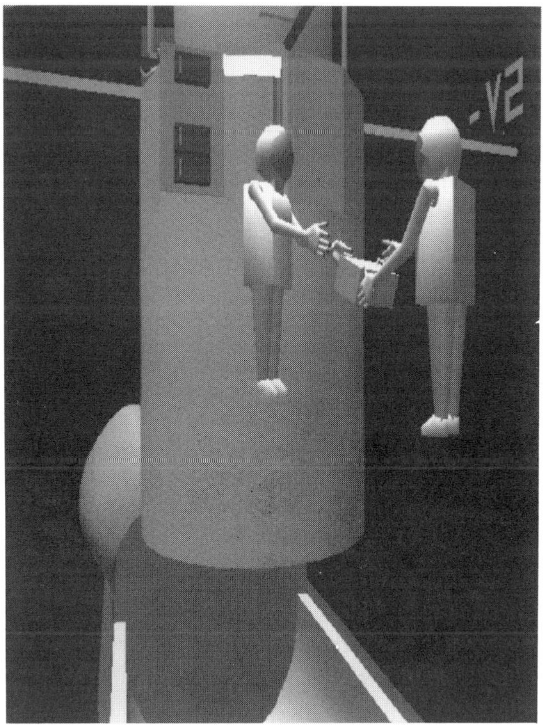

Figure 5. Astronauts Bernard Harris (in Houston) and Ulf Merbold (in Darmdtadt, Germany) prepare to carry out a cooperative task within a shared virtual environment.

In addition to models of elements of the HST, the training scenarios also contained a models of the Space Shuttle payload bay and the maintenance/replacement hardware necessary for the user to complete the major procedural steps associated with the planned maintenance activities. Six EVA scenarios were developed, coinciding with the six primary Extra Vehicular Activities scheduled for the actual mission:

1. Solar Array (SA) change-outs,
2. Rate Sensor Unit (RSU) change-outs,
3. Corrective Optics Space Telescope Axial (COSTAR) replacement,
4. Wide Field/Planetary Camera (WF/PC II) change-out,
5. Solar Array Drive Adapter Electronics (SADE) replacement, and
6. Magnetic Sensing System (MSS) Magnetometer installation over original Magnetometers.

The specific procedural steps associated with each of the EVA tasks were determined from the written procedures used for mission training and operations and from extensive reviews of video recordings of astronauts undergoing training in the Weightless Environment Training Facility.

RESULTS

After the completion of the HST mission a survey instrument was delivered to all members of the flight team that received training in the virtual environment. Perhaps the most important result of this survey concerned the overall effectiveness rating of training. Users graded overall effectiveness at "slightly over effective" or 4.08 (out of a range of 0 - 5). Graph 1 shows these results for both individual scenarios and the overall effectiveness. Written comments showed that users found that the use of the virtual environment enabled accurate visualization of the HST, its components, and the mission activities. Other comments also noted that efficiency in training delivery was increased. The audio and ICAT support in the system received an average rating of 4.2 (out of a range of 0–5) for its enhancement of the training effectiveness of the experience (see Graph 2).

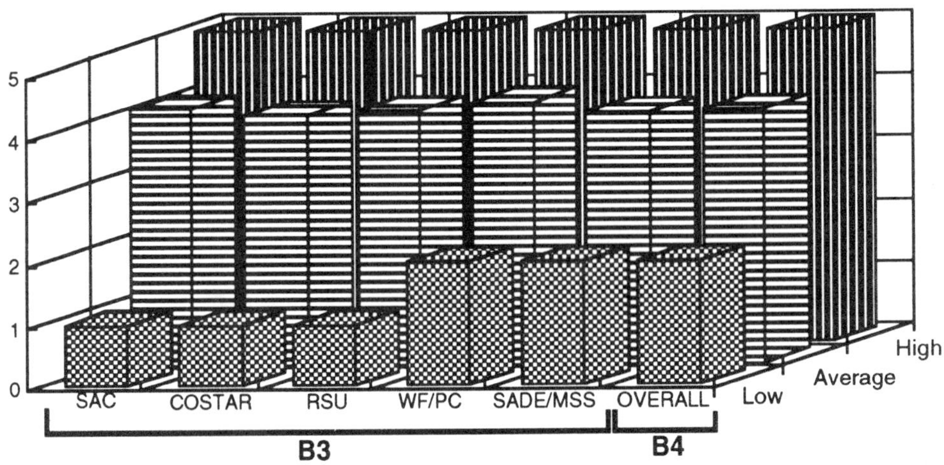

Graph 1. Effectiveness of individual scenarios and overall rating.

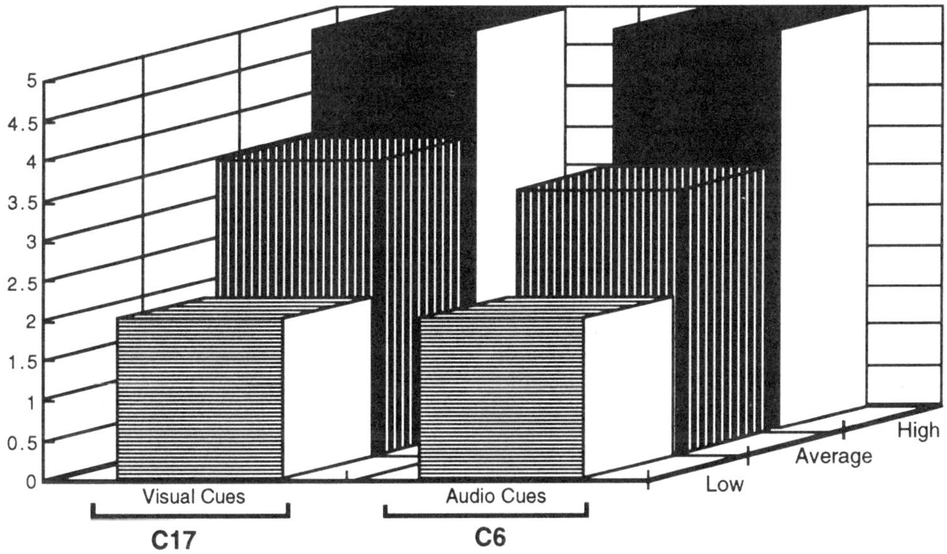

Graph 2. Effectiveness ratings of audio and visual instructional aids.

An interesting trend from the survey dealt with physical side-effects such as nausea, oculomotor problems, and disorientation resulting in mild cases of simulator sickness. Graph 3 summarizes the results of the simulator sickness questionnaire [Kennedy, 1993] that was administered. Apparently, compared with current and past simulator sickness studies, these trainees reported relatively lower rates of the various side-effects described by Kennedy [1992].

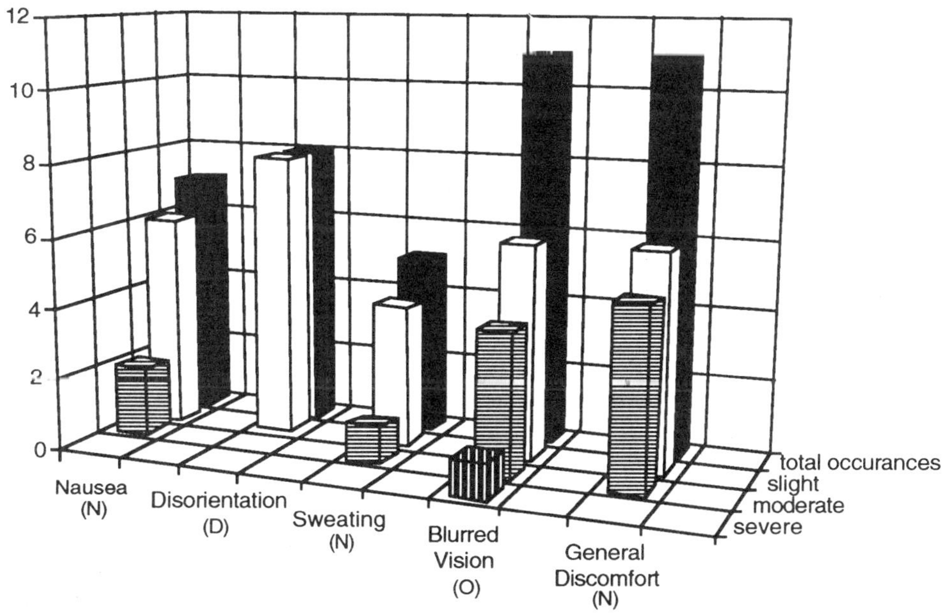

Graph 3. Simulator sickness symptoms and instances.

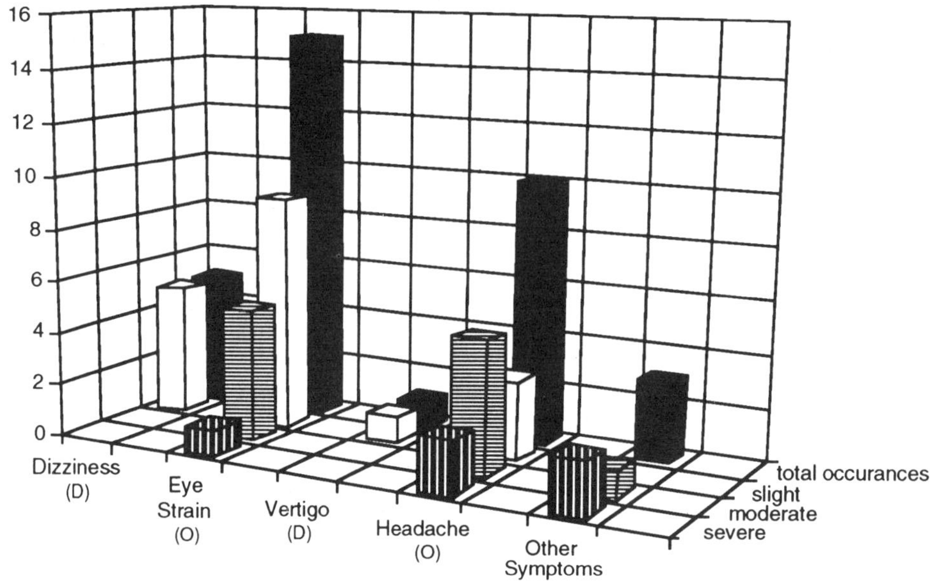

Graph 3. (*Continued.*)

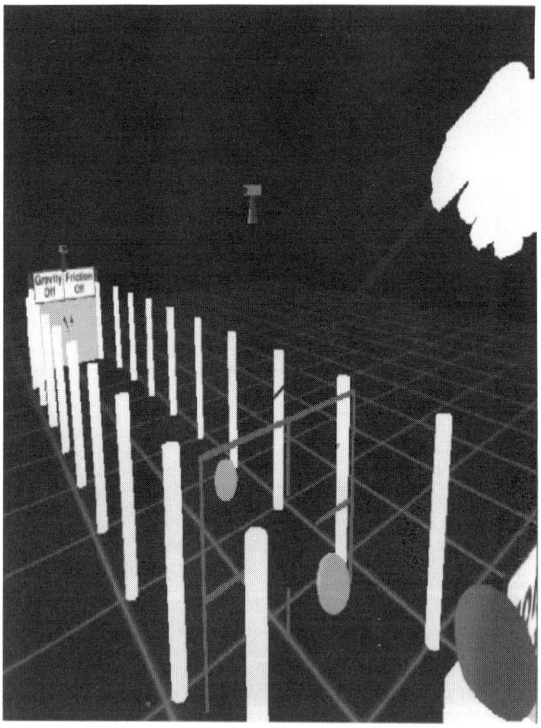

Figure 6. NewtonWorld: A user is "perched" at a camera view located atop a wall at the end of the corridor and is preparing to translate to a view from within the selected ball.

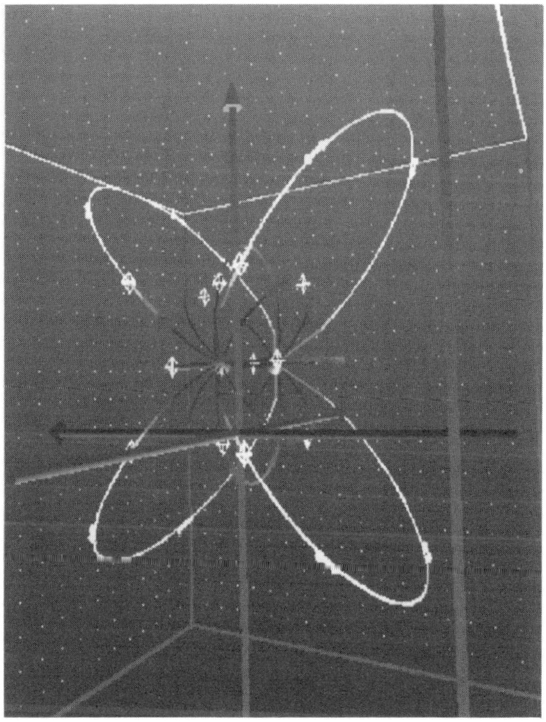

Figure 7. MaxwellWorld: A view from outside the world showing an electric dipole with both force vectors on positive test charges and a number of electric field lines.

Figure 8. PaulingWorld: A model of the cabbage protein is shown with some amino acids represented by labeled boxes and others in ball-and-stick form.

A more detailed description of the training scenarios, the training process, and the post-mission survey results is contained in the paper by Loftin [1994b] and in an internal NASA Report (available from the author).

CONCLUSIONS

As the results reported above demonstrate, members of the flight team judged, on the average, that the use of virtual environments for training had a positive effect on their job performance during the HST repair and maintenance mission. These positive experiences have broadened and deepened the interest of NASA in the use of Virtual Environment Technology as a training tool. Perhaps just as important is the ability that VEs afford for the training of personnel who currently receive little or no experiential preparation for their assigned tasks.

ACKNOWLEDGMENTS

The authors gratefully acknowledge the support of the HST flight team in both providing data essential to the construction of the HST virtual environment and for their willingness to participate in an experimental training program. The work report here involved many NASA civil servants, contractors, and students. This work was supported, in part, by the NASA Office of Space Systems and by NASA Grant NAG 9-713.

REFERENCES

Batter, 1972] J. J. Batter and F. P. Brooks, Jr., "GROPE-1," *IFIPS Proceedings 71*, 759.

Brooks, 1987] F. P. Brooks, Jr., "Walk Through—A Dynamic Graphics System for Simulating Virtual Buildings," *Computer Graphics 21* (1), 3 (January, 1987).

Brooks, 1988] F. P. Brooks, "Grasping Reality through Illusion—Interactive Graphics Serving Science," in *Proceedings of ACM SIGCHI*, Washington, DC, 1–11, 1988.

Chung, 1989] J. C. Chung, M. R. Harris, F. P. Brooks, Jr., H. Fuchs, M. T. Kelley, J. Hughes, M. Ouh-Young, C. Cheung, R. L. Holloway, and M. Pique, "Exploring Virtual Worlds with Head-Mounted Displays," in *Proceedings of the SPIE Conference on Three-Dimensional Visualization and Display Technologies*, Los Angeles, January 18–20, 1990, 42–52.

Dede, 1994] C. Dede, M. Salzman, C. Calhoun, R. B. Loftin, J. Hoblit, and W. Regian, "The Design of Artificial Realities to Improve Learning Newtonian Mechanics," in *Proceedings of the East-West Conference on Multimedia, Hypermedia, and Virtual Reality*, Moscow, Russia, September 14–16, 1994.

Fuchs, 1989] H. Fuchs, M. Levoy, and S. M. Pizer, "Interactive Visualization of 3-D Medical Data," *IEEE Computer*, 46–50 (August, 1989).

Hall, 1963] M. R. Hall and J. W. Miller, "Head-Mounted Electro-Ocular Display: A New Display Concept for Specialized Environments," *Aerospace Medicine*, 316- 318 (April, 1963).

Kennedy, 1992] R. S. Kennedy, N. E. Lane, M. G. Lilienthal, K. S. Berbaum, and L. J. Hettinger, "Profile Analysis of Simulator Sickness Symptoms: Application to Virtual Environment Systems". *Presence, 1*, pp. 295–301.

Knerr, 1993] B. W. Knerr, D. R. Lampton, J. P. Bliss, J. M. Moshell, and B. S. Blau, "Assessing Human Performance in Virtual Worlds," Proceedings of the 1993 Conference on Intelligent Computer-Aided Training and Virtual Environment Technology (Houston, TX: NASA/Johnson Space Center), Vol. II, p. 270.

Kozak, 1993] J. J. Kozak, P. A. Hancock, E. J. Arthur, and S. T. Chrysler, "Transfer of Training from Virtual Reality," *Ergonomics 36*, pp. 777–784.

Loftin, 1992] R. B. Loftin and R. T. Savely, "Advanced Training Systems for the Next Decade and Beyond," *Proceedings of the AIAA Space Programs and Technologies Conference* (Washington, DC: American Institute for Aeronautics and Astronautics) AIAA Paper 92–1626.

Loftin, 1993] R. B. Loftin, R. B. Loftin, M. Engelberg, and R. Benedetti, "Applying Virtual Reality in Education: A Prototypical Virtual Physics Laboratory," *Proceedings of the IEEE 1993 Symposium on Research Frontiers in Virtual Reality* (Los Alamitos, CA: IEEE Computer Society Press), pp. 67–74.

Loftin, 1994a] R. B. Loftin, L. Wang, P. Baffes, and G. Hua, "General Architecture for Intelligent Computer-Aided Training," U.S. Patent Number 5,311,422, awarded May, 1994.

Loftin, 1994b] R. B. Loftin, P. Kenney, R. Benedetti, C. Culbert, M. Engelberg, R. Jones, P. Lucas, M. Menniger, J. Muratore, L. Nguyen, T. Saito, R. Savely, and M. Voss, "Virtual Environments in Training: NASA's Hubble Space Telescope Mission," to appear in *Proceedings of the Interservice/Industry Training Systems and Education Conference*, Orlando, Florida, November 28-December 1, 1994.

McGreevy, 1991] M. W. McGreevy, "Virtual Reality and Planetary Exploration," in *Proceedings of the 29th AAS Goddard Memorial Symposium*, Washington, DC, March, 1991.

Minsky, 1990] M. Minsky, M. Ouh-Young, O. Steele, F. P. Brooks, Jr., and M. Behensky, "Feeling and Seeing: Issues in Force Display," in *Proceedings of Symposium of 3-D Interactive Graphics*, Snowbird, Utah, March, 1990.

Orr, 1989] J. N. Orr, "Exotic CAD," *Computer Graphics World 12* (7), 88–89 (July, 1989).

Ouh-Young, 1988] M. Ouh-Young, M. Pique, J. Hughes, N. Srinivasan, and F. P. Brooks, Jr., "Using a Manipulator for Force Display in Molecular Docking," IEEE publication CH2555–1/88, 1824–1829.

Regian, 1992] J. W. Regian, W. L. Shebilske, and J. M. Monk, "Virtual Reality: An Instructional Medium for Visual-Spatial Tasks," *J. Communication 42*, pp. 136- 149.

Sutherland, 1968] I. E. Sutherland, "Head-Mounted Three-Dimensional Display," in *Proceedings of the Fall Joint Computing Conference 33*, 757–764 (1968).

Vickers, 1970] D. Vickers, "Head-Mounted Display Terminal," in *Proceedings of the IEEE Int. Computer Group Conference*, 102–109, 1970.

11

VE AND TRAINING, LIMITATIONS, AND OPPORTUNITIES

W. A. Lotens and J. B. J. Riemersma

TNO Human Factors Research Institute
P.O. Box 23, 3769ZG Soesterberg, The Netherlands

VE TECHNOLOGY

Virtual Environment (VE) is a combination of traditional, existing and new technologies, rather than a technology by itself. Therefore it is hard and probably useless to draw sharp borders between what belongs to VE and what not. In the integration of technology in society there is a gradual transition from data files to multimedia (MM) and from there to VE. Relevant for implementation in training is not whether a technology is identified as VE, but what it adds to the functionality of a training system. The central topic of this paper is what the new functionalities are and how they can be exploited.

Characteristics of VE Functionality

In a typical VE a 3D world is created, which surrounds the observer more or less. The visual and auditory senses are stimulated and in some occasions also the tactile system. By means of real actuators the observer communicates with the system, for instance with a joystick or a data glove. In some applications the activator is indirectly used, not to control a system, but to handle a virtual device. Grabbing and moving an object in a VR by means of a data glove is such an application. Despite the appeal of the idea to experience a non-existing environment this is not the most powerful use of VE-technology. The essential of VE technology is that all aspects of the environment are under digital control and of the user under digital monitoring, stored in databases, controlled by efficient constructs such as models. In this way all that happens in the VE is determined by a tiny flow of information. Using the same information, two completely different VE's could be presented, which are fundamentally identical, but differ in appearance. As an example: the spatial location of an object may be communicated to the observer by a light source, a spatial sound or a tactile sensation on his back. Another way to express this feature is to state that dramatically different interfaces may be set up for the same system and that switching between interfaces is easily done. The characteristic of the VE is thus that the tiny information flow is expanded to full size environments.

Virtual Reality, Training's Future? edited by Seidel and Chatelier
Plenum Press, New York, 1997

This requires a lot of computing power, but very modest networks.

Traditional technology, such as video does the opposite: the equipment is simple, but the bandwidth requirements excessive for the magnitude of information that is transmitted.

A VE works also the other way around. The actions of the user are registered and are available for analysis. This is not a slight advantage, since training effect has to be evaluated and feedback during the training is essential for the control over the learning process.

Contrast to Existing Technologies

The VE functionality is added to the power of existing and traditional technologies for training. Such technologies are education science, simulation (a real system with a simulated environment such as driving and flight simulators), computer supported training (programmed instruction, individual training programs, diagnostic systems) and multimedia (adding motion, sound and various viewing angles to text and static images). The probably largest difference between this category of technology and VE technology is the level of interaction: with existing technology preprogrammed chunks of information are selected and presented in desirable order (a typical CD-i or CD-ROM approach), with VE technology the system reacts precisely to the commands of the user, because the system is exactly modeled and controlled by means of input parameters. This allows for variable points of view, control of speed and amplitude, change of lighting conditions, unlimited range of initial conditions, runs of indefinite duration, etc.

TRAINING

Transfer of Training

A training system should be designed to train specific skills. The better the aim of the system is defined the more specific the design can be and the better the transfer of training to the real task. The trainer need not necessarily Be realistic, as long as the essential skill is right. Excellent trainers have been demonstrated for electric welding, where the metal work was a monitor screen, the welding tool a lightpen and the heat a white spot on the screen. Despite this lack of realism the essential skill, to control the heat by maintaining the right distance to the work, was trained well. For other tasks the demands may be different and some may even require realism. In recent research on the perception of virtual workspaces (technical centre of a frigate) it was found that visually empty environments (flat shading, flat colours, large surfaces) are perceived less accurate than environments with detailed texture (Werkhoven and Kooi, 1994).

Perceptual-Motoric Trainers

VE based systems are designed for real time interactions and therefore in principle suited to train perceptual-motoric tasks. In particular with VE the training of those tasks can be done that require motor control over vehicles that move in space. The 3D vision ability of a VE is helpful for this purpose. In some environments, specially those that closely surround the user's body, computer generation of detailed images is cumbersome and undesirable. An example is a task in which an observer can see his own hands. Modeling these hands would require data gloves to sense finger posture and trackers to monitor position and orientation of the hands. The computer has to generate a robot-like hand (like the Thing of the Adams Family) that mimics the actions of the real hand and this robot hand is visually presented at the position where the real hand is. It would be much easier to just show an image of the real hand or use see-through glasses. Mixing real images with virtual components is called Augmented Reality (AR) and we regard this as a useful compromise between VE and real life. A second and very urgent argument is that for correct feedback of forces (sitting on a chair, leaning on a surface, putting objects down) some physical structures are indismissable. In general, in a perceptual motoric trainer there will be some real controls, like a wheel, (force feedback) joystick, pushbuttons etc.

Perceptual Cognitive Trainers

Purely cognitive training is not dependent on the specific features that VE provides. However, many cognitive tasks depend on information collection and the presentation of this information many profit from VE features. Data retrieval and representation has links to imaginary spaces, containing the structure of the data (the mental map). Retrieval procedures depend on the mental map and the other way around, data storage requires structure and creates a mental map. This becomes particularly evident when navigating through a space. When the vesibular system keeps up with the turns that are made in a maze, orientation is not lost. The way out may be hard to find, but observers know where the exit is. If the maze is navigated by means of a virtual or teleoperated vehicle, such that in rounding a corner the head remains in a fixed direction, but the image sweeps by, people get lost very quickly. Apparently the development of the mental map depends strongly on sensorial input.

Mental maps are extensively exploited in exploratory learning. In contrast to cursory instruction, exploratory learning puts the responsibility for the implementation of the learned material on the student. The student has the difficult task to uncover the relationships between the newly gained knowledge, which demands a high degree of interaction. Conventional interfaces put during heavy interaction a high workload on the student, which goes at the expense of the learning process. VE interfaces can decrease the workload by easier recognition of objects, spatial ordering, large size environments as compared to some monitor screen, etc. This becomes obvious in the example where a student has to assemble a device from parts that have to be retrieved from a store.

The conventional interface would be that he has to look up parts in listings, collect them and mount them by selecting instructions, mount substructures and then assemble the device, carefully stating the order.

With a VE interface he would recognize the parts in the racks around him, pick them with a selection tool and mount by manipulating the parts manually. Not only would the cumbersome procedure be simplified, also would the essential skill of fitting shapes be developed.

The use of mental maps tends to develop with the increased experience of the observer. Inexperienced observers explore routes, whereas experienced observers rely less on routes and jump between familiar places. The interface of the system should for optimal training systems adapt to the achieved level of experience, which is a very advanced topic in current training science.

LIMITATIONS OF VE

Current VE systems provide a limited range of perceptual stimuli. Visual and auditory presentation is better developed than haptic or vestibular. In the following list the state-of-the-art is summarized.

- *Vision.* There is a trade off between field of view (FOV) and pixel resolution, governed by the total number of pixels in the display. High end systems provide IM full colour pixels, low end systems about 30k monochromatic pixels. Even a high end system can only provide good resolution over a 20 degree FOV, or alternatively low resolution (visus .15) over a good FOV. Peripheral vision is troublesome, since displays have flat surfaces, which hardly can reach into the peripheral visual field. Colour reproduction and brightness of the screen are limited but useable. Stereoscopic vision on displays is limited by optical constraints (the stereo volume is not so large, limited to the overlap of the two eyes and the allowed disparity range) and viewing is unnatural and tiring.
- *Hearing.* Quality sound can be produced, but spatial orientation depends on subtle differences between the shapes of individual ears and heads and therefore requires individual calibration. Distinct localization of virtual sound sources is difficult. The creation of multiple virtual sound sources requires additional hardware. Extensive sound generation techniques are available, including synthesizers and digital samplers.
- *Feeling.* Tactile displays are in their infant days. The skin contains four different types of tactile sensors, and these together produce a rich spectrum of tactile experiences. Integration over surface area and time is an important feature of the tactile system. Tactile displays are small in number of pixels, in skin area stimulated (usually only finger tips) and in variety of tempero-spatial patterns. The only realistic option at this time is to provide tactile feedback for collision detection (like in grabbing an object). This done by pneumatic or vibro-tactile elements.
- *Force.* Primitive devices have been developed to enable body parts to exercise forces relative to other body parts. A well known example is the set of pneumatic cilinders that allows fingers to squeeze a virtual ball. Exerting forces to the environment (like simulating weight) is cumbersome, involving mechanical constructions and wires. The mechanical feedback devices are expensive, sensitive to failure, and potentially hazardous when malfunctioning. The best developed application is in force feedback joysticks. (See the sections on sensory feedback in the IEEE VRAIS conference, Seattle, Sept. 18–22, 1993).
- *Vestibular.* Moving bases provide some vestibular stimulation in concert with visual motion cues. Moving bases may have six degrees of freedom, but usually with limitation to 20 degrees of rotation and a few decimeters of translation. Wider ranges are available a fewer degrees of freedom. Since low accelerations cannot be noticed, moving bases are most effective in the high end of the frequency spectrum. Slow movements are better presented in a visual mode. The physical limitation of the moving base can thus in part be compensated by visual stimuli. Simulator sickness is a mode of motion sickness, related to discrepancy between vestibular and visual (and probably haptic) perception. The latest view on the cause of simulator sickness is that a deviation of the subjective vertical (estimated by the senses) and the real vertical (gravity) is critical (Bles and Bos, 1994). Such a deviation may result from time lags in the system, in particular from the head tracker and due to computation time, and from disorientation. Simulator sickness is potentially a threat to effective training, since it affects the motivation of the student.

MERITS OF VE

Team Training

One thing that VE can do effectively is to simulate large scale exercises, that would be too expensive to perform life. Such exercises are command and control training, battlefield simulation, disaster control, and basically all exercises that involve large staff, expensive vehicles, environmental concern and dangers to the participants. Such exercises can seldom be repeated in real life, if succeeding at all. Yet this would be desirable, in order to provide the participants not only with the experience, but to also allow them to optimize their performance. In small groups like military units typical performance increments of tasks with fixed procedures have been measured of 40 to 50%, developing in 3 to 4 replications (mortar groups, aircraft loading crew, artillery group, Holewijn, 1990). There is little reason to believe that for larger groups the required number of repetitions may be smaller, since the critical tasks are often more complicated. Experiments on company level showed larger learning effects, with similar timing (setting up a chemical decontamination street). In particular training of teams that do not work according to rigid procedures may take long learning times.

Exploration

A second excellent use of VE would be the exploration of unknown environments. The aim will often be the planning of activities, involving judgment of locations, checking on availability of resources, estimate space requirements, plan transport, etc. Examples are space flight rehearsal, planning of military actions and evaluation of equipment design. In the latter example enemy aircraft can fight with current or future own aircraft to develop tactics, set requirements for weapons, estimate losses, prepare for repair and replenishment, etc.

Being Up to Date

Although not explicitly assumed, usually VE will share databases between participants, mostly on-line, assuring that they have the latest update available. This may require networking. The network also allows participants to be geographically spread, without further complications.

CONDITIONS FOR EFFECTIVE TRAINING

Controlled versus Interactive Learning

What opportunities do multi-user simulated exercises offer in terms of training? In conventional training the learning goal is fixed and the learning process is directed towards developing skills that meet that specific goal (controlled learning). In large scale training the goal is not fixed, but depends on the reaction of the opponent (interactive learning). That is not an ideal learning condition and learning may be slow, but it allows for developing intelligence. Intelligence in this respect is the aggregation of experience, as in artificial intelligence research. The success of the process depends on the various links in the command chain. If the lower skills are not developed, the exercise will fail. Thus a condition for success is that an order of development of skills is maintained:

1. individual skills such as control behavior of weapon systems, navigation
2. explicit team training on group level (communication, mutual correction, trust, support)
3. using the environment properly for tactical purposes (terrain, weather, camouflage, etc.)
4. only then variable goals may be trained with success. It is not certain that the training process will converge to a set of stable higher order strategic rules. Little data is available on the conditions for convergence.

In a networked VE training system the use of synthetic partners may be considered to create the right conditions for the development of strategic skills.

Training with the Right Means

Training conditions need to be identical to operational conditions. It is tempting to provide the commander with VE visualization technology, which is probably an excellent means to express the result of the work of the intelligence officer, but this should only be done if the commander will have the same tools available in operational conditions.

Instruction

Another consideration is that a training system need not only provide the training condition, but also the support with actual instructions. These may be presented by voice or as hypertext. Augmented reality techniques are useful here. By approaching an object data can be brought up about it, including text, schematic drawings, spatial characteristics (for instance possible movements, effect predictors) and moving images. Instruction can be presented this way. The instruction needs to be structured according to a student model, which is the aim of computer supported education. Instruction systems with an intelligent diagnosis of errors of the student are under study, but not yet far developed. Including an instruction system in parallel to the instruction condition requires an adapted interface, with possibilities for highlighting information, providing global versus detailed information, etc.

EXAMPLES

In the following a few relevant examples of military training situations are commented upon with respect to VE technology opportunities

Weapons Recognition

Studies in weapons recognition show that detection is a more relevant problem than recognition(..). Once detection took place, recognition and identification follow quickly. VE's tend to be flat in structure in order to simplify the calculation of the images and that is not what is needed here. Emphasis should be put on camouflage, concealment, lighting conditions, environmental circumstances (dust, smoke, visibility, noise) etc. Recognition depends largely on typical features of the weapons, such as size, gloss, motion characteristics and other details. That requires a lot of detail, which is not the strongest point on VE's. However, showing various aspects of the weapons in an environment that really requires searching, integrated in a scenario with realistic likelihoods, may outweigh the shortcomings mentioned. Also the ability to zoom in on possible targets and to simulate instrumental images from combined sensors are useful additions.

Networked Exercise

Networked exercise imply two essential elements, the first that the exercise involves other participants and the second that the other participants need to be at the same location. Networks have a limited bandwidth, so reduction of information flows is important. With SIMNET only position information is sent to partners when the error between real and predicted position exceeds a threshold. The information can be interpreted by the receiver in many ways, depending on the definition of his own equipment. This provides a great deal of flexibility. It has been estimated that the real information exchanged between communicating persons is no more than few tens of bytes per second; 35 of these persons would be able to have a teleconference over a single telephone line (Lotens, 1995). In that view ATM networks, with bandwidth up to 150 MB per second seem a waste. ATM aims at transferring moving digitized images, which do not allow for much transformation. SIMNET is thus a more future oriented approach than ATM, despite the seemingly opposite. Networked exercises save a great deal of transport and logistics and allow interactive work between participants. To achieve training goals the elementary skills need be at level, as explained before. The goals are harder to define, compared to a single student system. At this time the goals are not well defined and consequently a choice between systems cannot be made. It is well possible that a distinction between different levels of training has to be made. Such a distinction could be:

- Technical skills: learning how to control equipment, communication and procedures; stand alone system.
- tactical skills: use of circumstances and terrain, handling losses and failures, achieving limited goals; playing against a synthetic opponent, not necessarily networked.
- group performance: working together with other friendly units towards a mutual goal, against a synthetic opponent; networked system.
- strategic skills: working together against a real opponent; networked system.

Given the current state of perceptual quality of VE's it is important to match this quality between participants. Unequal detection chances or unequal accuracy of actions may lead to learning of wrong behavior, which in turn may result in negative transfer of training.

Mission Rehearsal

Mission rehearsal or planning is one of the most suitable applications VE to training. In particular when equipment is mobile and can be installed at location the advantages are great. In action, missions cannot be trained without risk to crew and equipment or without the risk of uncovering tactics to the enemy. Geographical databases are available for most of the earth surface, providing 100 foot resolution. The accuracy for altitude is better, but may be not as accurate as desirable for ground vehicle tactics (order of meters).

For air missions the resolution is good enough. In fact, large commercial aircraft manufacturers are developing synthetic panoramas for cockpitless aircraft, based on VE technology. For flying in at airports more detailed databases are included, that show runways, buildings, etc.

For many mission rehearsals the sight conditions are extremely critical. An accurate idea of the lines of sight should be developed. In comparison to the cognitive effort involved in imagining a view from a viewpoint from abstract information like a map with altitude errors. The importance of visualization as a support of the user also points at the importance of providing geographically correct information. If this information is inaccurate, the whole system turns into a disadvantage.

CONCLUSIONS

VE technology can add functionality to training, compared to traditional technologies, including multimedia. A training system should consist of a presentation system, along with an instruction and evaluation system. The measure of success will be the transfer of training and not the realism of the presentation. However, the perceptual quality of the presentation system can be very relevant for its function. Some presentations depend heavily on the accuracy of the database involved and the flexibility of the image generator. Communication of haptic, force and vestibular information is very limited with the current state of technology. Much of the functionality of a VE comes from the possibility to replicate large scale exercises, to learn in a exploratory way, to carry out interactive training with a human opponent and to manipulate basic information, instead of sound, images etc. It becomes possible to merge synthetic and real environments and to adapt training systems to the level of the student.

REFERENCES

Blex, W. And J.E. Bos (1994). A spatial orientation model. Report TNO Human Factors Research Institute, 1994 A-58, Soesterbert.

Holewijn, M. (1990) Loss of performance due to IPE. What's known. AGARD Conf Proce. 457, p 361–367.

Lotens, W.A. (1995) Real human factors research in a virtual environment. Report TNO Human Factors Research Institute, in preparation.

Werkhoven, P.J. and F.L. Kooi (1994). Spatial perception in a virtual operations room.
Report TNO Human Factors Research Institute 1994 A-53, Soesterberg.

12

VIRTUAL REALITY ISSUES IN TRAINING ENVIRONMENTS

Summary of Current State of Office of Naval Research (ONR) Efforts

Helen M. Gigley

Cognitive and Neural Science and Technology Division, Code 342
Office of Naval Research

ABSTRACT

Advances in the use of virtual environments (VE) for Navy operation and training have been made along several dimensions. Chiefly, the emphasis in the initial stages has been on building virtual environments. Emphasis has been on developing several different virtual reality situational displays where different levels of immersion can be provided. These include cave environments, head-mounted displays integrated with other immersive interaction capability displays such as data gloves or the PHANToM device to study what is effective VR. Initial investigations have shown that VR is not a solution for all rehearsal and training problems. Sometimes the technology does not provide a suitable environment for the desired outcome.

A brief overview of what has been achieved, the need for evaluation of all aspects of the work, from level of fidelity or granularity of display to different interaction devices and capabilities will be presented. In conclusion, preliminary information concerning the *cost* of doing business in VR will be raised as an important part of the approach.

BACKGROUND OF ONR VR PROGRAM

The ONR program in Virtual Environments for Training, Targeting and Teleoperation (VETT) began with a basic research option plan in 1994. The basis for proposing the new start at that time was that VE interfaces were claimed to provide a unique property which can create for the human user, the sensation that they are immersed in a tangible environment where they can move, interact with, and manipulate objects as if they were real. The technology was at a formative level and basic research questions regarding its

Virtual Reality, Training's Future? edited by Seidel and Chatelier
Plenum Press, New York, 1997

useability, effectiveness, and efficiency needed to be addressed. The suggested methods of study included the collaborative interaction among multidisciplinary teams of perceptual and cognitive sciences, computer science, and mathematics.

Of primary concern was determination of when virtual reality environments need to replicate reality as there are many times when they should not. The goals of the research program included 1) understanding what information virtual environment displays must supply to the human perceptual and cognitive systems to support human needs to carry out the complex tasks being synthesized, at the skill level, for spatial reasoning, and remote object manipulation, and 2) devising the computational resources to enable this functionality within the virtual environment.

Of import to this is the notion of immersion and its degrees. What is the relation of the granularity of the displays and the reality of their perception to the role the system is to play for the human user? How "real" does the feedback to the human perceiver need to be to make the system effective for the task? The answers to these issues are beginning to emerge. Some types of information can be acquired with 2-D representations or with lecture and pictures as well as they can be acquired in a virtual view of reality . An extensive overview of video, interactive video, audio and studies related to their role in systems can be found in Wetzel, Radtke, and Stern (1994).

VEs address key Navy needs such as Realistic Mission Rehearsal and Planning, Teleoperation, and Targeting, and they can provide simulated environments to enhance training. In order to develop the technologies and answer basic research questions regarding the perceptual and cognitive and mathematical demands to support them, the program has focused on understanding what spatial information VE displays must supply to human perceptual and cognitive systems for the tasks, and developing the basic computational and theoretical methods to enable their creation and integration into the virtual systems.

The effort within the Navy VE programs is related to other on-going research and development. Several approaches will be listed here to point them out. They are: the ARPA program on head tracker and head mounted display development; modeling and simulation development being supported through the Defense Modeling and Simulation Office (DMSO); the NASA program in VE for Space application, one related project being that of Dr. Bowen Loftin at the University of Houston; and the Army (ARI and ARO) programs in battlefield management (SIMNET) that focuses on integrated multiple displays to provide common battlefield scenario across geographically distributed platforms.

TWO NAVY VR APPROACHES

Two systems have initially been built in the VETT program and are being studied for their effectiveness. These are a Submarine Officer of the Deck (OOD) Shiphandling Training system and one to teach Electronics Troubleshooting.

In the *Submarine Officer of the Deck Shiphandling Training,* the goal is to use visually immersive technology to provide practice in guiding a submarine into a port. The view is via a head mounted display. There is a head tracker to determine the viewing position. There is no involvement of haptics but there is simple positional auditory information such as buoy bell rings that are included. It has two different fields of view, one is "wide angle" and the other is as if the person is using binoculars.

It has become immediately apparent that the task demands must be decided along with the features that form the critical components of the environment to convey the task in a meaningful way before any implementation begins. One needs to think about not only what should be visually presented but also about how the visual presentation will change under the user's interaction and what that interaction will assume. Will the means of interacting be natural as in the real world task? For instance, will speech be used or will parts of the task which require language inputs be simulated using text inputs. Here, speech recognition of the OOD voice commands is included in the simulated environment. Related to the input side is what levels of feedback is the user being trained to expect and how will these be provided? These are hard questions and in this context initial integration of solutions has been achieved to enable a first pass at evaluating the results. Definition of the evaluation methodologies to go along with this task presents another thread of the research.

The *electronics troubleshooting task* is based on real classroom training situation in the Navy. It includes the development of a virtual visual display of an actual piece of equipment used in troubleshooting and correcting electronics problems. The goal is to integrate correct feedback responses using a haptic interface device along with the high resolution simulated visual presentation to provide the same "equipment" as currently is available in shore-based training classrooms. By achieving this virtually, the intent is that the training will be done on location.

Issues being resolved are the actual implementation of the virtual device. The levels of fidelity to the real equipment are being assessed along with the feedback for lever motion and button presses. Scenarios must be developed to capture all of the critical lessons in the text book to drive the equipment correctly in response to the student inputs. With linkages to data collection, a means of student evaluation can also be developed. This system is currently under development and will be tested and evaluated in several scenarios. A related matter in using these systems for training is determining what is a suitable paradigm for testing knowledge gained and for determining the transfer of this knowledge to real world situations. Also of critical import is whether there really is a cost saving provided or if not, are the training results substantially increased for the same cost.

RELATED NAVY EFFORTS IN VR—INTERFACE DEVELOPMENT AND DESIGN

Other new starts in a related Focused Research Initiative include work by Imetrix and MIT to develop a VE training system for teleoperation of an underwater vehicle. Lockheed-Martin is the primary contractor on an effort with the University of Southern California to integrate the RIDES authoring system into the virtual reality capabilities of Lockheed which have been demonstrated in assessment of ship design. This effort includes use of a virtual classroom where student interactions with the virtually driven scenarios can be observed and modified by the author or instructor. The third new start is the project at the University of Houston and George Mason University where inclusion of artificial humans in the systems is being developed using the Army Jack model results and experience in the successful system design of the Hubble repair training virtual environment. These efforts have just started.

Summarizing the advances within the current efforts, VR is a bi-directional problem. In design, one needs to continually think about what to display, how it is perceived , by what perceptual system(s), how it can be manipulated, if at all, and what are the "right" responses from the system for the user? An important result is the realization that visual simulation is NOT the whole VE problem! The answers to questions regarding the actual presentation and the related interaction can subscribe to differing levels of reality.

Whether consistent adherence to reality is necessary or not is yet to be determined. Some levels of mismatch have deleterious effects such as seasickness when the induced motion from a visual presentation is inconsistent with real world feedback as encountered in everyday life.

Factors found important in the design of a VR system: 1. The need to decide what the task is for the human; 2. How real must the VR environment be to be useful?; 3. What are appropriate interactions for VR situations?; 4. Evaluation of transfer to real world environments after training in VR ones; 5. The need for authoring tools to enable prescribed development to cover the intended role of the VR environment; and 6. The definition of interdisciplinary requirements to do it right and have confidence in what is created.

What is the task? Is it for training? for rehearsal? The demands of levels of granularity need adjustment depending on the goals of the exercise. There is also the related problem of equipment and tethering of movement and its affect on performance. Related issues concern definition of the role of video and animation of what is observed, learned, retained and can be transferred to the real world. Previous evidence in the 2-D realm where use of real models and or video explanations has shown that there are mixed results in using these other presentations over standard lecture, demonstration class rooms. The results depend on how the presentations are integrated and depend on the nature of the task at hand. To date there are no confirming studies of increased retention of information or of increased transfer to task using these techniques (Wetzel, Radtke, and Stern, 1994). Another question becomes one of cost which will be mentioned later. There seems to be a sense of better transfer during rehearsal and visual recognition of real world situations such as recognition of terrain and locale. However, the information is introspective at this point and has not been supported by careful evaluation.

A task where VR has received anecdotal support is in demo training for the Damage Control Assistant (DCA). Again, there is no clear evaluation but everyone feels that the situation induced stress is real under the simulated condition. It is not clear that officers exposed in the demo system gain any better skills in managing different levels of problems during damage assessment and control but the impression from those going through the system is that it is *real.* and gives them a more confident picture of what to expect. Problems with this demo include difficulty in modifying the scenarios or controlling the scope of the simulated environment for training. This will be discussed below in issues for authoring, design and control of situations, within VR environments.

Where is the Reality? What degree of mimicking of real world physics and phenomena is necessary within any VR environment? What are the payoffs to enhancement or can we get by with a 2-D display and have the same effectiveness? Is this a game or edutainment? If training is for a task that assumes automatic motor skilled reactions then the system needs to respond in a manner that provides the necessary correct operational feedback to the trainee. How to scope this out for a real situation is still under investigation.

Appropriateness of the display and interactive capabilities for VR situations implies that we have criteria for determining how to build and use these systems. This is leading edge research. Current investigations include development of new interaction techniques which give the user direct control in a *natural* way with an environment that includes some level of real reaction capability. In other words, when things fall, they fall at an expected speed and they go in the *right* direction. In addition, appropriate feedback to the participant mimics what they expect in the real world. An example of this includes the introduction of force feedback to data glove manipulation so that a virtual object does not get crushed on grasp. Current visual displays have refresh rate problems if the participant moves too fast. This can affect the performance and the gains in the system use. It is characterized by the narrow view in the submarine shiphandling system. However, in large screen VR situations such as the cave these effects seem to be less of a problem although it is not clear that this is the case.

Evaluation methods to determine the effectiveness of VR in the real world are being developed. As stated earlier, evaluations in 2-D situations where video or model manipulation were included showed mixed results in transfer to real world problems. The case in Virtual Environments is yet to be determined. To date most evaluation is introspective and anecdotal. Some non-immersive systems (IMAT) exist that are currently being evaluated as to their effectiveness but the results are not in yet (Ellis and Parchman, 1994). Methods for evaluation will need to be developed. Current practice of a multiple choice test to ascertain the knowledge of the lesson will not suffice as the new system emphasis changes to recognition of a real world situation that has been studied from within instead of observed second hand and learned only by reference. Another related concern is that these systems can quickly get boring. How much *game playing* is assumed in the context of the situation training and to what extent are the related skills of the game similar to what is to be learned in the task?

How to develop appropriate situations and scenarios to achieve adequate systems is the focus of authoring tool development. It is critical that after one knows what levels of granularity need to be controlled for the real world transfer and has an idea how to assess performance in the VR environment, one needs to be able to make sure that critical situations are encountered during exposure. What is the necessary context of situations relevant for the task? This can be viewing a scene under different weather conditions if the goal is situation recognition in a rehearsal or it can be related to assessing a skill level of performance and controlling exposure to guarantee a certain level of performance on a skilled task such as a mechanical fix for a device. The visual, auditory, haptic and other displays need to be manipulatable in prescribed, coordinated ways and capability to edit the 3-D images into coherent visual real world reactions in a dynamic way need to be developed.

The DCA VR demo briefly described above is a prime example where these critical authoring capabilities can be described. The video was collected from a fabricated scene using actors. It is a single scenario and provides the content of the entire training segment. This has carefully integrated displays that are generated to enact the situation and to convey the sense of stress in the situation. Mostly, the concern is in presenting what it is like to see everything that is happening and to hear the noise and communications among the team that is fighting the damage. However, the actual displays do not exist currently in the DC environment and the demo was built as a one-time endeavor that is carefully crafted. Currently there is no index into the video which captures the critical aspects of its content in ways that would enable it to be spliced with different reactive situations. There is also no means for dynamically reacting to the commands from the DCA. It is at best a fragile example of what might be done in the future.

Authoring systems need to be developed to allow correct manageable control of what is being displayed to mimic the real world in ways that allow one to capture critical aspects of the task, that allow one to react to the system responses in real ways, and that include means to follow alternative paths in the interactive environment task space to cover what is considered by experts to be the critical level of knowledge to perform the skill or have adequate training to command. This level of effort is just beginning. Indexing of video on content is current basic research; editing speech with video for different effects does not generally exist; being able to edit speech from recognized speech signals is in its infancy; definition of suitable display situations to capture a task environment are just being built. Once they exist, we can begin to develop a more skilled capability in putting the VR parts together in a systematic manner. Currently it is extremely costly from the hardware end through the system integration and design.

VR requires interdisciplinary teams to adequately build and control the task environments. While lip-service to interdisciplinary activities has existed from many years, this particular endeavor will need the integrated teams of researchers to be able to cover the complex situations which need to be controlled and manipulated to be effective. System design will need the integration of knowledgeable persons who know about software building and have expertise in human factors and in task modeling. In addition, after determination of what the goal for the VR environment is, it will need evaluation as to its effectiveness for the task at hand. This requires extensive evaluation within the psychological or human factors paradigm of study to know whether the system conveys what is intended. A worst case example is that a system is built to train for situation a, and that it trains expectations in situation changes and reactions that are counter to the desired performance. We currently do not know how to detect such anomalies.

COST of VR is a critical concern. Anyone anticipating integration of VR for embedded training or for rehearsal needs to be aware of the up-front costs to get the systems in place. Hardware is coming down in cost but the level of refresh rate still is a problem unless fast machines with good graphics capabilities are available. This requires much more than an off-the-shelf PC or Mac platform provides. The granularity is significantly different for the cost. This gets back to the issue of how much reality is needed for what kinds of training or rehearsal. Large screen environments such as caves are expensive costing millions of dollars. Their benefit is not clear. The nature of shared knowledge spaces in team environments where even now we have large screen displays in the CIC is not clearly understood.

Speech understanding systems currently are trained for a specific domain and are not easy to modify. In addition, they are closed microphone and have problems in variable noise environments. Tank environments have been used as proof of concept for the future as tank noise is more consistent and special filters for it have been developed. The *general* noise in a Navy command center currently interferes with what the technology can do. Even in aircraft it is not clear what a suitable role for speech interactions with controls and displays might be, as speech is already extensively used for other things. The microphones in speech understanding interfaces often are switch controlled because of ambient voice communications that are not intended for the device. This remains a problem.

The role of non-speech auditory information is being studied with respect to what types of information can be separately recognized and whether it can be used as an additional channel for discrete information presentation. Problems with it include that it is one-time, unless it is recorded in which case playback facility must also be given (yet another control), that it is used naturally more as a situation monitor than as explicit conveyance of information except with speech. All of these special device systems require additional hardware. The need for real-time response dictates that many of these parts of a given VR system exist on separate devices. Their time coordination with integrated update rates and reaction is under development. This is costly from the hardware perspective and affects the complexity of the software needed to carry out the functions as well as the software for the scenario situation authored information content of the VR environment. In addition, computer support staff are required to make sure the system networks that underlie the environment remain operational and provide maximum performance. This is not a technology that you download and run. It will require continual supervision and maintenance of the software and the run environment from the computational perspective.

Summary. Initial investigation has demonstrated that there is potential application of different levels of VR capabilities in situation rehearsal and training. The current investigations are in their infancy. There are many aspects of development of underlying technology that must continue to be explored as well as the evaluation of them within different contexts where they may be applied. The technology is presently being explored and investigated as to its usefulness under different contexts. How to define a context and make sure the VR environment matches it to a necessary level of granularity is under investigation. Each immersive system deployed in the immediate future is being independently constructed. The SIMNET environment provides interactive functionality at a global level and is modularly designed, but is only partially immersive. Even with SIMNET the evaluation of its effectiveness has not been complete. Whether edutainment is the goal or whether more reliable measures of credibility for use of VR remains a question.

REFERENCES

Virtual Reality Scientific and Technological Challenges, Nation Research Council, National Academy Press, Washington, D.C., 1995.

Ellis, J. A. and Parchman, S. *The Interactive Multisensor Analysis Training (IMAT) System: A f Formative Evaluation in the Aviation Antisubmarine Warfare Operator (AW) Class A School,* Approved for Public Release, Navy Personnel Research and Development Center, San Diego CA 92152–7250.

Instructional Effectiveness of Video Media, Wetzel, C. D., Radtke, P. and Stern, H. Lawrence Erlbaum Associates, Publishers, 1994.

13

INTELLIGENT ARCHITECTURE

Desktop VR for Complex Strategic Design in Architecture and Planning

Alan Penn,[1] Nick Dalton,[1] Laura Dekker,[2] Chiron Mottram,[1] and Meyer Nigri[2]

[1] The Bartlett School of Architecture
[2]Department of Computer Science
University College London
Gower Street, London WC1E 6BT
Tel: +44 (0)171 387 7050 ext 5919; Fax: +44 (0)171 916 1887
a.penn@ucl.ac.uk
WWW: http://doric.bart.ucl.ac.uk/web/Pangea/IntelligentArchitecture.html

ABSTRACT

The most difficult problems in architecture occur on the boundaries between different disciplines where solutions to problems in one domain create problems in others. These interdomain problems are also amongst the most difficult to train designers to deal with since no one understands properly the dynamics of the interactions. Currently, computers are widely used in the later stages of managing construction production information, but tend only to be of limited use early on for design decision support.

The Intelligent Architecture project aims to bring forward the use of computing to the earliest stages of design when the most critical strategic decisions are taken that affect the resolution of interdomain problems. By using three dimensional object based representations of the design, linked to a range of analyses using 'intelligent' techniques (Neural nets, Genetic Algorithms, Fuzzy Logic) and OLE/DDE/AppleEvents communications to allow the program to draw on external applications and databases, the project provides simultaneous visualisations of the functional outcome of a proposed design from a range of points of view at once. Predictions are made, for instance, of energy use, construction cost and likely communications patterns between workers, and then presented to the designer in graphical or simple numeric form. This enables him to optimise the design from a number of points of view at once at the same time as getting a full, real time, interactive visualisation of what the building will look like.

The system is implemented on Mac and PC level hardware to ensure that it arrives on the decision taker's desk, using the latest 'games' software real time renderers to make interactive 3-d modelling and navigation intuitive enough for them to master. Our experience of these kinds of analytic tools in design suggests that one of the most useful aspects of the program will be in training designers to become intuitive about the way the different domains interact and we believe that the links to interactive 3-d representations will allow a closer link between intuition, experience and analysis in design. Early prototypes of the software are currenly under test.

THE PROBLEM OF COMPLEX DESIGN

The design, construction and management of the built environment through its life cycle brings a large and varied group of organisations into contact. Although all are concerned with the same physical design, each have their own views of the object at hand, their own representations and tools for dealing with it and their own domains of expertise which are brought to bear on its evaluation. Even within each discipline individuals appear to use different modes of working (Powell, 1994). Essentially we believe, the built environment sector has evolved this division of labour as a means of handling the complexity and apparent indeterminacy of its subject matter. By bringing together different approaches and knowledge domains based on fundamentally different world views more complex problems can be tackled than when a team is composed of people who share the same approach or view. However, as the size and complexity of projects has increased and project time scales have decreased, the organisational divisions implied by this system have become a source of problems in their own right.

Often the most difficult problems occur at the boundaries between the knowledge domains of the organisations concerned in the process, where solutions to one person's problem create a problem in another's domain. In these situations there is little for it but to resolve problems around the meeting table, often with a three dimensional physical model sitting in the middle as the main reference source. These meetings revolve around 'what if' questions regarding the effects of 3-D physical designs on a series of outcome variables—microclimate, energy, traffic, construction cost, rental premium and so on. Strategic solutions are thrashed out around the table depending on the experience and knowledge of the various people concerned, possibly backed up by computer analysis applied to their own specialist domain. However, the main form in which knowledge is exercised, particularly in early strategic design, is through intuition, and since both the knowledge and its application is vested in individuals, the resolution of conflicts between domains becomes a communication problem.

Problems also occur where one team passes responsibility for a project to another at key points in the project lifecycle. At these points investment in human knowledge and experience is for the most part lost. This happens when drawings pass from the designer to the subcontractor and shop drawings pass back, where transactions happen mainly in paper form. It happens again at project handover when operation and maintenance manuals and as-built drawings are passed on from the project managers to the facilities managers. The knowledge and data loss at these transitions is enormous, as is the learning curve for the new team. Again these can be seen as largely communications problems.

In each of these situations problems are exacerbated by organisations using different software running on different platforms. Whilst file transfer using de-facto standard formats (DXF, IGES for example in CAD) between organisations is possible, it is problematic and at present forms a bottleneck in any attempts at improving communications.

Where software representations are widely different, for example between CAD and Project Management software, de-facto standards for data transfer have yet to emerge.

Currently, where a single design is to be analysed from different points of view, each consultant tends to duplicate data entry. Since this is obviously wasteful a number of approaches to the problem of integration are being explored. While some of the larger CAD systems offer their own customised links to central DBMS and analytic packages, they tend not to be the tool of choice for all organisations in the team. Part of the problem is that different analytic applications require different forms of representation, levels of detail or abstraction and attribute data associated with the description of the design. Structural analysis for example requires data on loading, fairly rudimentary descriptions of building geometry, and only the geometry of those parts of the fabric which form part of the structural system, whereas HVAC analysis requires a spatial representation of the building, its orientation, geographical location, thermal properties of the fabric and expected occupancy and equipment heat gains. Even in those situations in which a single building element takes part in more than one functional system (the structural and thermal performance of walls for instance), it often requires different attribute data in order to perform the specific form of analysis. In each case the simplest description of the building for the purposes of one analysis is fairly independent from the others. Since software for different applications has tended to be developed in isolation, the representations adopted support their own application with minimal data requirements. This is one of the reasons why software that aims to support more than one application domain often seems too complicated to *all* its domains of users, and seems to gather little support from anyone. Currently the 'all singing and dancing' package is so hard to use and requires so much data entry that only the CAD expert can actually interact with the system. In many design offices yet another 'division of labour' has been produced in the form of the CAD bureau to handle the complexity of current software. This only serves to remove the potential of IT from the decision takers around the table. Multiple data entry is still the practical solution for many design teams since it allows each member to use the software of first choice for their own 'world view'.

COMPUTERS IN AN ARCHITECTURAL PRACTICE

Traditionally computers have been thought to be particularly useful for the performance of mundane and repetitive tasks. As such architectural offices have successfully adopted IT to handle the chore of tedious graphical production. This falls into two areas: visualisation used both during design and to 'sell' a design to the client and planning control authorities; and the drafting of production drawings for use in procuring and constructing the building. Computers are now being used widely for both of these tasks. However, there is a new trend emerging in advanced architectural practice, in which soft ware is playing a much more central role in the creative part of architectural design. A number of common 2D drawing programs like FreeHand, MiniCad, AutoCAD and page layout software like Pagemaker and QuarkExpress are used increasingly interchangeably and synthetically with 3D design oriented software such as Modelshop, Designers Workshop and the 3D functions in MiniCad to produce design drawings and feasibility/competition entry 'conceptual design' presentations. In a sense this is exactly what these kinds of software and the flexibility of operating system level information sharing (cut, copy and paste) were designed for. Now, though, we are seeing image manipulation programs such as Adobe Photoshop take their place alongside the photocopier and the pencil as a means of graphical transformation that is being used integrally in the 'generation of form' part of the design process. This is a new phenomenon and may pave the way for future developments in design software.

We believe that this development is of interest for two reasons. First, it highlights an important aspect of the way we believe architectural design teams to work. That is, there seems to be a basic asymmetry in design between 'form production' and 'form analysis', and it suggests that there may be different kinds of software needed for each of these activities. Form production is a highly personal activity, and different designers have quite different methods of working to arrive at proposed built form. Pencil and paper, or wax and wire work for some, but software is now beginning to be used—and misused—as a creative artistic medium in much the same way that photocopiers and faxes have been for some years now. The fact that Photoshop should have emerged as a favoured tool for this kind of work is not just chance. It is because it provides a set of tools and 'plug-in' functions that in no way pre-suppose a fixed method of working or a kind of design solution, that it is open to the innovative kinds of use to which it is being applied in architectural design. It is essentially a generic creative graphics tool and as such has found application in architectural form production just as other artists media have before. Second, it suggests that there may be a powerful role for IT in the creative aspects of design, in addition to its current use in the automation of repetitive tasks, if only we can find the right way of getting it developed.

Why is it that so little software has been successfully produced to help in creative form production? We think that in part it stems from the approach adopted by IT developers to the process of software design. The dominant model is of a linear process from specification writing through design as a problem solving activity to a final piece of software (Carrara et al, 1994, but see Richens, 1994, for a critique with which we concur). This means that software has tended to be developed with most success where the task is well specified, and that, by and large, is for mundane and repetitive tasks. Where problems and their solutions are ill defined, as in software to support the creative parts of architectural design, we believe that a different software specification and development approach is called for. Architectural design itself, where problems are often ill specified and designs are carried out by those who do not necessarily have complete knowledge of the client's domain in exactly this way, provides a possible model. Here a form of working has evolved in which the definition of the brief emerges as the design is developed. As often as not the lay client is unable to provide more than a sketch statement of intent at the start of a project. The brief itself is often developed by the design team and forms one of the key negotiating documents in the design process in which the client is asked to 'sign up' to a design strategy in 'physical' sketch form as well as the brief, a textual description of the functional requirements the design is aiming to fulfil.

Whether or not a specific physical design fulfils those functional requirements is a matter for analysis and this is where the different domains of knowledge encompassed by the design team come in. Design iterates between these two activities. In the first designers generate form—'let's make the building round'—in the second they criticise the form from a number of standpoints—'high volume to surface area ratio, means low energy gains and losses—good', 'round buildings are tricky to construct—costs more', and so on. Engineers and other specialists know a lot about the effects of a proposed form for the outcomes in terms of their domain of knowledge, and a lot of this knowledge is systematised in terms of calculations, rules of thumb and analytic computer packages. The problem is that many of these analyses need the specialist to interpret their results, and so the form in which the software is produced tends to reinforce the divisions in the team. It is possible that by using graphical visualisation methods these techniques of analysis could be brought into the designer's frame of reference, not as a set of analytic results, but as a part of the medium the designer is manipulating during the synthetic and creative 'form generating' phase of work. The proposition our research aims to test is that by bringing more of the analytic potential of computing into the intuitive ambit of the 'form generation' activity, design intuition may be harnessed to produce not only innovative forms, but innovative solutions to complex inter-domain functional problems of that sort that have proven virtually intractable to current techniques. The Intelligent Architecture project (DTI/EPSRC ISIP 8003) is founded on this basis.

PANGEA

The Intelligent Architecture project is developing a generic 3D workbench called 'Pangea' which is designed to provide a fluid interface for modelling 3-dimensional 'worlds' and for navigating around them. We do this using the simple notion of cameras with associated windows. Cameras can be selected and moved either in a separate window in which both camera and the world are visible, or from within the camera's view itself—the 'tank driver's body centric view'. Cameras also provide a simple metaphor for analysis. By linking a particular form analysis—say energy—to a camera, that view always carries with it the particular tools needed to construct and view an energy analysis of the design. As many analyses as you might need can be run simultaneously over a particular design. As the design is changed the views update themselves and give graphic feedback on the results of analysis for that particular aspect of function so allowing the designer to try and optimise for more than one parameter at once. By making the visualisations graphic our hope is that designers will begin to internalise the dynamics of the way changing the form of the design affects its functional outcome—they will be able to begin to use multiple analytic views as a 'material' with which to create—a sort of 'intelligent' modelling putty.

For instance, about 80% of the energy consumption of a building is determined in the earliest stages of a design when the buildings size, orientation, window to wall ratio, number of floors are defined. After a basic site strategy has been determined most other energy design decisions can be considered as 'retro-fitting'—using special thermal glass to reduce solar gain, or increasing the insulation of the external walls really only has the other 20% to play with. It is to aid the designer in the earliest strategic design decisions that methods like the Lighting and Thermal (LT) Method have been developed. The design of the LT method (Baker, 1993; Baker & Steemers, 1994; Baker, 1994) is based around the sketch design process and combines the results of heating, lighting and cooling analysis to construct at total picture of energy consumption. What differentiates the LT method from more traditional methods of energy calculation is its emphasis on the qualitative difference between alternative designs rather than the absolute accuracy of its predictions. At strategic design stage it is important that design A is inherently more energy efficient than design B but it does not matter too much what the precise consumption figure will be. Actual energy consumption will depend on decisions that have yet to be taken in the design process as well as on factors outside the architects immediate control such as patterns of building occupancy and usage. At the earliest stages of design too much detail is not only irrelevant, but can also be misleading suggesting a level of accuracy that is not realistically achievable.

In Pangea the LT camera is designed to be placed within a design 'world'. It creates a window which contains the controls and main outputs of the analysis (Fig. 1). The primary inputs to the analysis are extracted from the geometry of the model. On screen controls allow the other inputs to be modified interactively. The primary results of the analysis are presented graphically as a pie chart representing the heating, lighting and cooling energy loads on the building, and numerically as a print out of the energy efficiency per unit area as well as total energy consumption. In this case the LT analysis and the graph and numeric feedback are all carried out in an Excel spreadsheet using Apple Events/OLE to link directly from the Pangea 3-D objects and supply the information on building geometry. The energy analysis can be put on automatic (recomputed every time an object is modified) or manual modes, with recalculation only carried out when the user clicks on a button in the energy window. The objective is that as the user modifies the building the energy consumption view of the building is updated. The results are fed back overtly in the energy window as a colour change in the model.

The next stage is to create several different camera views each giving analytic feedback on different aspects of the design. To date we have developed early prototypes for cameras to optimise shell/core arrangements to maximise workstation layout efficiency using simple rule based techniques, and to analyse circulation layouts to maximise communication between workers in office environments using 'space syntax' techniques (Penn & Hillier 1992). By analysing the same sketch design from all these points of view at once, as well as by evaluating it aesthetically and intuitively in the normal way, we hope at least to help designers to internalise the dynamics of how several functional systems interact with building form.

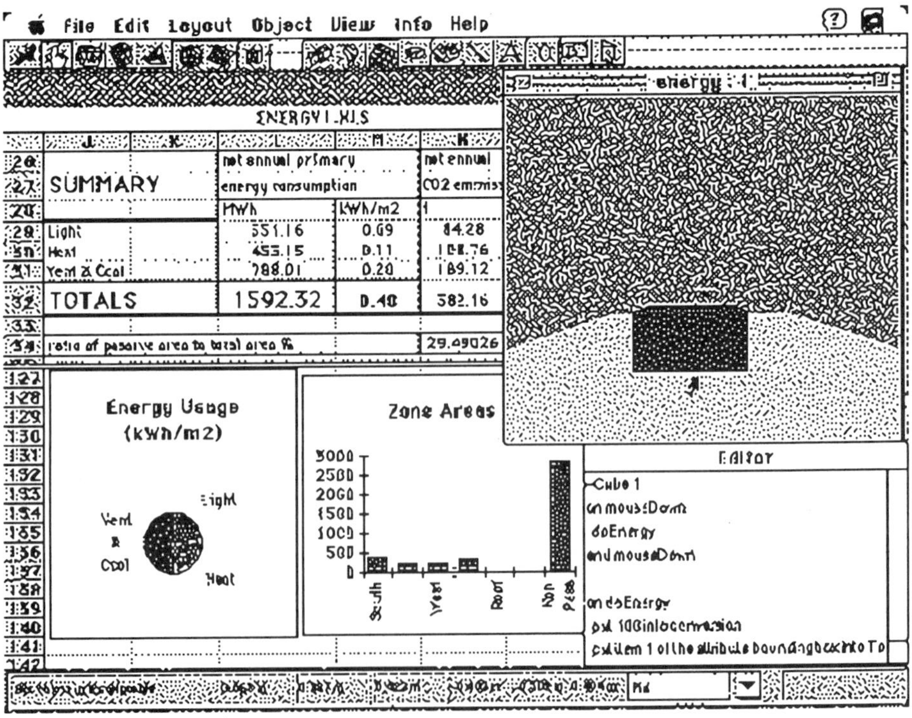

Figure 1. Pangea energy camera (top right) feeding information to an LT analysis in an Excel spreadsheet.

So, what functionality do we need to carry out this kind of analysis? First, it is clear that modelling and navigation must be achieved easily and fluidly if the computer interface itself is not to present a barrier to early stage sketch design. For a medium to be used in creative design it has to be attractive as a material in its own right, and in the case of software that is largely a matter of apparent fluidity of use. It is particularly important that analytic software makes the break out of the CAD bureau and onto the designing partners desk, and this sets high standards for interface design. Second, objects in the real world are mainly three dimensional solid or spatial objects, and have a large number of properties (mass, density, Young's modulous, colour, texture and so on), and for any kind of behaviour a different list of these properties is required knowledge. It is therefore important that the medium be based on 3-D objects with an arbitrary list of properties. Finally, real world objects have behaviours: you push on a chair and it slides; you push on a door and it swings. And more generally, systems (structural, energy, transport) operate through the interactions between component parts which can also be thought of as behaviours. This means that we need a way of coding behaviour and the ability to respond to external actions into our objects. Essentially, we treat behaviour as a special kind of object property, and in this way have defined a very minimal representation that allows us to create highly complex 'worlds'. In this approach we differ from the main thrust of knowledge based design support systems currently under investigation (Carrara et al, 1994; Eastman, 1994; Watanabe, 1994), as well as the current development of international standards for product information exchange (ISO STEP, 1994). Instead of concentrating on the implementation of meta-models of the built environment that seek to capture the important aspects of buildings within a relatively fixed (if general) model schema, we are developing a generic software tool that could in principal be used to implement a broad array of underlying model schema.

ATTRIBUTE ENTRY AND INFERENCING

Although the basis of Pangea is simple and aims to be generic, the need for objects to carry within themselves additional information could be seen as a drawback. The designer during the 'form generation' phase of work is mainly interested in form. To interrupt that activity by requiring him or her to type in attribute data for every form would lead to the system not being used. However, some of these attributes are geometric: size shape, location; others are material properties, and both of these are of interest to the 'form generator' in 'creative' mode. For most forms of analysis knowledge is required of both material properties and geometric information about the shape and location of the various components of a design. In addition, knowledge is often required of the topological relations between different components: 'window 209 is in wall 153'.

Although this may seem simple enough in principle, Pangea faces the problem of collecting information for many forms of analysis at once. This poses a problem for users who don't want to have to fill in a form for each and every component they create, especially in the strategic design phase where much of the information may not have been determined. This is a classic problem for traditional algorithmic computing which finds it difficult to cope with incomplete or inconsistent data sets. Most analyses require all the input variables to be filled in before any sensible results can be computed, but at the earliest stage of design the designer tends to have the least ability to fill in that data, and they are loathe to 'waste time on something that's going to change anyway'. The solution Pangea uses is to infer as much information as possible, with any missing information marked on the model in red (this is similar to the real world situation where an engineer redlines the architect's drawing where errors or ambiguities appear). The inferencing is performed by a mix of rule based expert system, fuzzy logic and neural network tools, using hybrids where appropriate (Fig. 2). After a shape is created it is analysed by a 'smart attribute assistant', the assistant has access to a number of local geometric properties of the object, for instance it's size, arrangement of faces, ratios of dimensions and type. This is then combined with the local relational information about the object—what is it embedded in, what is it supporting, what is it supported by. The relational information is stored in the object during its construction as a biproduct of the use of a 'smart cursor'. If the user confirms the 'smart cursor's' suggestion that two faces on different objects should be aligned, that constraint is built into each object's knowledge of itself—by being added to the object's attribute list ('object A aligns with object B, object B aligns with object A'). In this way topological and relational information is constructed with virtually no overhead to the user.

The inferencing engine then runs over the full list of object attributes, including their local topological relations to other components, and infers what kind of element they are most likely to be: a slab, window, column etc. These guesses can then be used to add default attributes and values to objects where these are missing, to spot and flag-up inconsistencies or possibly to propose standardisation of components. By using a high level intermediate, the computer can label components as it goes which in turn helps it to label other components. The user is free to disagree with a label and provide a new label, and the learning part of the assistant can then use the parameters of the component to improve its recognition of other components without user intervention. By holding one central

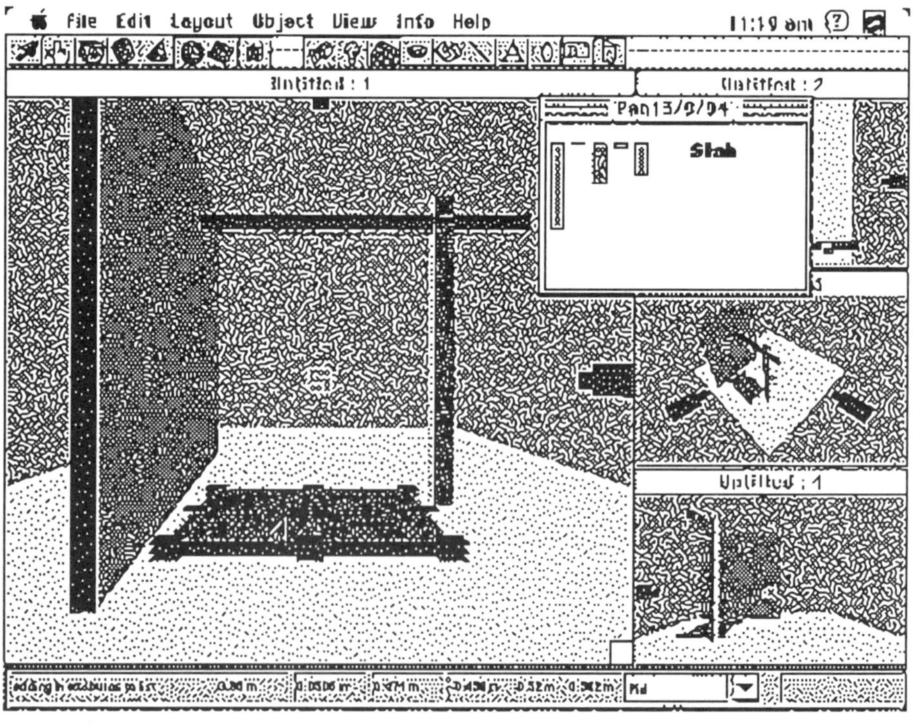

Figure 2. Pangea uses a neural network tool to infer that the selected object is a slab.

source for the attributes Pangea also gains through the ability to use one attribute for many analyses. For example, the wooden door can be used for rendering, sound analysis, and fire hazard analysis. When the door is changed then all the forms of analysis can be updated or marked up as 'in need of recalculation'. The main aim of this part of the Pangea system is to enhance the knowledge of attribute properties of objects on the basis of the computer making suggestions and the user confirming them. The aim is to move from purely geometric visualisation towards enhanced knowledge of other attributes of objects in the world needed in order to model aspects of their function as real world systems: structural, in terms of energy or light, and so on.

OPTIMISATION

The ability to visualise the design in terms of more than one analysis raises the possibility of trying to optimise the design from more than one point of view at once. Pangea gives access to a generic 'optimisation' toolkit. The purpose of the optimiser is to allow the user to propose constraints on the system and then allow Pangea to find a best solution to those constraints. The built world is inherently three dimensional and the primary constraint on the layout of objects is normally intersection, for example putting the maximum number of tables in a room implies a constraint that no two tables can intersect. When three dimensional information combines with attribute information and possibly time, the parameter space of the problem becomes highly irregular (implying a large number of local minima). If the problem space is enlarged to solve multiple problems—minimum cost for construction, heating, and maintenance over the building's life for instance—then simple hill climbing will not necessarily be sufficient. Pangea gives access to a range of optimisation tools, including Genetic Algorithms and dynamic hill climbing. The cost functions for the optimisation have access to a number of attribute and spatial primitives which can be specified in terms of the analysis defined by one or more of the camera views of the world (energy, cost etc.). This provides a relatively simple metaphor for the hard part of most optimisation problems—that of defining the cost function.

CONCLUSION

In his review of CAD developments over the last 30 years Bill Mitchell (Mitchell, 1994) identifies three paradigms for design: design as a problem solving activity (after Simon); design as a knowledge based activity; and design as a social activity. He stresses the importance of the latter as it is here that multiple autonomous intelligences are brought to bear on the design problem at hand. To these paradigms we would add a fourth: design as a problem eliciting activity, and it is here that we believe the particular strengths of VR—or more precisely 'virtual abstraction'—will be best placed to make an impact in architectural design. This fourth activity is inherently social since designers and their clients are usually different people, and it is the client who has the problem (although all too often at the inception of a project they cannot specify it with any precision, if at all) and the designer who takes responsibility for its solution. The strength of visualisation software and VR in particular is that it makes it possible for a client to use their intuitive understanding of the built environment to better evaluate and give feedback on an evolving design. The strength of virtual abstraction as we have proposed it is that it promises to help the 'form generating' designer to capture, and bring their intuition to bear on, the analytic evaluation of form from a wide range of different domain points of view as an integral part of the earliest stage of form generating activity. We believe that most knowledge in architectural design is brought to bear through the 'intuitive' application of principles acquired through experience, rather than through a 'well understood' logical progression. It is here that the immediacy of VR and the potential of IT to abstract and simplify offer the potential for a quite novel kind of design aid.

One of the most promising areas in which we believe these sorts of tool will find application is in the training of design team members. We have found that so long as feedback is graphic designers are very quick to internalise the principles of how a particular outcome varies with a proposed form—say the way energy utilisation varies with shape and orientation of building blocks. Our hope is that the more complex dynamics of more than one outcome variable will also prove open to being 'internalised' in this way, and that through using tools like Pangea we will begin to train designers to use their intuition in complex systems where traditional logical reasoning often leads to spurious results.

In any virtual reality which is related to real world objects, there is a necessity to include the behaviour of the objects at some level of abstraction. For strategic design the level of abstraction is necessarily high—we only know of design constraints at a relatively rough way at that stage. In this sense Pangea is an experiment in a less 'real' virtual reality. By abstracting the properties of objects in a world, and inferring from the properties we have—their geometry and topology for instance—Pangea is testing the use of virtual realty as a design aid in the synthesis of complex interacting systems such as those found in the built environment. Pangea can be seen as a first step in the process of constructing a general purpose virtual reality tool which can quickly be redesigned to simulate different systems in the real world, but its real test is in the use of simultaneous multiple simulations in strategic design by offering the creative designer a new plastic, yet analytic, medium.

REFERENCES

Baker, N.V., *LT Method Version 2.0* - Cambridge Architectural Research Limited, Royal Institute of British Architects, 1993, London.

Baker, N.V., and Steemers, K., *The LT Method 2.0 An energy design tool for non- domestic buildings*. Cambridge Architectural Research Limited, 1994, Cambridge.

Baker, N.V., *Energy and Environment in Non Domestic Buildings* - Cambridge Architectural Research Limited, Royal Institute of British Architects, 1994, London.

Carrara, G., Kalay, Y.E. & Novembri, G., *Knowledge-based computational support for architectural design*, Automation in Construction 3 (1994) 157–175, Elsevier, Amsterdam.

Eastman, C.M., *A data model for design knowledge*, Automation in Construction 3 (1994) 157–175, Elsevier, Amsterdam.

ISO STEP, *Draft International Standard Version of the Initial Release of ISO 10303*, (1994)

Mitchell, W., *Three paradigms for computer-aided design*, Automation in Construction 3 (1994) 157–175, Elsevier, Amsterdam.

Penn, A. & Hillier, B., *The Social Potential of Buildings: spatial structure and the innovative milieu in scientific research laboratories*, Corporate Space and Architecture 2, 39–43, Ministère de l'Equipement, du Logement at des Transportes, Paris, 1992

Richens, P., *Does knowledge really help? CAD research at the Martin Centre*, Automation in Construction 3 (1994) 157–175, Elsevier, Amsterdam.

Watanabe, S., *Knowledge integration for architectural design*, Automation in Construction 3 (1994) 157–175, Elsevier, Amsterdam.

PART 2

LESSONS LEARNED OR LESSONS NOT YET LEARNED (BUT OFTEN REVISITED) ABOUT THE DESIGN, APPLICATION, AND MANAGEMENT OF LEARNING TECHNOLOGIES

RSG-16: Advanced Technologies Applied to Training Design,
Dr. Robert J. Seidel, Chairman

FOREWORD

This report is based on data provided and discussed at our past four workshops, discussions and presentations made at the RSG 16 meetings, and papers provided at our final workshop. A collection of these papers is attached as Appendix A to this report. We, the members of RSG 16 appreciate the opportunities that Panel 8 and the Defense Research Group has given them to improve our collective state of knowledge concerning military training. In recognition of the fact that training is almost our sole peacetime endeavor and is directly responsible for military readiness, we look forward to being able to work with the DRG and Panel 8 again. The current and projected advances in technologies that are and will be made available as tools to permit more efficient and effective training will skyrocket in the next decade. These changes will quickly make the results of our past workshops historical data points awaiting revision and documentation.

Médécin-en-Chef Paul Gorzerino (France)
Dr. Jodi Krol (The Netherlands)
Commander Anthony Mizen, RN (United Kingdom)
Dr. Gian Paolo Noja (Italy)
RDir Dr. Rolf Otte (Germany)
Dr. Robert J. Seidel (Chairman) (United States)

I. INTRODUCTION

Background: This Section Provides a Brief History of How the RSG Was Formed, a Summary of Its Activities and of Its Products

As a result of three symposia on military training, held by Panel 7 (Defence Applications of Operational Research) and Panel 8 (Defence Applications of Human and Bio-Medical Sciences), a NATO Research Study Group (RSG) was formed on Advanced Technologies Applied to Training Design. The specific technologies that would be reviewed were identified by the members with inputs from industry and academia. A final selection was made based on our collective vision of which ones would have he greatest beneficial impact on military training in the future. It was our success at technology selection that helped develop the learning part of the agenda for this past years DRG seminar.

The principal objectives of RSG 16 is to establish an active exchange of data, methods, models, and media that will bring advanced training technologies into greater use for team and joint force training. It does this with focused workshops that provide an in-depth review of specific advanced technologies. Building on data and knowledge derived from RSG 16, technologies such as embedded training, AI, and authoring tools were reviewed and applications examined to determine their payoff. In addition, special coordination was accomplished with the other NATO bodies [e.g. Advisory Group for Aerospace R & D (AGARD) and TTCP (The Technical Coordination Program)] that focus on Virtual Reality, Networking, and Simulation and Gaming.

The following are some of the accomplishments of RSG 16. Each of the workshops, except for the last one on "lessons learned" have resulted in a book published by Plenum Press. A list of these books is provided in the Scientific area of this report in response to the questions asked by Panel 8.

Workshop on Computer-Based Instruction in Military Environments, Held in Brussels, Belgium April 15–17, 1985

The proceedings were published by Plenum Press, 1987. This workshop addressed the advances in microprocessor technology that would revolutionize how and where military training could occur. During this symposium there were exhibits to demonstrate the various applications of computer based training techniques. There were twenty-three papers discussing and describing data and experiences from the use of advanced computer based technologies. The workshop clearly showed how truly international in character the advances are and how important it is to share experiences and data.

Workshop on Advanced Technologies Applied to Training Design, Held in Venice, Italy October 22–24, 1991

The proceedings were published by Plenum Press in 1993. This workshop occurred during the time that many changes were occurring in Eastern Europe and world wide. The need to identify training technologies for maintaining a capable and ready force during times of decreases in military force structure was, and is currently , our challenge. This workshop maintained its focus on technology and applications regardless of the specific user. The workshop focused on 6 technological areas that could provide both researchers and practitioners with ready sources of information. The six technological categories were

(1) Authoring Systems, (2) Models, (3) Embedded Training & Simulation, (4) Advanced Hardware technology, (5) Use of Cognitive approaches , and (6) Expert Systems.

Workshop on Technology to Support Distance/Distributed Learning; Learning without Boundaries Held in Munich, Germany September 29–October 1, 1993

The proceedings were published by Plenum Press, 1995. This workshop addressed the issues arising from the restructuring and down-sizing of our military forces, along with the decreasing funds available for resident training at multiple locations. Distance/Distributed Learning relies on the availability to network computers, people, and data bases locally and/or over a distance. The maturity of the internet as well as the increased power of computers allows training or occur anywhere and at any time. While this subject is continually to advance, this workshop allowed the alliance to share current and future activities that would reduce the need for extensive travel to training sites and would allow access to data and situations which might otherwise be unavailable. Twenty-two papers were presented and discussed. The workshop clearly showed that interactive, electronic technologies can provide the opportunities for eliminating physical boundaries as a requirement for learning. The reports showed that what is needed now is a continuing discourse, exchange of information, and a vision which can stipulate that, under the right circumstances and with the appropriate technology, Distributed Learning will provide a necessary and significant component of any comprehensive training and educational system.

Workshop on Virtual Environments...Training's Future? in Portsmouth, UK March 7–9 1995

The report is currently at the publisher (Plenum Press). This workshop provide a forum for both practitioners and researchers to learn from each other and develop opportunities for collaboration and further coordination with other international R&D groups. The workshop's agenda provided papers and discussions for those wanting VR R&D information related to: (1) research and development; (2) current capabilities and opportunities, (3) current applications, (4) education and learning knowledge infrastructure, and (5) transfer of this knowledge and technology from military to civil applications. Discussion sessions focused on providing good data and information on costs, effectiveness, availability, risks, and implementation issues (software portability, policy, authoring, logistics, etc.) Demonstrations of relevant UK programs and systems were provided by the Royal Navy.

Most of the topics seemed to encompass discussions on those technologies associated with virtual reality which allows training to be brought to the user rather than having to transport the user to the training environment.. Much emphasis in NATO is being placed on those learning technologies that allow the trainee to virtually leave the classroom and electronically interact in the simulated "real world." The interactive insertion of the learner into "real life experiences" using computer aided technologies can now be an integral part of what is often called "learning by doing." The emergence of Virtual Environments technologies appear to make this opportunity readily achievable. Looking to the future the workshop discussed obtaining relevant training data and training experiences on constantly emerging technologies such as virtual reality, shared presence, surrogate travel, and others technologies being pursued by the entertainment industry. While intuitively these might seem to be highly relevant to individual, team and joint forces training, the feasibility as well as the training/cost-effective value or value-added contribution of these technologies must be identified, questioned, discussed and summarized by a workshop of peers.

The VR/VE workshop was a natural extension from past workshops. From the extended classroom to the individual or team immersion in a distributed, virtual and collaborative environment is an easy conceptual step. Technically however, we need to know the feasibility and the amount of added value of VE in order to make cost-effective decisions concerning the use of VE as a part of our training or educational systems. The workshop provided data on how we can perform required tasks without the physical pressure of either fellow performers or actual equipment, by creating a workspace environment which is virtual. This enables learning without physical boundaries. The sense of identity within this environment by the performer is her/his reality, a virtual reality. This sense is then vastly heightened by immersion through the use of pseudo 3-D displays on a flat panel or through the use of helmet mounted displays (HMD). Unfortunately our workshop only touched on a part of the many technologies related to VE such as human language (voice recognition); telemedicine and the ability to train medical technicians anywhere and anytime, haptic feedback, and new advances in expert system tutors, or multi-user domains seen as MUDs or MOOS.

The DRG Seminar, September 1995 at the Institute for Defense Analysis in Washington, DC

The DRG symposium, sponsored by Dr. Anita Jones the Director of Defense Research and Engineering, allocated thirty-three percent of this seminar education and training. Not only were workshop topics the basis for these demonstrations and papers, but distance learning, virtual reality, the use of expert systems for tutoring, voice recognition and synthesis, interactive CD technology for bio-medical training, advanced authoring systems and helmet displays integrated with a belt computer were all shown and their great potential for education and training within the alliance was discussed.

Lessons Learned Workshop, 19 September 1995 in Genoa, Italy

A small workshop was held to meet the requirements of the Defense Research Group (DRG) request for a report which captured the experiences and findings of the RSG. Because of the dynamic nature of training technology, it was decided by the RSG that the only reasonable way to obtain comprehensive data was by having a workshop. Appendix A contains the final papers provided for this workshop. It was these papers plus the past 4 books and numerous meetings, faxes, and phone calls that make up the repository of data contained in this report.

SUMMARY OF LESSONS LEARNED FOR ADVANCED TECHNOLOGIES APPLIED TO TRAINING DESIGN

The following is a summary of RSG-16 findings and issues that are deemed relevant to the DRG by the members of RSG-16. We have divided the findings into two categories;

administrative and *scientific* to make it easier to focus on the output in terms of relevance and application.

I. Administrative

A. Suitability of the Procedures for the Conduct of Cooperative Research?. The DRG process and procedures do not lend themselves to achieving the most cooperative or collaborative research possible. Since there is no joint (NATO) money to stimulate and reinforce collective research, each RSG has to be very inventive and they must do this within the constraints of their national political and financial positions. Effective collaboration requires frequent contact, narrow focus on specific subject areas that must occur over a number of years. While training and simulation are certainly one of the most open and mutually required technologies for military readiness, the DRG implicit (if not explicit) procedures require short term, interesting subjects and reports. This procedure restricts over all productivity and value to the alliance which could otherwise occur if the subject could be revisited and new data analyzed subsequent to a workshop. For example, the topic of Distance Learning was just emerging when we held our workshop in Munich. By the time our book was published, many new networking and collaborative software tools were becoming available. Yet RSG-16 had to claim success and move on rather than continue as a viable group and establish a truly collaborative R&D program. For it was only after the workshop that many of the member countries actually began to promote distance learning as a cost-effective method for training as well as education. This same experience is true for virtual reality and for curriculum authoring systems. Each topic urgently calls out for more collaboration and discussion, but policy requires that the RSG by terminated. An alternative policy in order to satisfy such obvious needs would be to allow on a case by case basis for continuation of an RSG contingent on its potential increasing contribution to the NATO military. (See recommendations in the scientific section)

B. Comments on the Level of Bureaucratic Load. The bureaucratic load has not been too extensive. As a matter of fact the administrative requirements from DRG has been thoughtful and helpful. If anything a few more constraints would be helpful. For example, if one could standardize on software packages and data base applications, life would be much easier. Trying to exchange word processing files or data base files causes many problems and restricts active and participative cooperation. It would also be of great help to send more information from DRG and the Panel directly to the chairperson of each RSG or EG. This combined with an active electronic mail capability at DRG Headquarters would greatly help cooperative R&D within the alliance and communication within the DRG and its subordinate bodies.

C. Problems and Solutions in the Conduct of the RSG. The major problems are solved during the first two years of the RSG. After that each member has developed rapport with the other and the chairperson knows how to best communicate with the members. Probably the most difficult part of conducting an RSG is to obtain feedback quickly and in sufficient detail to plan the meeting/workshop and to then do an after action review. Those members who are on an electronic mail system make this problem trivial. The use of fax machines has also helped alleviate many communication problems. However, it is only after a year or so of working together and visiting each others facilities is it possible to know where, how and when to fax materials. This finding has implications for recommended minimal durations of RSGs.

D. Recommendations for Revisions to DRG and/or Panel Policy. What we are proposing is a modification to the all or none procedure that the DRG seems to have in place for RSGs. Rather than broadly apply a sunset rule, what we would like to see modified is that depending upon the timeliness and successes that an RSG had with its topics, continuation of the RSG should be dealt with based on its potential for incremental contribution to the NATO military. For example, we have held workshops in broad areas of advanced technologies and have found that there are certain topics which require revisiting and would benefit from successive workshops. After the various workshops were held on advanced technologies, distance learning, CBI, and VR, we have now found that distance learning as an embodiment of new technologies for training provides a perfect opportunity for revisiting the advanced technologies that can be applied to distance learning, such as new ways of authoring and networking, the advanced development of CBI tutors, and from the Virtual Reality workshop the findings that the creation of virtual environments through the use of MUDS and MOOS and other time and space spanning virtual capabilities. All provide the basis for a very productive and forward looking distance learning workshop and an RSG that would continue to focus on these emerging technologies as they become available. But it would require a fundamental change to the administrative procedures for RSG s and their sunset rules; i. e., that an RSG (whether it was RSG 16 or any others) should be allowed to continue depending upon (a) the quality of its output, (b) emerging nature of the technologies involved and (c) the willingness for the members to continue participating. An alternative policy would be to designate certain core RSG's as standing groups, such as Training, Human Factors, and Biomedics. Their job would be to maintain a futures watch. Then when new technologies appeared, special topic RSG's with narrow and time-limited focus would be created.

II. Scientific

A. The Value of the Completed Activity to

1. *NATO.* For over two decades, the NATO alliance has been continually adjusting to the many trade-offs involved with a changing economy, increased population, increased technology, increased cost of new weapon systems, and a decrease in military requirements. The only activity that has maintained itself as a priority is education and training. Education as it relates to adult learning to keep current on emerging technological and information opportunities, and training as it relates to job transition or learning to operate new systems whether they are for military or civil purposes. RSG-16 is the only NATO effort which was focusing on learning technologies. It has provided workshops on Computer Based Training, Advanced Technologies for Training Design (Authoring), Distance Learning, and Virtual Reality as it applies to learning. Each of these have resulted in a commercial book published by Plenum Press as well as individual NATO reports on the subjects. In order to maintain coordination and reduce the opportunities for redundant or duplicative work, RSG-16 has worked with AGARD, the EuroNato Training Committee, and The Technical Cooperation Program (TTCP). The activities of RSG 16 truly meet the goals of NATO. It provides application oriented data on advanced training technologies that help the military alliance obtain and maintain their military readiness. In addition it provides continuous technological data and knowledge to assist NATO as it consults in other non-military fields. The recent NATO seminar in Washington, DC is an example

where RSG-16 technologies were demonstrated and made up one-third of the seminar.

2. *Individual Nations.* Each of the participating nations have benefited in at least three ways. First they have gained directly from the data and experience gained from others (members, guests, and workshops) on the development of training systems that were of immediate and future interest to the nations. Many of the findings have not only found their way into the military via the RSG representative but have also found their way directly into the forces via the EuroNato training organization. Second, the research and its results have been shared in the open literature so that practicing and graduating scientists are kept abreast of international developments and can better assist their own nation, and third it has supported the economic base by allowing international training companies to emerge with competitive capabilities which were previously found in only a few of the nations.
3. *Laboratories, Institutes, and Individual Researchers.* With the world wide downsizing of the active military forces, there is an "keepers" of the science and data relevant to each Nation's military readiness and military security. Since all a nation does during peacetime is to train, training and the technologies, tools, and devices that are used are the most important aspect of maintaining a strong and ready military (active and reserves). Each of the representatives to the RSG had at least one counterpart who was from one of its laboratories and/or institutions. In addition these laboratories and institutions were many of the primary contributors and discussants at the four workshops held by the RSG. Finally, two of the committee nations, U.S. and NL, directly provided for research personnel cooperation and exchange. This constant the advancements of training technology by those National representatives responsible for long term military assistance is one of the best contributions that this RSG could provide any nation.
4. *The Industrial Base.* The training industry is at least a $2 Billion business in the United States. It has only been within the last decade that the NATO countries have seen an increase in their own training industry. The annual simulation and training conference held in the spring each year somewhere in Europe has had an exceptional growth curve. In addition the telecommunications industry has seen how distance learning can increase its business base 1000 fold. The use of computers in classrooms and homes for education and training has turned what we used to call a cottage business into a large, profit making business throughout Europe. This was evidenced by the number of European companies participating or desiring to demonstrate their capabilities at our workshops. All of this advanced training technology began with the military to meet defense requirements. And one of the first showcases for these learning technologies was at our RSG16 workshops. A good case in point is distance learning. When we began, there was little awareness of distance learning outside of those thinking of teleconferencing. However two years after our report is out, distance learning is now becoming one of the few known ways to reduce costs while increasing the availability of quality instruction. Here is an example where the military drastically needs to have another NATO workshop because the technologies of networking, authoring, course conversion, collaborative learning, etc. have grown and changed so rapidly that the work of two years ago is no longer of much value.

B. Problems and Solutions That Would Improve the Value (Perhaps Alternative Approaches). What we are proposing is a modification to the all or none procedure that they seem to have in place for RSGs. Rather than broadly apply a sunset rule, what we would like to see modified is that depending upon the successes that an RSG had in that the topics that an RSG deals with be dealt with on a case by case basis for continuity. For example we have held workshops in broad areas of advanced technologies and have found that there are certain training technologies that require revisiting and would benefit from successive workshops. This then would mean that an RSG whether it was RSG 16 or any others should be allowed to continue depending upon (a) the quality of its output, (b) emerging nature of the technologies involved and (c) the willingness for the members to continue participating. If we take RSG 16 as a specific example after the various advanced technologies, distance learning, CBI, and VR workshops were held, we have now found that distance learning as an embodiment of new technologies for training provides a perfect opportunity for revisiting the technologies of authoring, networking, the advanced development of, CBI tutors, and from the Virtual Reality workshop, the findings that the creation of virtual environments through the use of MUDS and MOOS and other time and space spanning virtual capabilities. All could provide for a very productive and forward looking distance learning workshop and an RSG that would continue to focus on these emerging technologies as they become available. But it would require a fundamental change to the administrative procedures for RSG s and their sunset rules(see Section D below for specific suggestions) .

C. Identification of Products and Successes. There have been four books published as well as numerous papers, working notes, and presentations that have been shared with the DRG members plus AGARD, and the EuroNato Training Group. The books published by Plenum Press are:

1. *Computer-Based Instruction in Military Environments*; Plenum Press, 1987.
2. *Advanced technologies Applied To Training Design*; Plenum Press, 1993.
3. *Learning Without Boundaries: Technology to Support Distance/Distributed Learning*; Plenum Press, 1994.

D. Recommendations for Future Activities. There are three areas where the RSG should revisit as the result of extreme advances in training technology.

1. The *first is distance/distributed learning (DL).* This area has such a major impact on the military active and reserves that we must hold another workshop as soon as possible. There are a number of reasons that this cost-effective method of learning can fail. It is up to the research and development community to maintain a viable technology watch and to make sure that up-to-date methods and tools are provided to help the user as technology pulls military training to use new opportunities. For example, the ability to author distance/distributed training materials has not been addressed in light of our current ability to transmit object and real-time video over the internet. Nor have we addressed the methods we must develop for effectively and efficiently transitioning old curriculum into the new DL format. However, all of this is minor to the fact that we have not focused our combined knowledge on how to evaluate performance over a distance/distributed learning system. Military downsizing is forcing us to use DL yet we have not advanced our evaluation process to make sure we are able to determine if learning and performance has been achieved.

2. The *second is virtual reality as applied to training*. This imersive technology allows surrogate travel within engines to permit maintenance training, it allows field doctors experience traumatic wounds before having to encounter them in real life, it permits vehicles to go into restricted spaces and practice otherwise inaccessible training experiences or environments, and it allows individual reserves to practice as teams even when they are kilometers apart. While this is often seen as a type of distance/distributed learning, it is much more. It is a combination of the use of synthetic environments which might be locally presented and used for instruction and practice and networks which can be used for data, tutoring, in the future remote operations. Again this technology requires increased attention on authoring and evaluation systems as well as ways to best handle tutoring of complex instruction using visual objects and synthetic environments.
3. *The third area is embedded training*. While this has been a training technology that has been discussed for years, it has been only recently that the computer and software have developed enough to permit training to be embedded as part of the actual system. However, this integration of training and actual systems offers a number of challenges to the training community. Some of these changes relate to how we do instruction system development, how we measure performance, how we maintain/update curriculum as system changes are being made, how we use instruction (real people with an instructors console or intelligent tutoring)? Others relate to job patterns and employment patterns which mitigate against widespread use of this capability. In short, the basic technology exists for embedded training but design and operational usage patterns along with the lack of specialized instructional development procedures and tools can prevent the cost effective utilization of these training opportunities.

All of the above plus many more are issues that the DRG and Panel 8 must be prepared to answer for the military if we are to continue to contribute to the readiness of our military forces.

III. DETAILED LESSONS AND PRACTICAL GUIDELINES

This Section contains detailed lessons learned and practical guidelines when applying the technologies studied by RSG-16. First, there are a few general technology principles which cut across all of the topics covered by this RSG. They are lessons "not yet learned" but need to be continually revisited as more and more data and new technology becomes available. Following this, the technology principles are organized by specific topics as follows: Training the Individual and Individualizing Training, Intelligent Tutoring Systems, Instructional Development, Architecture, Authoring Systems, Distance Learning, Virtual Reality and Training, Training Evaluation-cultural and intercultural aspects, and Cost/Effectiveness.

A. Generic Technology Principles

1. Do not allow technology pull to drive us to reach new heights of capabilities and costs before we have sufficient data on performance effectiveness, user knowledge or willingness to take the risk of this new technology, or the cost of ownership.

2. The "front end analysis" required during training system development should include trade-off analysis and specification of types of media and technologies needed.
3. Address the issue of fidelity and realism early and with data which directly relate to the desired performance required by the user(s). The importance of fidelity and/or realism to the training task is the question which must be answered during the analysis phase if the outcome is not to be biased. Fidelity levels required for enhancing the learning process are often lower than that for generating realism.
4. The use of embedded training has many opportunities to provide highly effective training in the work environment. But use it with care and only after thorough front end analysis. There is considerable potential to incorporate training in operational equipment but lead/development times are long. Provisions really needs to be made early design phases.
5. Advancements in microprocessors, helmet displays, voice recognition software, and telecommunications allows one to train or have job related aids anywhere and at anytime. The development of "wearable" computer systems for one-site maintenance and repair now allow training and job aiding to be integrated into a system that can go with the person.
6. Design for interoperability from the beginning to avoid the expense of adapting either the architecture or the learning system after the fact (e.g., a universal BUS with pluggable components). Since simulation and many other learning technologies are not mature enough to predict their use or effectiveness, issues can be solved as they occur if one is prepared for iterative changes throughout the development of the system.

B. Specific Technology Principles

The following is the list of specific lessons learned. While they have been placed under a given heading, the reader is cautioned that some of them do intersect other areas and headings. The headings have been used principally to help focus the many items on the list.

Training Individuals and Individualizing Training.

1. Instructional efficiency can be accomplished by tailoring instructional sequence, content, pace, and style to the needs of each learner. This is becoming an economic necessity in military training since the economics of group instruction are reducing the effectiveness of such group instruction.
2. Before beginning a new program for individualized instruction, develop an organized body of principles based on the current literature and technology since technological advances can quickly what is available or supportable.
3. Increased student interactivity provides increased student achievement.
4. The use of computer based instruction will provide at least a 30 percent reduction in instructional time.
5. The use of computer based instruction has its greatest savings from shortening the training time thereby allowing personnel to have more operational (work) time available.
6. The use of two-dimensional representations (simulations) of three-dimensional equipment allows students to learn as well or better than with real equipment.

Favorable cost ratios are obtained when personal computers are substituted in training for actual equipment. Savings were in the 1–3 orders of magnitude better without sacrificing instructional achievement.

7. If large amounts of practice are required to master a subject matter, CBI may be the most feasible and cost-effective way to provide it. Training based on CBI has the often noted qualities of patience, privacy, and economy.
8. If equipment costing substantially more than desk-top computer systems can be simulated adequately to meet the training objectives at hand, then it is likely that CBI simulations used partially or wholly in place of actual equipment will both lower costs and increase training accessibility. Training using such simulations is both more reproducible (students can try one set of decisions, observe their consequences and try again) and more visible (students can see the invisible in simulations and they can focus on training relevant experience) than is training using actual equipment.
9. Experiences that students need in order to achieve training objectives may be too dangerous to provide without simulation. Such experiences are particularly common in military training. Many such experiences can be provided using training technology.
10. Computer Based Instruction (CBI) can be provided outside of classroom settings, presented at arbitrary times and places (including barracks, workbenches, and homes), and delivered cheaply. It can be a cost effective tool therefore for distance learning.
11. Privacy, closely monitored progress, or both. Many students in military training — particularly those who pursue full military careers — are highly motivated and would benefit from frequent progress monitoring. Daily, even hourly, monitoring and privacy can be provided by CBI.
12. Standardized, less variable training outcomes. Because of the assessment that can be built into CBI, its outcomes can be standardized and even certified. This feature has been observed in classroom instruction using CBI where achievement variability is reduced because fewer students are "lost" — students are more likely to reach criterion levels of performance when CBI is used in place of more conventional classroom approaches. Equivalent results for job site training seem likely.

Intelligent Tutoring Systems (ITS).

1. Only start an ITS project if there is a need to have an added training value as compared to conventional CBT.
2. Always start with a thorough domain analysis using knowledge based analysis techniques
3. Make a clean separation between domain knowledge and instructional logic.
4. Use an ITS only when highly tailored training is necessary or is cost justified
5. ITS development demands a merging of AI with training strategies, task-analysis, and multi-media and therefore particularly emphasizes the need for multi-disciplinary development teams.

Instructional Development. The art and techniques of training design are well enough developed. Their adaptation to new training technologies; e.g., networked training, virtual reality, is lagging behind traditional training. What is needed are the broader application of rules and design guidelines which have been well developed for manual use but which can and should be adopted by software engineers for computer use.

1. Define a generic courseware structure to reduce development time
2. Keep interfaces simple to use (e.g. do not overdo use of colors, sound, etc.).
3. Use one rich data type (video, animation, etc.) at a time.
4. Use multidisciplinary development teams with domain experts, courseware developers, video specialists, instructors, project managers, etc.
5. Refine the Instructional Development procedures to apply to: cultural and social learning objectives, simulation networks, and virtual reality.
6. Perform an evaluation with users of different expertise levels in order to investigate whether the system can be used by a broad or narrow class of users.
7. Choose a proper checklist to evaluate the functionality of a system or to select the proper system. A checklist is a good first indication if a system complies with the functions that should be present in general in a system.
8. Provide an introduction in which the ins and outs of the system and the purpose of the evaluation is explained.
9. Increase the degree of difficulty with each subsequent exercise.

Architecture. Assumption: There are normally, according to ISO (International Standards Organization) , a standard seven layers of architecture for a system. Since we are nominally dealing with only software associated with training, we are excluding from our concern those layers which are associated with mathematical or software principles or hardware/software interface models or even the interface models associated with distributed systems.

Our use of the term architecture is focused on that which can be affected by the developer of learning software or the user/manager of this software. The issues of re-use, shared use, and interoperability are the core concerns of architecture. Inherent in the logic of an architecture or infrastructure as it is sometimes called is whether it is an open or a closed system.

1. It is necessary to adapt extant information technologies and their components to achieve interoperability or re-use whether they are for a closed or open system. Develop and maintain a robust and a flexible architecture. Remember, one size does not fit all. In the last 5 years we have seen three distinct types of simulations used for training; (1) Real (e.g., instrumented real combatants), (2) Virtual (e.g. networked simulators and semi-automated forces), and (3) Constructive (e.g. traditional algorithmic aggregate war games). Significant strengths and weaknesses have been found in all depending on their use.

   Caveat: Current limitations on simulation types rest in the fact that the spontaneity in battle possible in actual maneuver and free play virtual exercises frequently have a high payoff or a high cost consequence that so far cannot be programmed.
2. Do not be tempted to "fix" or dictate standards based upon what is known today. It can hamper your being able to take advantage of breakthroughs in technology which might vastly reduce costs or provide new capabilities.

   Caveat: Users who attempt to force a standard before there is adequate intellectual discovery face the high probability that the accepted standard(s) will soon be obsolete (e.g. VHS and Beta video format)
3. Allow the respective participants to develop expertise by taking advantage of the value added of shared or common user knowledge. This is very important in

the areas where technology is maturing so rapidly that real knowledge is dispersed among many.

4. Put the bulk of the computing power with the user. Digital libraries or "virtual collections of information" are constantly increasing in size and content. It is more cost effective to go to the source than maintain it locally. To take advantage of this requires a lot of computing power which must be constantly available to the ultimate user.
5. Establish reliable databases of performance characteristics of "objects of interest." These databases need to contain a variety of valid operational characteristics of equipment of interest to the users.
6. Databases for joint or combined training activities using networked simulations, will need to contain the "official" operational characteristics of objects of common interest to the users.
7. Develop a common taxonomy of characteristics for various objects so that objects developed by different builders can be used with confidence. This will also develop a need to fit the overall architecture with models and data that are compatible to that architecture.

   Caveat: If it is not possible to require immediate compliance with an official taxonomy, have the developers identify to what extent they can comply with the official standards implicit in the taxonomy. This way users will know how functional their developments are in terms of its intended use and/or reuse.
8. Models should be built to meet the purposes of their design as well as their operational use (e.g., It is now recognized that models that work perfectly by themselves for their intended purposes may not behave accurately when networked with other models). The intended use of models significantly influences the quantity and the accuracy of the characteristics required for reliable results. Models designed for training will be different from models designed for operational military systems.
9. Try it before you adopt it. Compliance with a protocol or standard DO NOT necessarily produce desired performance. No matter how well understood the protocols are nor how stringent the quality control system, networked simulations are not compliant until they interact in a realistic setting.

Authoring Systems.

1. Have an updated set of evaluation criteria to permit the training developer to make systematic judgments about the type(s) of authoring tools needed for their specific applications.
2. Obtain a general survey of information about currently available authoring systems.
3. Select a small number (3–5) candidate systems from available databases for examination.
4. Evaluate the candidate systems with a comprehensive set of criteria, which include various graphics and text editors, built-in instructional design and development (programming) aids, expandability of the system, user friendliness, and cost/affordability.
5. Final selection should be based on the unique needs of a given situation.
6. Present realistic cases for exercises that have to be prepared with the authoring system.

Distance Learning (DL).

1. Personal and organizational privacy and security of resources are of prime concern and must be taken into account from the very beginning.
2. Distance Learning is a flexible learning strategy that provides learning on demand at a significant cost savings/avoidance since travel and the need for instructors is reduced.
3. An interoperable network should be used for transmitting the variety of media and technology since it allows for constant injection of new and emerging capabilities.
4. The many forms of distance learning have all been successfully tested in both education and training settings with a variety of content areas.
5. Distance learning provides for a tailored reduction in residence based training to meet specific user and organizational needs.
6. Distance learning allows for almost immediate access to NATO and other international resources and assets relevant to mission needs.
7. The use of interconnectiveness can significantly reduce and/or avoid duplication of effort.
8. Distributed/Distance learning technologies allows the users to maintain flexibility and coordination with their peers and supervisors in order to tailor the learning program to meet changing needs.
9. It permits readiness training to occur at any location, any time, and with varying degrees of sophistication. Without it, reserve forces might not be able to receive such training and hence be unable to perform their job safely and effectively.
10. Developers and administrators need to make sure that residency requirements are considered when offering courses over a network.
11. With the increased use of digital, multi-media instructional resources and associated compression capabilities, make sure universal access tools are available to the users.
12. The use of distance learning does not eliminate the need for qualified instructors. Remote site instructors will be required to administer to the students and support materials provided by subject matter experts.
13. Prepare to compensate educators for handling larger student loads. Such compensation can take the form of an accelerated path to tenure, designing, predicting and presenting new courses, and other forms of non-monetary incentives.

    Caveat: The costs of converting courses for use over a distance learning system is a significant funding challenge. It is necessary that NATO provide consistent and meaningful cost formulae to ensure reliable, credible, and accountable data when planning and/or modifying distance learning systems.

Virtual Reality (VR) and Training. The current knowledge base is limited. The field of VR is quite dynamic. Studies completed to date suggest great potential. However, so far the bulk of the use of VR has been focused on design and not for training. Applications of different levels of VR capabilities in situation rehearsal and training are in their infancy. There are many aspects of development of underlying technology that must continue to be explored as well as the evaluation of them within different contexts where they may be applied. Therefore the following guidance is a mixture of general guidelines and cautions to be used when trying to apply VR to training.

1. Decide what the task is for the human.

2. Determine how real to make the VR environment for it to meet training needs.
3. Identify the appropriate interactions that are required for the VR situations.
4. Evaluate the transfer to real world environments after training in VR ones.
5. Determine the need for authoring tools to enable them to cover the intended role of the VR environment.
6. Identify the interdisciplinary requirements to do it right and to have confidence in what is created.
7. Let the users get sufficient time to experiment with the system, especially when the system is complex.
8. Use questionnaires after each application to gather information about a certain topic and afterwards to get general information.

Design for VR & Training. The answer to questions regarding the actual presentation and the related interaction can subscribe to differing levels of reality. Whether consistent adherence to reality is necessary or not is yet to be determined. Some levels of mismatch have deleterious effects such as seasickness when the induced motion from a visual presentation is inconsistent with real world feedback as encountered in everyday life.

1. *Location of the immersed operator's position.* In order to give the subject the illusion of being immersed in the world created through computers, we must provide the computer a series of real time data about instantaneous position of the body. This will provide the subject a virtual world, related to his own spatial and temporal references.
2. *Interfaces.* For each interface, various answers are appropriate in the military area depending on the application. Importance should be given to the cost/quality and performance trade off to choose the best solution for each specific application. Physiological constraints are essentially related to the technical possibilities of providing a sufficient visual field and a stereoscopic illusion.
3. *Visual interfaces.* Digital representational progress permits very high quality numerical images. The remaining decision concerns the way to present these images to the operator in order that he get the sense of immersion without physical, physiological and psychological constraint. Current experiments are showing that sense of immersion is directly related to the size of the visual field. Effort should therefore concentrate on getting displays with the biggest possible field. Stereoscopic vision is important for tasks taking place in a space smaller than ten meters.
4. *Reality/fidelity.* We must focus on providing information in terms of virtual space of activity rather than in terms of picture realism with the reality. From this perspective, techniques of image enrichment have a lot to offer. "Enhanced reality" is one important point to look at for applications regarding training, teleoperation or remote battle. Cost/Effectiveness tradeoffs must be considered when deciding to use enhanced 3D reality in VR vs. a 2D display. If training is for a task that assumes automatic motor skill reactions then the system needs to respond in a manner that provides the necessary correct operational feedback to the trainee. How to scope this out for a real situation is still under investigation.
5. *Auditory interfaces.* Actually there are two possibilities: stereo sound and 3D sound. In terms of practical application, 3D sound is interesting only when we want to improve the presentation by giving more information.

6. *Haptic interfaces.* Providing the operator with information on physical aspects of environment other than visual and auditory is an absolute necessity. The problem is then related to how: by stimulating the relevant organic sensor without simulating real surroundings or by simulating real surroundings without any specific interface (e.g., electrical excitation of thermal sensor or acclimatization of the room). The decision should be made on a cost-effective basis but within the context of the operators task requirements.
7. *Psychological issues.* Virtual reality impact on the operator has to be considered seriously. As with each new technology, virtual reality will probably change our way of life. Some effects will be positive, teleworking will probably reduce the traffic as well as the stress. But there is also some risk of negative effects. Unit further research is completed, expert opinion should be sought for each application in order to get a better grasp on the impact of VR immersion, cognitively and emotionally.
8. *The task.* Is it for training or for rehearsal? The demands of levels of detail need adjustment depending on the goals of the exercise. There is also the related problem of equipment and tethering of movement and its effect on performance. Related issues concern definition of the role of video and animation of what is observed, learned, retained and can be transferred to the real world.

   Caveat: To date there are no confirming studies of increased retention of information or of increased transfer to task using real models and/or video explanations (Wetzel, Radtke, and Stern, 1994). There seems to be a sense of better transfer during rehearsal and visual recognition however it has not been supported by careful evaluation. Previous evidence in the 2-D realm has shown that there are mixed results over standard lecture and demonstration classrooms. The results depend on how the presentations are integrated and on the nature of the task at hand.

   Virtual Reality has received anecdotal support in some military training applications (e.g., demo training for the Damage Control Assistant (DCA)) but there is no clear evaluation. Problems with this demo include difficulty in modifying the scenarios or controlling the scope of the simulated environment for training.
9. *Appropriateness of the display and interactive capabilities for VR.* This implies that we have criteria for determining how to build and use these systems. This is leading edge research. Current investigations include development of new interaction techniques which give the user direct control in a natural way with an environment that includes some level of real reaction capability. In other words, when things fall, they fall at an expected speed and they go in the right direction. In addition, appropriate feedback to the participant mimics what they expect in the real world. An example of this includes the introduction of force feedback to data glove manipulation so that a virtual object does not get crushed on grasp.

   Caveat: Current visual displays have refresh rate problems if the participant moves too fast. This can affect the performance and the gains in the system use. It is characterized by the narrow view in the submarine ship handling system. However, in large screen VR situations such as the cave these effects seem to be less of a problem although it is not clear that this is the case.
10. *Evaluation methods to determine the effectiveness of VR.* The case in Virtual Environments is yet to be determined. To date most evaluation is introspective and

anecdotal. Some non-immersive systems (IMAT) exist that are currently being evaluated as to their effectiveness but the results are not in yet (Ellis and Parchman, 1994).

Caveat: Methods for evaluation will need to be developed. Current practice of a multiple choice test to ascertain the knowledge of the lesson will not suffice as the new system emphasis changes to recognition of a real world situation that has been studied from within instead of observed second hand and learned only by reference. Another related concern is that these systems can quickly get boring. How much game playing is assumed in the context of the situation training and to what extent are the related skills of the game similar to what is to be learned in the task?

11. *How to develop appropriate situations and scenarios to achieve adequate systems is the focus of authoring tool development.* It is critical that after one knows what levels of granularity need to be controlled for the real world transfer and has an idea how to assess performance in the VR environment, one needs to be able to make sure that critical task situations are encountered during exposure. The visual, auditory, haptic and other displays need to be manipulatable in prescribed; coordinated ways and capability to edit the 3-D images into coherent visual real world reactions in a dynamic way need to be developed.
12. *Authoring capabilities need to be developed to allow correct manageable control of what is being displayed to mimic the real world.* They should include ways that allow one to capture critical aspects of the task, to react to the system responses in real ways, and include means to follow alternative paths in the interactive environment task space. This approach will cover what is considered by experts to be the critical level of knowledge to perform the skill or have adequate training.
    Caveat: This level of effort is just beginning. Indexing of video on content is current basic research; editing speech with video for different effects does not generally exist; being able to edit speech from recognized speech signals is in its infancy; definition of suitable display situations to capture a task environment are just being built. Once they exist, we can begin to develop a more skilled capability in putting the VR parts together in a systematic manner. Currently it is extremely costly from the hardware end through the system integration and design.
13. *Virtual Reality requires interdisciplinary teams to adequately build and control the task environments.* While lip-service to interdisciplinary activities has existed from many years, this particular endeavor will need the integrated teams of researchers to be able to cover the complex situations which need to be controlled and manipulated to be effective. System design will need the integration of knowledgeable persons who know about software building and have expertise in human factors and in task modeling. In addition, to its effectiveness for the task at hand. This requires extensive evaluation within the psychological or human factors paradigm of study to know whether the system conveys what is intended.

    Caveat: We do not know how to detect anomalies in a system that is built to train for a given situation and that trains expectations in situation changes and reactions which are counter to the desired performance.
14. *Cost of VR is a critical concern.* Anyone anticipating integration of VR for embedded training or for rehearsal needs to be aware of the up-front costs to get the systems in place. Hardware is coming down in cost but the level of refresh

rate still is a problem unless fat machines with good graphics capabilities are available. This requires much more than an off-the-shelf PC or Mac platform provides. The granularity is significantly different for the cost.

Caveat: The issue is how much reality is needed for various kinds of training or rehearsal. Large screen environments such as "caves" are expensive costing millions of dollars. Their benefit is not clear. The nature of shared knowledge spaces in team environments where even now we have large screen displays in the Command Information Center is not clearly understood.

15. *Speech understanding systems currently are trained for a specific domain and are not easy to modify.* In addition, they are noise cancelling microphones and have problems in variable noise environments. The microphones in speech understanding interfaces often are switch controlled because of ambient voice communications that are not intended for the device. This remains a problem.
16. *The role of non-speech auditory information is being studied.* It is unclear whether or not it can be used as an additional channel for discrete information presentation.

    Caveat: All of these non-speech systems require additional hardware. The need for real-time response dictates that many parts of a given VR system exist on separate devices. Their time coordination with integrated update rates and reaction is under development. Therefore it is costly from the hardware perspective and affects the complexity of the software needed to carry out the functions as well as the software for the scenario situation-authored information content of the VR environment. In addition, computer support staff are required to make sure the system networks that underlie the environment remain operational and provided maximum performance. This is not a technology that you download and run. It will require continual supervision and maintenance of the software and the run environment from the computational perspective.

Training Evaluation: Cultural Aspects.

1. The training process should be designed and evaluated with sufficient knowledge and reference to the cultural and social circumstances of training. Culture, we broadly define as the range of values and social norms of specific groups like instructor, trainees, officers, enlisted personnel, or of different NATO countries. This definition becomes critical, if distance learning and networked simulation are to make it possible to conduct inter-cultural training. If we understand inter-cultural training, we will be able to design and use networked and distributed training systems to their fullest advantage.

   Caveat: Inter-cultural training may become a problem, when the general acquisition of norms and values by a person (learner or instructor), his so-called acculturation, dominates his learning and training behavior (at least his micro-behavior) and therefore may conflict with the behavior of persons who were acculturized differently. Educationally speaking, it is not the bridging of long distances by communication lines, that constitutes a training problem. It is the inter-cultural training between nations, populations or even stratification's of a given society, which we should understand and master. The problem of inter-cultural military distributed training is a rather new area and there have been few if any attempts to address it.
2. What we should know in more detail are the structure of inter-cultural training, furthermore strategies to obtain knowledge, and of course hypotheses about the

extend of inter-cultural differences in the learning and training behavior. Let me elaborate this a bit further:

Training Evaluation: Inter-Cultural Aspects.

1. Inter-cultural training may roughly be structured according to the basic social relationships in any given training environment: student-to-student-interaction, student-to-teacher-interaction and teacher-to-teacher-interaction. The influence of the different social status of soldiers and of different leadership styles on training and instruction may certainly be worth researching.

2. Inter-cultural competence should be a qualification at least of instructors; behavior in inter-cultural groups should be a general training objective at least in leadership training. Sources of knowledge are public education in heterogeneous and multi-cultural societies and officers courses with participation from foreign countries. As for the public education, inter-cultural education is widely researched. As for the military training, This problem has not been attacked.

3. In order to maximize the inter-cultural appropriateness of training system design, human factors analysis should be applied to the full range of training interactions. Every simulator, trainer, and CBT-specification should comprise a section which addresses specific ergonomic attention dealing with communications, environment, and infrastructure. Apply these methods not only on the higher command level (where training is planned) but also on the training course and training unit level and adapt the methodologies accordingly. The new key words are "just in time training" and cost performance responsibility of the unit commander for the allocation of training funds. The latter, known also as "self supporting units", will be new for some European NATO forces.

Caveat: There is too little or no empirical research known concerning the acceptance of simulators, as judged by instructors and students on ergonomic grounds. The "ergonomic" tests, which may be part of the technical evaluation at the end of the development phase, concern mostly basic MMI evaluations. The ergonomics of social learning in and with simulators remains unexplored.

Cost/Effectiveness.

1. To make training cost/effective on the micro level a new approach must be taken. This new approach is called "activity based cost accounting for training". The challenge is elaborate an educational activity list of military training and to associate money to educational decisions on the micro level.

   Caveat: Although most NATO forces know more or less well, what a particular training course costs, every instructor and every person is responsible for the planning of military training but has a limited knowledge about the effects of certain educational activities. We have little or no knowledge about the impact of educational "micro"-decisions on the **cost** of a given training course. Some examples of educational micro-decisions are:

   a. selection of training goals according to the training level of the students
   b. selection and application of certain training strategies and methods for a given training group
   c. the application of motivational measures on training of a given individual or group

d. organizational decisions, such as the distribution of training load over time, the ration between "training in advance" and "training on demand".

2. The evaluation methods and measures should be consistent with the purpose of the application (e.g. a cost-effectiveness comparison of different methods must retain the same objectives and criteria. This is different from an application which is designed to provide additional training value to the old way of training. In this case new objectives and new criteria must be designed to fit the new value..

APPENDIX A

Individual Papers from Lessons Learned Workshop

THE NEED FOR EVALUATION AND ASSESSMENT IN TRAINING AND SIMULATION

Alexander von Baeyer

Industrieanlagen-Betriebsgesellschaft
Training Systems Department
Ottobrunn, Germany

INTRODUCTION

The purpose of the this paper is to present a "policy" paper on military training research. The ultimate goal of military training research is be to safeguard the long term qualification of military personnel. To achieve this goal research must have itself a long term strategy. My aim today is to contribute to this strategy.

Following this introduction I shall present six requirements that should be met in order to assure a high standard of military training through the advances of research. My contribution focuses on educational and social aspects of training and simulation.

Each of the six requirements is defined by four categories:

- situation that needs improvement
- definition of the requirement
- state of the art and what we know
- what we don't know

The requirements are mainly described on the basis of results produced by this RSG and other NATO sponsored research. The knowledge gaps are described as far as they can be filled realistically. Therefore, no daydreams, but reasonable goals will be submitted for discussion. I ask you, the participants of this workshop, to comment especially on the feasibility of my proposals.

The six requirements concern:

1. Training design and total quality management
2. New approach to the evaluation of training
3. Special ergonomic requirements for simulators
4. New cost/effectiveness evaluations
5. Better analysis and use of the open learning environment
6. The allocation of funds

The requirements are interlinked, as you will notice at once.

Virtual Reality, Training's Future? edited by Seidel and Chatelier
Plenum Press, New York, 1997

1. TRAINING DESIGN AND TOTAL QUALITY MANAGEMENT

Situation: Military training is or should be planned, designed and implemented following the already established rules of the ISD, SAT or similar procedures. These procedures always start with a task analysis and work down to the implementation of training courses or other training measures.

This requirement is trivial but, nevertheless, not realized in all cases. The fact that the rules of training design are not always followed has two important reasons:

- training areas with cultural, social and emotional learning objectives are difficult to fit into the SAT/ISD rules, but this is not impossible
- new emerging training technologies are still predominantly the domain of scientists and engineers; they are far too little researched by human factors and education experts.

Requirement: Training design must become TQM of training, if the rules of systematic planning and designing are extended to the cultural, social and emotional areas of military training as well as to the newly emerging training technologies and therefore if it is done within the framework of HSI/MANPRINT*.

Status: The art and techniques of training design are well enough developed. Their adaptation to new training technologies, e.g. networked training, virtual reality, is lagging behind traditional training. What is needed, are not new rules, but the broad implementation of the rules through the following means:

- refining the SAT/ISD procedures to cope with cultural, social and emotional learning objectives
- applying the SAT/ISD procedures to simulation networks and virtual reality.
- implementation of a HSI or MANPRINT approach, in order to place training design between fully undertaken manpower analyses, ergonomics and logistics (for most European NATO countries this is a new approach)
- familiarsation of those military leaders with the methods of HSI/MANPRINT and training design, who define the framework of training; those who are responsible for military technology, organisation, logistics and budget must know, how training is designed and how difficult this is.

What we don't know, are three things:

a. We need more empiric research and evaluation, concerning the application of training design procedures: concerning especially the degree of proceduralization, the validity for non-cognitive and non-psychomotor objectives.
b. We need the inclusion of front end analyses according to SAT/ISD procedures into the experiments with networked simulations and virtual reality. Definitively we need more human factors expertise in these new and emerging technologies.
c. We don't know, how to sensitize the non-training community for HSI/MANPRINT and particularly training problems. But this is not a task of training research. It is a task of the organisational change in and around the training community.

---

* Human Systems Integration or Manpower Personnel Integration. Cf. the results of RSG 21: Workshop on Liveware Integration Needs, Dec. 1992, AC/243(Panel 8)TP/5; "Liveware Integration - Final Report", AC/243(Panel 8)TP/18.

2. NEW APPROACH TO THE EVALUATION OF TRAINING: SOCIAL AND ORGANISATIONAL CONDITIONS OF TRAINING AND SIMULATION

The second requirement is closely connected with the preceding.

Situation: Training success has been evaluated (if at all) as to how well students retained, what they have been taught. The evaluation of the increase of individual and group performance through training is necessary, but does not constitute the entire scope of evaluation. The circumstances, under which successful training was delivered, must be evaluated as well. This is done, more or less systematically, by cost and effectiveness analyses of training devices[*], training infrastructure and other tangible elements of any one training system. But there is something left for careful evaluation:

Requirement: The training process should be designed and evaluated with good knowledge and reference to the cultural and social circumstances of training[†]. This becomes necessary, if distance learning and networked simulation make it possible to conduct inter-cultural training.

Inter-cultural training may become a problem, when the general acquisition of norms and values by a person (learner or instructor), his so-called enculturalization, dominates his learning and training behaviour (at least his micro-behaviour) and therefore may conflict with the behaviour of persons who were enculturalized differently.

Educationally speaking, it is not the bridging of long distances by communication lines, that constitutes a training problem. It is the inter-cultural training between nations, populations or even stratefications of a given society, which we should understand and master. If we understand inter-cultural training, we will be able to design and use networked and distributed training systems.

Status: As far as I know, the problem of inter-cultural military distributed training[‡] is a rather new area and there are few attempts known, to address it. May be, you know more about it.

What we should know in more detail are the structure of inter-cultural training, furthermore strategies to obtain knowledge, and of course hypotheses about the extend of inter-cultural differences in the learning and training behaviour. Let me elaborate this a bit further:

- Inter-cultural training may roughly be structured according to the basic social relationships in any given training environment: student-to-student-interaction, student-to-teacher-interaction and teacher-to-teacher-interaction. The influence of the different social status of soldiers and of different leadership styles on training and instruction may certainly be worth researching.
- Sources of knowledge are public education in inhomogeneous and multi-cultural societies and officers courses with participation from foreign countries. As for the public education, inter-cultural education is widely researched[°]. As for the mili-

* Cf. Workshop-Reports and Final Report of Panel 7 RSG 15 on Cost/Effectiveness and the Military Value of Training.

† Cf. S. Bagnera's contribution to the RSG 16 workshop in Munich in Sept. 1993 entitled "Organizational Requirements For Educational Technology Development and Use" and the author's paper for the RSG 26 workshop in Brussels in Sept. 1995 entitled "Training Strategies and Networked Simulation - A Conceptual Analysis".

‡ Cf. C. Hack's contribution to the RSG 16 workshop in Munich in Sept. 1993 "Attitudinal Considerations in Distributed Training".

° The research is oriented in two directions: training for (multi-)cultural competence and training of multi-cultural target groups.

tary training, I am not sure that this problem has been attacked. Anyway, inter-cultural competence should be a qualification at least of instructors; behaviour in inter-cultural groups should be a general training objective at least in leadership training.

- The hypotheses about the extent of inter-cultural differences in military training may concern the fact that there are differences to be observed or measured at all, and that these differences concern the micro-behaviour in organizing one's one knowledge acquisition as well as the macro-behaviour in the instructor performance. Another hypothesis may be that leadership and command, control and information are the training areas, where inter-cultural differences matter most and therefore inter-cultural training and instruction may have problems.

3. SPECIAL ERGONOMIC REQUIREMENTS FOR SIMULATORS

Situation: Simulators, trainers and CBT systems are planned and designed on the basis of training concepts, which specify the appropriate training objectives and training strategies. The wider ergonomic circumstance, under which technology based training takes place, is oftentimes overlooked.

Requirement: Every simulator, trainer, and CBT specification should comprise a section which addresses at least the following issues with specific ergonomic attention:

- the educationally adequate communication between instructor and student
- the communication between instructors and/or operators in larger simulation systems (including networks)
- the communication between the students and the social learning (e.g.) in CBT classrooms: how it can be improved and when the individual learner must shielded from other learners
- the environment in the instructor station (noise, vibration, air, radiation)
- the infrastructure of an educationally valid briefing, debriefing, after action review and observation by non-active students

Human factors analysis should be applied to the full range of training interactions.

What we know: Instructor station ergonomics are researched since a few years*. The cognitive and perceptive requirements of simulation are researched also for many years but need still considerable effort†.

What we don't know: There is too little or no empiric research known concerning the acceptance of simulators, as judged by instructors and students on ergonomic grounds. The "ergonomic" tests, which may be part of the technical evaluation at the end of the development phase, concern mostly basic MMI evaluations. The ergonomics of social learning in and with simulators are unexplored. If you have better knowledge please tell me.

The descriptions the following two requirements will be shorter, because they deal with well established problems, which lack however a redefinition.

---

* For instance: M. Goode and M. Simpson: "I Want to Spend 90 % of My Time Facing Forward" A User-Centered Approach to Instructor-Station-Design, Proceedings ITEC, 1992.

† For instance the work done by the MASTER-consortium under the leadership of the Human Factors Institute TM-TNO of the Netherlands, sponsored by the EUCLID RTP 11.1.

4. NEW COST/EFFECTIVENESS EVALUATIONS: COST / PERFORMANCE RESPONSIBILITY, "KAIZEN" AND JUST IN TIME TRAINING

Situation: Training is still the most costly military activity in peace time. There are various cost-effectiveness methodologies to be used for predictive and post factum analysis of training*. These methods are applicable on a rather high planning and decision level.

Requirement: Apply these methods not only on the higher command level (where training is planned) but also on the training course and training unit level and adapt the methodologies accordingly. The new key words are "just in time training" and cost performance responsibility of the unit commander for the allocation of training funds. The latter, known also as "self supporting units", will be new for some European NATO forces.

What we know: Most NATO forces know more or less well, what a particular training course costs. Every instructor and every person responsible for the planning of military training has a more or less developed knowledge about the effects of certain educational activities. But this is not enough anymore.

What we don't know: We have little or no knowledge about the impact of educational "micro" decisions on the cost of a given training course. Educational micro-decisions are (e.g.):

- selection of training goals according to the training level of the students
- selection and application of certain training strategies and methods for a given training group
- the application of motivational measures on training of a given individual or group
- organisational decisions, such as the distribution of training load over time, the ration between "training in advance" and "training on demand".

To make training cost/effective on the micro level a new approach must be taken. This new approach is called "activity based cost accounting for training". The challenge is elaborate an educational activity list of military training and to associate money to educational decisions on the micro level.

5. BETTER ANALYSIS AND USE OF THE OPEN LEARNING ENVIRONMENT: MERGING THE CIVILIAN AND MILITARY RESOURCES: HOW TO PROCEED, INTER-NATIONAL AND INTRA-NATIONAL SHARING OF RESOURCES

Situation: Despite many declarations to unburden the national training load, real attempts of burden sharing in military training are still the exception rather than the rule. The problem is to harmonize national training requirements, to coordinate resources and to cope with the cultural differences (see above). However, there are training areas, where national military training philosophies and cultural differences do not matter too much. These areas are almost all technical and many logistical basic qualifications.

* See fn 2

Requirements: NATO should consider a new and broad burden sharing campaign for inter-national and civilian-military cooperation in training. The scope of this campaign should be to identify the training areas and topics, where cooperation is feasible and the NATO forces are willing to cooperate.

What we know: The framework of joint training and standardisation is available (Euro NATO Training Group, STANAGs, DEAs, bilateral training agreements). As far as I know, these activities are insular attempts and do not include the civilian training available in each country.

What we don't have, is a NATO-wide inventory of military and civilian training resources, which could be used. Furthermore we have so far no idea, what would be the organisational prerequisites and consequences of such a broad cooperation effort. The cultural problems I have already mentioned. Notwithstanding considerable difficulties, NATO should adopt a global approach to cooperation in training. The tremendous cost of military training and the new defence postures after the end of the east-west-confrontation leave no other choice. Creating a data pool and data management infrastructure for a lessons learnt systems would be a first step.

6. THE ALLOCATION OF FUNDS: THE NECESSARY ADVANCES AND THE ALLOCATION OF FUNDS IN PROMISING RESEARCH PROJECTS

Situation: There are more problems than there is money.

Requirement: Define research priorities, where advances are imminent **and** results lead to cost reductions.

Status of knowledge: NATO-wide there are plenty research projects concerning training and simulation.

What we don't know: There is no long term NATO research strategy for military training and simulation (at least known to me). This RSG may contribute to setting up a strategic research plan.

My proposal is the following:

First option with imminent payoff: Research on the efficiency of TQM methods in training, including the cost-performance responsibility approach on the training unit and training course level. This is not training research sensu structu, but research about the necessary organisational change in and around military training.

Second option with middle to long term payoff: Research on the cultural differences in training with special emphasis on networked simulation and burden sharing.

Both options concern the optimisation of training management. If research funds are allocated to issues of management and burden sharing, they will become a multiplier of funds that are invested in the theoretical research.

COST OF FLEXIBLE AND DISTANCE LEARNING

Jef Moonen and Betty Collis

University of Twente
The Netherlands

1. INTRODUCTION

Improving productivity is a permanent goal in the business world. In order to improve productivity, production procedures as well as the skills and expertise level of employees are crucial variables. Training is therefore a central issue for most companies.

Training, however, is expensive. In the traditional situation when an employee is sent to a training course, there are three aspects that constitute a major part of the costs:

a. the registration fee for the training course
b. travel and accommodation costs
c. opportunity costs: the employee is away from work and therefore is not productive.

Bringing down the costs of training can be looked upon as bringing down the costs of each of these components.

In principle, the registration costs can be brought down when a course can be delivered to a large audience. In this respect the economy of scale should do the work. Travel and accommodation costs can be lowered when the training course can be delivered near the working place of the employee. Using a distribution mechanism that takes this aspect into account can be a solution in this respect. An obvious direction for a solution is the use of communication technology (using video via television-broadcast, satellite, ISDN, Internet, or even via videotapes sent through regular mail; e-mail and computer conferencing) or using the traditional distance delivery of printed material. The loss of productive time for the employer could be dealt with when an employee is willing to attend the training in his/her own 'free' time.

All of these aspects and/or combinations of them, constitute a more 'flexible' training situation than what is done in a more traditional situation. The target of such a more-flexible training situation is to present a more cost-effective solution to the training problem.

Virtual Reality, Training's Future? edited by Seidel and Chatelier
Plenum Press, New York, 1997

2. THE TELESCOPIA PROJECT

To illustrate how more-flexible learning can be realised, the Telescopia (1995) Project is taken as example. The Telescopia (TransEuropean Learning System for Crossborder Open and Interactive Applications) project is a one year project funded by the Commission of the European Community.

Investigating cost-effective solutions is one of the main objectives of the Telescopia project. The target of the project is to realize a communication technology infrastructure comprising interactive television, interactive audio-video connections using ISDN, and a variety of facilities, such as computer conferencing, not requiring an ISDN connection.

Six course providers participated in the project offering a diversity of courses to students and trainees. Each course provider offered a variety of communication technology facilities. Two aspects are of specific interest: (a) how is the prime information of the course distributed?, and (b) how can students interact with the teachers (and with other students)? In very global terms these provisions can be described as follows (each course provider will be mentioned by a capital letter A-F; for further details see the final report of the Telescopia project): course A offered WWW-facilities and videoconferencing; course B offered lectures to students who were distributed through an internal video-conferencing distribution system, e-mail, telephone and connections between lectures and students via microphones; course C offered interactive television and videoconferencing via ISDN; course D offered television-broadcasting via satellite, regular mail, fax, telephone, and e-mail; course E offered computer conferencing, interactive TV, telephone, e-mail, and fax; course F offered via ISDN connections the Pro-Share desktop conferencing application. The main reason for this description is not to go into specific technical details. The reason for mentioning the technologies is to illustrate that each of the course providers used a rather different set-up and telematics platform.

An important aspect of the project was to gather data about the cost-effectiveness of the different course provisions. Originally the intention was even to find a relationship between the level of cost-effectiveness of each approach and the technical configurations used. However, given the demonstrator approach of the project, and given the limited number of participants in the courses that were offered by the course providers, trying to find a valid and reliable measure of effectiveness cannot be very successful. Therefore, the focus of the investigation is mainly on the cost issue.

3. DATA COLLECTION

Method

Within the Telescopia project various questionnaires were dispersed. These included course provider questionnaires, learner questionnaires and tutor questionnaires. In addition to the questionnaires the checklist for course providers has been used.

The results of these questionnaires are summarized in the Final Report of Telescopia (Köhler & Collis, 1995). These results however, only gave a global insight in the issues. Therefore, to get a more detailed insight in the costs, an interview with a cost expert in every course provider's organization was organized. Such interviews were held with five of the six course providers. Although many attempts were made, no interview nor (reliable) quantitative data could be gathered from one course provider. Therefore this course provider is left out of the further quantitative analysis.

Method for Analysis

The course provider questionnaires and the checklist for course providers yielded primarily qualitative data about costs and effectiveness. These data were looked at and taken into account when considering the data yielded by the interviews. The interview data were both qualitative and quantitative. The latter were used to calculate the costs per student per hour which was further taken as the unit of comparison.

The data yielded by the learner questionnaires were also primarily qualitative. These data were looked at to get some understanding about how learners view the costs and effectiveness of the course they took at the course provider's organization.

4. RESULTS

Course Provider: Questionnaire Data

All six course providers returned the Course Provider Questionnaires (Parts I and II). Course providers were asked about the importance of costs and effectiveness in the context of the TeleScopia project. Costs were mentioned as important for two course providers and not important for another two. From the remaining two, no clear answer was received. The two course providers who found that costs were an important issue were both operating on a more-or-less commercial basis. The two course providers that mentioned that costs were not important gave as an explanation that the costs were provided on a project basis. Costs are only an important issue when they are part of a real commercial enterprise.

Four course providers responded that effectiveness is an important issue. However, asked for further explanation, none of them clearly described how they interpreted effectiveness nor how they were going to measure its impact. All of them gave some broad description of activities that probably could be related to effectiveness issues without being exact or precise. One course provider said for instance: 'WWW was chosen in order to increase effectiveness and bring in more flexibility in learning, tutoring and coordination'. Effectiveness is seen as something that is 'good', and therefore should be aimed for. Unless clear statements about measurable objectives and criteria are formulated in advance, the effectiveness issue will remain at a very global, almost philosophical level. Therefore it was said before that in this report and given the circumstances of the project, it was not sensible to go into further detail about effectiveness.

Learner: Questionnaire Data

The return rate of the Learner Questionnaires (Parts I and II) was 30 % (73 out of 243 questionnaires). Within the questions related to costs, a distinction was made between external and internal costs. External costs are equal to the registration fee for the course. Internal costs are all other costs made by the learner, such as costs for traveling and for the acquiring of devices necessary to participate in the course.

Most learners considered the external costs inexpensive. This result is not surprising because only a very small number of the learners had to pay a fee. When there was a fee, this fee was approximately 500 ECU. Internal costs were estimated being around an average of 447 ECU, while for 60% of the responders the amount was below 200 ECU. A total of 80% of the respondents found these internal costs reasonable or inexpensive.

A high percentage (75%) of the respondents found the courses (moderately) effective. As no criterion was given to indicate what was meant by 'effective', respondents expressed only their general feelings with respect to this issue.

Costs Per Trainee/Hour

In order to get a comprehensive and comparative overview of the costs for the respective course providers, Table 1 was produced. An interpretation of those data is provided as well as some tentative conclusions.

Table 1 shows data from five of the six course providers. The figures in the tables were calculated or derived based upon the information given by the course providers. Most of these data were gathered during the interviews with the course providers. It cannot be excluded that, due to misunderstanding and/or miscommunication between the researchers and the course providers, some data deviate from reality or are not complete. The researchers take the responsibility for the data as presented.

It is the strong impression of the researchers that exact cost data are often not available. On the other hand, the researchers are convinced that the data provided represent a fair estimate of the costs. It is also the impression of the researchers that as course provision evolves towards a serious commercial enterprise instead of being in a kind of 'experimental' or 'subsidized project' stage, knowledge of the exact costs of activities becomes a more serious issue.

In Table 1 the following aspects are covered:

- *Course Provider*: The public or commercial organization that provides the course.
- *Development costs:* Costs to develop the learning material in such a way that the learning material does not need to be updated during the lifetime of the course.
- *Operating costs*: Costs needed to deliver the course during *one* round; exploitation and maintenance costs during or as a result of a round of the course.
- *Lifetime*: The *expected* number of course-rounds before the course material has to be updated or revised; the lifetime is given as an estimate by the course providers.
- *Total costs*: The sum of development and operating costs.
- *Contact time*: Time that trainees spend on contact-related activities (for instance: watching a video provided by the course provider, watching a broadcast by the course provider, communicating with a tutor in a face-to-face fashion or through using telecommunication facilities, etc.). These figures have been mentioned by the course providers.
- *Total study-time*: Time that trainees spend on the whole course. These figures have been estimated by the course providers.
- *Trainees* (expected): The *expected* number of trainees for one course-round as mentioned by the course providers.
- *Trainees* (TeleScopia): The number of trainees actually involved in the TeleScopia course.

With respect to the descriptions above, there are some difficult conceptual issues to deal with. One of these issues is how to give reliable indications of the 'total study time' a trainee spent on a course. It is clear that the total study time used by a student will vary to a large extent, so how to deal with this kind of variability? Courses delivered in a more-traditional situation (for instance a university) are often labeled by so-called study points or credits. A study point (SP) is a measure of the amount of time a student is expected to work on a course. For instance: 1 SP equals one week (40 hours) of work. A course worth

Table 1. Overview of costs calculations (in ECU)

Course provider	Develop-ment costs	Operating costs per round of a course	Lifetime (number of course rounds)	Total costs per lifetime	Contact time per course round (in hours)	Contact time per lifetime (in hours)	Total study time per course round (in hours)	Total study time per life-time (in hours)
A	76,000	132,500	2	341,000	25	50	135	270
B	20,000	10,000	3	50,000	12	36	40	120
C	726,000	113,000	5	1,291,000	40	200	70	350
D	30,000	40,000	10	430,000	5	50	60	600
E	30,000	115,000	10	1,180,000	18	180	84	840

Course provider	Operating costs/contact hour	Operating costs/ hour total study time	Total costs/ contact hour	Total costs/hour total study time	Trainees/ course round (expected)	Trainees/ course round (TeleScopia)
A	5,300	981	6,820	1,260	75	21
B	833	250	1,390	420	40	48
C	2,800	1,600	6,460	3,690	1,000	125
D	8,000	666	8,600	720	40	21
E	6,400	1,370	6,560	1,400	20	23

Course provider	Operating costs/ contact hour / trainee (expected)	Operating costs/ hour total study time / trainee (expected)	Operating costs/contact hour/trainee (Telescopia)	Total costs/contact hour/trainee (expected)	Total costs/hour total study time/trainee (expected)	Total costs/contact hour/trainee (Telescopia)
A	70	13	252	91	24	324
B	21	6	17	34	10	28
C	2.8	1.6	22	6.5	3.6	52
D	200	17	381	215	18	409
E	320	68.5	278	327	70	312

3 SP means that a student is expected to work a total of 120 hours on this course. This amount includes the contact time (following classes, maybe private face-to-face tutoring by a tutor, and the time needed to do the exam) and the private study time (reading and studying the book or notes taken, talking with colleagues, working in the library, preparing for the exam). All kind of detailed schemes can be worked out in order to relate the allocated study time of a course to the number of classes, number of pages of required reading, etc. This kind of approach could also be used to estimate the total study time that trainees spend on a course in the new situations as available in the Telescopia project. That information however is not available. Therefore the available figures are estimations by the course providers. In addition the question can be put forward if the measure of total study time should be related to a cost calculation. In a cost calculation both the costs for the course provider and the costs of the trainees should be taken into account (see earlier). This approach is based upon the philosophy of 'cost ingredients' as advocated by Levin (1983). With respect to the costs to be allocated to the trainee, these costs should (at least) consist of three parts: (a) external costs (course fee), (b) internal costs (costs in order to be able to take the course, such as travel time, technological provisions at home, etc.), (c)

costs connected with the time a trainee spent in order to follow the course. As has been mentioned above, there are some indications about the external costs and the internal costs of the trainees in the Telescopia project. It was also mentioned that in the case of the Telescopia project, course fees were not asked for. This is certainly not a situation that reflects a real-life situation. Further, there are no data available about the total time trainees spent on the course, nor whose time trainees were using (their own 'free' time, or regular 'work'-time). For these reasons, cost calculations in Table 1 only refer to costs made by the course providers.

Another difficult issue is the numbers of trainees that followed (or were expected to follow) the course. Normally this number is obvious: it is the number of trainees that paid the course fee. However in the case of the Telescopia courses, course fees were (in most cases) not applicable. In addition, the marketing of the Telescopia courses, due to the experimental nature of the situation, cannot be considered as a regular course provision for which elaborate marketing efforts would have been undertaken. For these reasons the cost calculations are based upon two kind of data: (a) the number of trainees that actually started with the courses, and (b) the number of trainees the course providers expect in a regular situation will register for the course when a normal marketing approach can be applied. Calculation of costs/hour/trainee takes as a reference the expected number of trainees. As these expectations vary a great deal per course provider, the obtained results show a large diversity of outcomes.

In order to be able to compare the different courses from a cost perspective, a number of measures have calculated:

- *Operating costs/contact hour*: The operating costs covered by the course provider to provide one contact-hour during a particular round of the course.
- *Operating costs/total study-time hour*: The operating costs covered by the course provider to provide one study-hour during a particular round of the course. As the costs for the students are not taken into account (see earlier), these figures are underestimations of the real costs. As at the same time the estimation of the total study time should be interpreted as less reliable, these figures should be interpreted with care.
- *Total costs/contact hour*: The total costs covered by the course provider to provide one contact-hour to during one particular round of the course. These figures take into account the development costs and the operating costs. The development costs are equally spread over the number of sessions as indicated by the course providers. These are the most interesting figures as they reveal the differences of the costs in comparison with the different delivery platforms.
- *Total costs/total study-time hour*: The total costs covered by the course provider to provide one study-hour during a particular round of the course. See earlier remarks with respect to total study time.
- *Operating costs/contact hour/per trainee*: The operating costs covered by the course provider to provide one contact-hour to *one* student during a particular round of the course. This measure can be used to make a comparison between the different course providers. At the same time it should be realized that the number of expected trainees is an estimation given by the course providers. A significant deviation of this number will change the results.
- *Total costs/total study-time hour/per trainee*: The total costs covered by the course provider to provide one study-hour to *one* student during a particular session. See earlier remarks with respect to total study time.

5. INTERPRETATION OF THE RESULTS

a. There is a significant difference between the cost figures of one course provider (B) and the others. It is unclear if this difference represent a real difference, implicating that the B approach is much cheaper then the others, or if the differences have occurred because of misunderstandings or misinterpretations of the cost factors that should have taken into account. Because of this uncertainty, the B figures are set aside with respect to the following conclusions.
b. The most interesting figure is the total cost/contact hour. Although the four remaining course providers each have a substantially different delivery approach, the total cost/contact hour is within a very small range around 7.000 ECU.
c. Another interesting figure is the total cost/contact hour/expected trainee. Because of the large variability in expected trainees, there is a large variability in these costs (range: 6.5 - 327 ECU). Given the specific circumstances and potential target groups, one can expect a broad range of course fees for different courses.
d. When an average and acceptable estimate is taken for a course fee/contact hour, a calculation can be made about the minimum numbers of participants needed in a course to reach a cost break-even point. It can be argued that in a commercial context 60 ECU/contact hour is a reasonable fee. In that case and taking 7.000 ECU as an average total cost/contact hour, the number of participants per session needed to reach the break-even point of a course is approximately 120. When we compare this amount with the expected number of trainees as expressed by the course providers, only one course provider is able to cover the costs of a course. Although 120 participants seems to be a rather small number when considering a European market, one has to realize that language barriers can act as a limiting factor, or when a language barrier is not an issue because the potential trainees are all fluent in, for instance, English then it could well be that the potential target group is probably highly specialized and therefore limited in numbers. If courses aim at a broader public and are provided on a much lower course fee (for instance 5 ECU/contact hour), the minimal number of students to break-even is around 1400 per round of the course.

6. CONCLUSIONS

Based upon these results the following conclusions can be formulated:

a. There is no significant difference in total costs/contact hour between delivery systems using different telematics platforms. The total cost/contact hour is approximately 7.000 ECU.
b. When commercial rates are used as course fees for courses delivered using different telematics platforms, a minimum of a 120 participants per course-session is necessary in order to reach the cost break-even point.
c. When non-commercial rates are used as course fees, a number of around 1000 participants per course-session is necessary in order to reach a cost break-even point.

Future research has to be done in order to get better and reliable cost data from the point of view of the course providers. In addition, insight in cost issues from the point of view of trainees needs an even a higher research priority. Finally, more fundamental research has to be set up with respect to the possibilities to obtain valid and reliable effectiveness data.

REFERENCES

Levin, H.M. (1983). *Cost-effectiveness: A primer*. Beverly Hills, CA: Sage

Köhler, H., & Collis, B. (1995). Issues Relating to Trans-European Course Delivery and Implementation Strategies: The Final Research Report of the Telescopia Project, WP1.6. Contact: Isabelle Dremeau, Deutsche Telekom AG, PO BOX 2000, D-53105 Bonn, Germany

WHAT HAVE WE LEARNED ABOUT COMPUTER BASED INSTRUCTION IN MILITARY TRAINING?

J. D. Fletcher

Institute for Defense Analyses
Alexandria, Virginia
Fletcher@ida.org

A number of papers prepared for NATO Research Study Group (RSG) 16, "Advanced Technologies Applied to Training Design," concern the direct, interactive use of computers in military training. For convenience, all these applications—which include drill and practice, tutorial dialogue, intelligent tutoring systems, tutorial simulations, interactive multimedia instruction, and similar approaches using computers to adjust instructional presentations to the needs of individual learners—may be called computer based instruction (CBI). Over a ten-year (1985–1995) period RSG 16 heard many papers of which about 31 concerned CBI. These papers were prepared for RSG 16 by 41 scientists in 8 different NATO countries. They presented valuable data and significant insights concerning the design, development, use, and evaluation of CBI in military applications. They introduced issues, some of which they answered and many of which remain unsettled. These issues and answers are summarized in this paper.

NEED FOR CBI

The challenges to successful training for military personnel have only increased since they were articulated by Wiggs and Seidel (1987). Workplaces in all sectors have become increasingly infused with technology, requiring workers to become increasingly "technology literate." The complexity of military operations has continued to increase along with the human performance needed to operate, maintain, and deploy the materiel, devices, and equipment they employ. At the same time, limitations in time, funding, training devices, training personnel, ranges, supplies, and other resources such as ammunition and fuel have made training missions increasingly difficult to accomplish.

Fortunately, technology may also provide a solution to these problems. It is being pursued in both civilian and military sectors as the key to meeting the challenges it, at least in part, has brought about. Military trainers, among others, are pursuing the use of computers in instruction because they must. In peacetime, they are unlikely to receive more resources than they have now to establish and maintain personnel readiness. Instead they must become increasingly efficient in obtaining value from resources at hand. CBI promises to provide a significant portion of this efficiency. Based on the evidence presented to RSG 16 and other forums, it can deliver on its promise.

INDIVIDUALIZATION

Research by Bloom (1984) suggests that the difference between those taught in classroom groups of 30 and those taught one-on-one by an individual instructor may be as great as two standard deviations in achievement. Unfortunately, individual tutoring is prohibitively expensive. In military training as in civilian education, the provision of a single instructor for every student is an economic impossibility. Yet the instructional efficiency that can be accomplished by tailoring instructional sequence, content, pace, and style to the needs of each learner is becoming an economic necessity in military training for the reasons discussed above. Computers in military training may replace some of the individualization lost to the economic necessities of group instruction. The approach is a classic economic solution in that it substitutes the capital of CBI for the labor of human instructors.

Several RSG 16 authors including Wiggs and Seidel (1987), Yasutake (1987), and Samarapungavan et al. (1991) stressed the need to develop an organized body of principles for individualizing instruction. Direct attempts to develop these principles have been pursued using two different approaches to development: artificial intelligence using principles of knowledge representation and optimization of instruction using optimal control theory.

Applications of artificial intelligence in CBI have involved direct attempts to imbue computer (or instructional computer software) with the capabilities possessed by a human tutor. These capabilities are usually said to be (a) subject matter knowledge, which among other things roughly represents the goal state for the learner, (b) knowledge of the student, which represents the current state of the student's knowledge and those characteristics of the student (e.g., ability, learning style, relevant background) that are required for tailoring instruction to meet his or her needs, and (c) tutorial knowledge, which the system can use to create an environment in which the student will progress from the current state to the goal state. Functionally, these applications may be characterized by an ability (a) to generate instructional presentations in real time in response to learner needs and (b) to allow mixed initiative instruction in which learners may freely interrogate the tutor, just as the tutor interrogates students in standard CBI.

Almost half of the CBI articles presented to RSG 16 concerned these knowledge-based approaches. Development of at least seven specific systems were discussed. These discussions are thoughtful and stimulating, but aside from student-computer interactions presented by Feurzeig (1987), no effectiveness or cost data were presented for these systems. This is characteristic of the field, which has been slow to produce data. It is notable that in addition to generating a level of individualization that would be unattainable without computer intelligence—or the presence of a human tutor—a second primary motive for developing these systems was to reduce the costs of instructional materials preparation—automation was sought to reduce these costs.

Four issues concerning these applications arise frequently and seem especially worthy of note:

- Role of instructors and formal instruction. If all military personnel can carry a "Ph.D in the pocket," that provides both job aiding and training anywhere, at any time, what is the role of formal schooling? What is the role of military instructors? How much training is really necessary if an expert advisor is always at hand—or in pocket? These issues were raised by many of the RSG 16 commentators. Answers were speculative.
- Overlay and misconceptions. On a more technical level, many RSG 16 commentators discussed overlay techniques for modeling student knowledge. What the student does to solve a problem is overlaid onto an expert's solution, and the mismatches are assumed to indicate what the student has yet to learn. Other commentators discussed student misconceptions. Wrong approaches are not assumed to be drawn at random, but to rise from at least partially well-constructed notions of the problem state. Overlays will not identify misconceptions. There is a widespread assumption that misconceptions must be directly addressed in an effective intelligent tutor. Is this true? Are time and resources better spent identifying misconceptions or simply presenting and re-presenting problems and their solution by experts? This is an issue that could easily be addressed by empirical study.
- Individual tutoring. Most research on instruction concerns group learning. Intelligent tutoring systems address a very different setting for instruction in which a single instructor attends to the needs of a single student. Far less is known about effective approaches for this setting, because it has received far less research attention. Again, this is an issue that could readily be addressed by empirical study.
- Coaching. Coaching generally concerns two issues: what to say and when to say it. A model of expertise may not communicate well to a learner whose understanding of the subject matter falls short of expertise. A computer coach must be able to articulate tutorial feedback and help to learners in terms they can understand. Secondly the timing of tutorial commentary is discussed by many authors. When should the progress of a learner be interrupted to provide feedback? Both of these issues have received more discussion than systematic research attention.

Applications of control theory were discussed by Marguin (1987) and von Baeyer (1991). In these applications the development of knowledge representations for instruction is finessed by taking a more behaviorist approach to instruction. Individualization is achieved by generating parameter values for student ability, item difficulty, and their interactions. For instance, the following transition matrix might be used in a three-stage theory of learning and forgetting in which items to be learned by student pass from an unlearned to a learned state:

Matrix A

State on Trial n	State on Trial n+1		
	L	S	U
L	1	0	0
S	c	1-c	0
U	a	b	1-a-b

Matrix B

State on Trial n	State on Trial n+1		
	L	S	U
L	1	0	0
S	0	1-f	f
U	0	0	1

This model describes the probabilities of transitions between unlearned (U), short term (S), and learned (L) states for learning (Matrix A) and for forgetting (Matrix B) of a specific item by a specific learner. Estimates of the parameters (a, b, c, f) can be used to choose items to present to a learner that can be proven by formal means to maximize achievement subject to such constraints as the amount of learning time available, number of items in the full set, and the parameters themselves.

EFFECTIVENESS

Student achievement using CBI is of natural interest, and five RSG 16 papers report data on the effectiveness of CBI. Dana (1987) reported reductions from 40% to 10% in washback rates, earlier screening of student suitability for training, and 1–2 week reductions in training time. Yasutake (1987) reported 24% to 35% time savings for four courses, positive (80–90%) student attitudes, and negative instructor attitudes for computer managed instruction. Noja (1987) reported reductions in training time from 8 to 5 weeks, equivalent student achievement for electronic theory and improved student achievement for electronic applications. In comparing results from a computerized, hand-held training aid with text-based workbooks, Wisher (1987) reported more course completions (91% as contrasted with 58%) and better test performance by a ratio of 2:1 for the computerized training aid. Noja (1991) reported 30% to 50% reductions in training time and per student per year savings of $5,500 for CBI.

Many studies comparing CBI with more conventional approaches have been reported in the literature. Meta-analysis is widely used in both education and medical research to combine, quantitatively, the results from many studies into a single metric, called effect size, for the overall effectiveness of some treatment or approach. Effect size is a standard score that measures standard deviations of difference between two means—one of which, for instance, might be derived from the performance of a group using instructional technology and the other of which might be derived from a group acting as an experimental control. It is calculated by dividing the difference of the two means by an estimate of the standard deviation of their combined distributions. In the cases discussed here, the larger the effect size, the stronger the case for using CBI.

Because standard deviations lack intuitive appeal as measures of population differences, effect sizes may be roughly interpreted as measures of the extent to which the performance of 50th percentile students may be raised or lowered by the experimental treatment or approach. For instance, an effect size of 0.50 obtained for some instructional

Table 1. Some effect sizes for CBI

Where	Effect size	No. of studies	50%tile to %tile
Elementary school[a]	0.47	28	68%tile
Secondary school[b]	0.42	42	66%tile
Higher education[c]	0.26	101	60%tile
Adult education[d]	0.42	24	66%tile
Military training[e]	0.40	38	66%tile
Overall	0.39	233	65%tile

[a] (Kulik, C-L Kulik, and Bangert-Drowns, 1985)
[b] (Bangert-Drowns, C-L Kulik, and Kulik, 1985)
[c] (C-L Kulik and Kulik, 1986)
[d] (Kulik, C-L Kulik, and Shwalb, 1986)
[e] (Johnston and Fletcher, 1995)

Table 2. Some effect sizes for interactive videodisc instruction[a]

Where	Effect size	No. of studies	50%tile to %tile
Military training	0.39	24	65%tile
Industrial training	0.51	9	70%tile
Higher education	0.69	14	75%tile
Overall	0.50	47	69%tile

[a](Fletcher, 1990)

approach might be interpreted as roughly equivalent to raising the achievement of 50th percentile students to that of 69% percentile students. Some effect sizes for CBI are shown in Table 1. As the table shows, effect size calculated across 38 studies of CBI applied in military training was 0.40, suggesting a raise in student performance from the 50th percentile to the 66th percentile.

Table 2 shows effect sizes for computer-controlled interactive videodisc instruction compared to conventional instructional approaches in three different settings: higher education, industrial training, and military training. As the table shows, the effect size for military training calculated for CBI with added multimedia capabilities was .39, suggesting an improvement in student performance from the 50th percentile to the 65th percentile. This is about the same as the effect size reported for CBI in military training. By contrast the effect size reported for CBI in higher education was 0.24 which can be compared with an effect size of 0.69 obtained for interactive videodisc instruction in higher education. Evidently there is more to be learned about the use and effectiveness of multimedia materials in instruction.

It is interesting to note that increased interactivity seems to buy increased student achievement. Among the interactive videodisc comparisons were three that compared branched approaches with linear approaches using the videodisc presentations. Their effect sizes were 0.85, 0.59, and 1.54, suggesting that branching and the individualization it accomplishes contributes to instructional achievement.

TIME TO TRAIN

Most of the effectiveness results presented by RSG 16 authors and summarized briefly above involve savings in time to train. Instructional time savings of about 30% for CBI is a stable and frequent result. It has been reported in independent reviews covering hundreds of evaluation studies by Orlansky and String (1977), Fletcher (1990), Kulik (1994), and Johnston and Fletcher (1995) as well as in specific assessments by Noja (1987), Yasutake (1987), and Noja (1991) writing specifically for RSG 16.

These results suggest significant savings in training costs through the use of CBI. However, in military applications the greatest savings that result from shortened training time may come from reductions in force structure that are possible when people are in training less and available for operational duty longer. Even though they result from reductions in training time, these force structure savings may dwarf those obtained from training. At present and despite its promise, CBI is only used in about 1% of the courses presented by the US military. A comprehensive analysis of personnel cost savings might motivate military planners who are responsible for personnel readiness to significantly increase their investment in CBI.

COSTS

A number of studies compared the costs of CBI with the costs of the instructional approaches it might replace. The costs of different instructional approaches have been assessed by calculating the ratio of the costs of instruction using technology to the costs of instruction using more conventional approaches. In these cases, the lower the ratio, the less costly, relatively, is the approach using CBI. Four classes of costs have been used in comparisons of this sort: research and development costs, initial investment costs, operating and support costs, and salvage costs. Of these four cost ratios are available for studies comparing initial investment costs and operating and support costs. A review of cost studies in military training reported that the ratio (CBI over conventional approaches) averages 0.43 for initial investment and averages 0.16 for operating and support.

Much of the savings realized in these studies of CBI costs arose from the use of simulation to present two-dimensional representations on computer display screens of (three-dimensional) devices that students were to learn to operate and/or maintain. Favorable cost ratios can be obtained when desk-top devices such as personal computers can be substituted in training for actual equipment costing 1–3 orders of magnitude more without sacrificing instructional achievement. These approaches provide only the fidelity that is necessary to achieve given training objectives. Several RSG 16 presenters discussed selective fidelity of this sort. The progression from discussions of high versus low fidelity to those concerning fidelity selected to meet specific training needs is notable in both RSG 16 and in military training circles in general.

COST-EFFECTIVENESS

The central question for decision makers may be that of cost-effectiveness. They may wish to compare the costs to accomplish a given level of achievement using a variety of instructional approaches—and most probably choose the least expensive approach while holding achievement constant. One comparison of this sort using empirically collected data appears to be available (Fletcher, Hawley, and Piele, 1990). It compared the costs to increase comprehensive mathematics scores (computation, concepts, and word problem solving) one standard deviation by using tutors, reducing class size, increasing instructional time, or providing computer based instruction.

The study found great differences in costs among the different approaches. The most cost-effective approaches were found to be computer based instruction or peer tutoring. It is notable that these approaches are not incompatible and that a very strong cost-effectiveness argument might be made for peer tutoring combined with computer based instruction, probably by presenting instruction to more than one student at a time on a single computer station. Studies of this sort have yet to be done for military applications of CBI.

Recommendations for cost-effectiveness analyses in military training have appeared frequently during the last 5–10 years. Orlansky (1992) summarized them as: (1) Include trade-offs between costs and effectiveness in cost-effectiveness evaluations; (2) Include factors of learning and forgetting in cost-effectiveness evaluations; (3) Develop databases on costs, effectiveness, and cost-effectiveness of training systems; and (4) Give high priority to investigations of military effectiveness. These recommendations seem valid and deserving of attention.

ENGINEERING OF TRAINING SYSTEMS

Training objectives usually represent a variety of training outcomes. These outcomes may include speed of response, accuracy of response, retention of either speed or accuracy, transfer of facts, procedures, or concepts to new devices or situations, motivation to continue learning about the subject matter, insight into the subject matter so that the learner can become the teacher, and so forth. To some extent these outcomes must compete for the scarce resources that are made available to implement the training system. Despite this range of intended outcomes, little has been done to develop information on ways to design training systems to accomplish specific outcomes and how to allocate training resources to resolve competition among outcomes. How, for instance, do we design a training system so that retention of accuracy of response is optimized subject to the constraints imposed by available training time and funding resources? Before the advent of computer technology and CBI, the design precision required for this sort of engineering of training systems was impracticable. Now, however, CBI has put it well within out technological reach. An engineering of instruction to obtain predictable, quantitatively specified outcomes is within our reach. We should pursue it.

ACCESS TO CBI MATERIAL, TECHNIQUES, AND DATA

One way for NATO allies to leverage their development of CBI is to develop ways to share CBI materials, techniques, and cost and effectiveness data on results. In an electronic age such sharing of resources usually implies creation and use of databases. Databases on CBI materials, techniques, and results shared among NATO countries would enhance the exchange of information on CBI, stimulate research, and motivate the implementation of this promising technology in military training systems. The need for such a database has been discussed in at least five papers prepared for RSG 16. Several ways for NATO members to access training information of this sort were discussed including agreements to provide direct access to NATO member country databases, development of a NATO gateway to the databases, development of a separate NATO training database, and development of a NATO directory of databases. Fletcher, Alluisi, and Chatelier (1991) suggest that development of a NATO directory of databases may be the preferred alternative. Such a directory would prove of value to researchers, training developers, system program managers, manpower planners, and policy makers concerned with training. The technical issues involved in creation of the directly are strictly routine. However, as Seidel and Chatelier (1991) pointed out, the issues involved in establishing resource sharing agreements among NATO countries are more difficult. Given the leverage and value to be obtained from such a directory, it may be past time to begin investigating the feasibility of these resource sharing agreements.

LESSONS LEARNED ON THE USE OF CBI IN MILITARY TRAINING

Based on the studies reviewed here, some practical advice for the implementation of CBI can be noted. CBI may be best, perhaps most cost-effectively used to provide:

- *Practice.* Training based on CBI has the often noted qualities of patience, privacy, and economy. If large amounts of practice are required to master a subject matter, CBI may be the most feasible and cost-effective way to provide it.

- *Simulation for expensive or inaccessible equipment.* If equipment costing substantially more than desk-top computer systems can be simulated adequately to meet the training objectives at hand, then it is likely that CBI simulations used partially or wholly in place of actual equipment will both lower costs and increase training accessibility. Training using such simulations is both more reproducible (students can try one set of decisions, observe their consequences and try again) and more visible (students can see the invisible in simulations and they can focus on training relevant experience) than is training using actual equipment.
- *Simulation for dangerous or expensive situations.* Experiences that students need in order to achieve training objectives may be too dangerous to provide without simulation. Such experiences are particularly common in military training. Many such experiences can be provided using training technology.
- *Stand-alone materials for physically dispersed learners.* Distance learning frequently focuses on the use of distributing classroom learning using video technology. In many instances, this is an appropriate approach. However, CBI can be provided outside of classroom settings, presented at arbitrary times and places (including barracks, workbenches, and homes), and delivered cheaply.
- *Privacy, closely monitored progress, or both.* Many students in military training—particularly those who pursue full military careers—are highly motivated and would benefit from frequent progress monitoring. Daily, even hourly, monitoring and privacy can be provided by CBI.
- *Standardized, less variable training outcomes.* Because of the assessment that can be built into CBI, its outcomes can be standardized and even certified. This feature has been observed in classroom instruction using CBI where achievement variability is reduced because fewer students are "lost"—students are more likely to reach criterion levels of performance when CBI is used in place of more conventional classroom approaches. Equivalent results for job site training seem likely.

FINAL WORD

On the basis of data and experiences both presented to RSG 16 and available elsewhere, it seems reasonable to conclude that CBI:

- Can be used to accomplish a wide range of instructional objectives across a variety of instructional settings;
- Is often more effective than other more commonly used approaches to military training;
- Is often less costly than other more commonly used approaches to military training; and
- Promises to be more cost-effective than other, more commonly used approaches to military training.

If these conclusions are true, then it is time to take CBI seriously. It should be routinely considered as a standard approach to be used in the design and delivery of military training programs. It should be allocated the necessary initial investment resources and made widely available in military training.

REFERENCES

Bangert-Drowns, R.L., Kulik, J.A., Kulik, C-L.C. (1985) Effectiveness of computer-based education in secondary schools. *Journal of Computer Based Instruction, 12*, 59–83.

Bloom, B.S. (1984). The 2 sigma problem: The search for methods of group instruction as effective as one-to-one tutoring. *Educational Researcher, 13*, 4–16.

Dana, D.K. (1987) The Use of Computers in Training in the British Army. In R.J. Seidel and P.D. Weddle (Eds.) *Computer-Based Instruction in Military Environments*. New York: Plenum Press.

Feurzeig, W. (1987) Cognitive Science, Artificial Intelligence and Complex Training. In R.J. Seidel and P.D. Weddle (Eds.) *Computer-Based Instruction in Military Environments*. New York: Plenum Press.

Fletcher, J.D. (1990) *The Effectiveness of Interactive Videodisc Instruction in Defense Training and Education* (IDA Paper P-2372). Alexandria, VA: Institute for Defense Analyses.

Fletcher, J.D., Alluisi, E.A., and Chatelier, P.R. (1991) A NATO Datebase on Advanced Technology to Aid Training Design. In R.J. Seidel and P.R. Chatelier (Eds.) *Advanced Technologies Applied to Training Design*. New York: Plenum Press.

Fletcher, J.D., Hawley, D.E., and Piele, P.K. (1990) Costs, effects, and utility of microcomputer assisted instruction in the classroom. *American Educational Research Journal, 27*, 783–806.

Johnston, B.R. and Fletcher, J.D. (1995) *Effectiveness of Computer Based Instruction in Military Training*. Alexandria, VA: Institute for Defense Analyses.

Kulik, J.A. (1994) Meta-Analytic Studies of Findings on Computer-Based Instruction. In E.L. Baker and H.F. O'Neil, Jr. (Eds.) *Technology Assessment in Education and Training*. Hillsdale, NJ: Lawrence Erlbaum Associates.

Kulik, C-L.C., Kulik, J.A., and Shwalb, B. (1986) Effectiveness of computer-based instruction in adult education. *Journal of Educational Computing Research*, 2, 235–252.

Kulik, J.A., & Kulik, C-L.C. (1986) Effectiveness of computer-based education in colleges. *AEDS Journal, 19*, 81–108.

Kulik, J.A., Kulik, C-L.C., & Bangert-Drowns, R.L. (1985) Effectiveness of computer-based education in elementary schools. *Computers in Human Behavior, 1*, 59–74.

Marguin, J. (1987) Consideration of Instruction and Training in Human Operator Models. In R.J. Seidel and P.D. Weddle (Eds.) *Computer-Based Instruction in Military Environments*. New York: Plenum Press.

Noja, G.P. (1987) New Frontiers for Computer-Aided Training. In R.J. Seidel and P.D. Weddle (Eds.) *Computer-Based Instruction in Military Environments*. New York: Plenum Press.

Noja, G.P. (1991) DVI and System Integration: A Further Step in ICAI/IMS Technology. In R.J. Seidel and P.R. Chatelier (Eds.) *Advanced Technologies Applied to Training Design*. New York: Plenum Press.

Orlansky, J. (1992) NATO Studies on the Military Value and Cost-Effectiveness of Training. In K. Ellis, J. Moraal, and A. von Baeyer (Eds.) *Workshop on the Military Value and Cost-Effectiveness of Training* (Technical Proceedings AC/243 (Panel 7) TP/3). Brussels, Belgium: NATO Headquarters. NATO UNCLASSIFIED.

Orlansky, J., & String, J. (1979) *Cost-Effectiveness of Computer Based Instruction in Military Training* (IDA Paper P-1375). Institute for Defense Analyses, Alexandria, Virginia.

Samarapungavan, A., Beishuizen, J., Brazier, F.T.M., and Sanders, A.F. (1991) Implications of Advances in Cognitive Science for Intelligent Tutoring Systems. In R.J. Seidel and P.R. Chatelier (Eds.) *Advanced Technologies Applied to Training Design*. New York: Plenum Press.

Seidel, R.J. and Chatelier, P.R. (1991) Advanced Technologies Applied to Training Design. In R.J. Seidel and P.R. Chatelier (Eds.) *Advanced Technologies Applied to Training Design*. New York: Plenum Press.

von Baeyer, A. (1991) The Optimisation of Training Systems. In R.J. Seidel and P.R. Chatelier (Eds.) *Advanced Technologies Applied to Training Design*. New York: Plenum Press.

Wiggs, C.L. and Seidel, R.J. (1987) An Overview of Computer-Based Instruction in Military Environments. In R.J. Seidel and P.D. Weddle (Eds.) *Computer-Based Instruction in Military Environments*. New York: Plenum Press.

Wisher, R.A. (1987) The Development and Test of a Hand-Held Computerized Training Aid. In R.J. Seidel and P.D. Weddle (Eds.) *Computer-Based Instruction in Military Environments*. New York: Plenum Press.

Yasutake, J.Y. (1987) Implementation of Computer-Based Training: A System Evaluation and Lessons Learned. In R.J. Seidel and P.D. Weddle (Eds.) *Computer-Based Instruction in Military Environments*. New York: Plenum Press.

LESSONS LEARNED ABOUT SYSTEMS ARCHITECTURE FOR TRAINING DESIGNERS USING ADVANCED TECHNOLOGIES

Steven L. Funk[1] and Del Lunceford[2]

[1]The National Science Foundation (USA) and
The Institute for Defense Analyses
[2]U.S. Army Simulations, Training and Instrumentation Command (STRICOM)

INTRODUCTION

Knowledge about advanced information technologies is a new emerging obligatory area of competence for commanders and staff officers to increase the probability of success in future military operations. Information technologies are beginning to decisively influence all aspects of command, control, intelligence and training. Commanders and training officers who develop or select advanced technologies for training are making systems architecture decisions that can increase or decrease the utility and life cycle costs of their training systems, whether or not they do so intentionally. Just as knowledge of the emerging state of the art of weapons characteristics and force capabilities of various countries is necessary for the planning, training and executing of successful military operations, some understanding of training systems architecture will assist commanders and training officers in getting the best benefit and value out of advanced training technologies. Contractors and outside experts are no substitute for an informed user.

A variety of breakthroughs in enhanced military proficiency have been demonstrated in recent years through the use of networked distributed simulations, from vastly improved land navigation to improved tank crew gunnery to improved training of a multinational allied army group. These improvements were achieved at lower cost than the use of conventional methods, with reduced demand on field training facilities and with reduced maneuver damage. While these technology enabled training opportunities are not substitutes for challenging field training, they can make the increasingly limited field opportunities more productive, provide training opportunities for which we have no equivalent field training facilities and provide opportunities to conduct training that would be considered too unsafe or too politically sensitive to conduct "on the ground."

While the cost trends for the hardware and communications components of these advanced technologies are falling rapidly, the costs of developing the training applications and proliferating them remain too high to be widely available for routine use throughout NATO.

Virtual Reality, Training's Future? edited by Seidel and Chatelier
Plenum Press, New York, 1997

The single most important factor in reducing these costs and readily incorporating future capabilities as they evolve lies in the "architecture" of developing advanced technology training systems. It is the architecture that provides or prevents having ready made "plug and play" families of applications as well as user developed models and scenarios that can interoperate and be shared and re-used. Architecture is a term that has been overused and under-understood. While the state-of-the-art of training systems architecture is immature, it's potential leverage is so high that we need to start to use the new techniques even while working to improve and evolve them (Hayes-Roth, 1995). This paper will briefly outline:

a. The payoff: improved military performance through the use of advanced technologies for training.
b. What is architecture and why should a commander or trainer care about it.
c. Lessons learned

THE PAYOFF: IMPROVED MILITARY PERFORMANCE THROUGH THE USE OF ADVANCED TECHNOLOGIES FOR TRAINING

Since the introduction of Simulation Networking (SIMNET) in the mid-1980's, a series of experiments and studies using advanced technologies to train military units have yielded a number of phenomenal results. For example:

a. Drastically improved tank gunnery scores resulting in winning the Canadian Army Trophy for tank gunnery without increased use of ranges or ammunition (Kraemer, R.E. and Bessemer, D.W., 1987).
b. A 60 percent reduction in land navigation errors among armored forces of the United Kingdom (Kelly, M., Anderson, T., English, N., Parkes, C. and Rees, D., 1994).
c. A 25 percent improvement in field tactical proficiency of U.S. armored platoons with a 25 percent reduction in training time, without additional maneuver damage or land use (Bessemer, D.W., 1991).
d. Exercise of a multinational allied army group equivalent to 175,000 personnel; 1,950 tanks and 12, 810 armored fighting vehicles for 36 percent of the cost of a REFORGER 1988, a 64 percent cost reduction (Defense Science Board, 1993).
e. Testing the battlefield impact of a new weapons system resulting in more comprehensive test results in one-eighth of the time (87.5 percent reduction) and two-thirds of the cost (36 percent less) than when using conventional methods (Defense Science Board, 1993).

While these capabilities have been, they are not yet widely available to NATO trainers. The applications have been limited, expensive and time consuming to produce. But commanders faced with an increasing array of types of missions, reduced forces and reduced finances are beginning to seriously consider how to use advanced technologies to achieve improved performance in military operations.

THE PROBLEM

Much of the time and cost of developing training applications is due to the labor involved to recreate similar software components and models because existing applications are not interoperable, reusable or transportable across systems, even on the same hardware configurations within the same country. This costly duplication of effort is caused by the use of a plethora of incompatible languages, design approaches and programming techniques which cause similar models to have to be continually recreated for each scenario or application. This incompatibility exists due to the lack of commonly shared design principles and techniques, and the absence of a suite of software design tools which would automate much of the process. In essence, every time a new application (e.g., model or scenario) is called for, the developers not only develop the application, they also create the tools for building those applications. While these expedient and unique (one-off) tools to some extent serve the commercial interests of the contractors and developers involved, the situation to a large extent is due to an immature state of the art. Until this diversity is overcome, breakthroughs in development costs cannot occur.

The development, evolution and understanding of shared design principles, practices and tools is what "architecture" is all about. As one of the largest customer groups, the military services can exert tremendous influence on the evolution in the state of the art by the way we state our requirements and the questions we ask.

ARCHITECTURE: WHAT IS IT AND WHY SHOULD I CARE?

Architecture is what can enable commanders to use advanced technologies to:

a. Train and rehearse participants under demanding, realistic conditions and then be able to analyze, replay and retrain using different speeds, conditions, decisions and configurations
b. Rapidly test trade-off decisions and alternative plans against realistic constraints and capabilities of a real or hypothetical mission, and ask "what if" questions under different conditions and assumptions
c. Train and test different components of a plan with selectable size, complexity and fidelity
d. Be able to "plug and play" different technologies and capabilities before committing to the development or employment of those capabilities

Trying to adapt existing software components for new purposes is expensive, technically challenging (if feasible at all) and can contain significant hidden faults that do not become apparent during use. Breakthroughs in new knowledge and practice in the area of architecture offer the highest potential payoff to making advanced technologies amenable and affordable to the trainer. Architecture provides the understanding and discipline required to make the training application development process reliable, repeatable, controllable and affordable. The issues of re-use, shared use and interoperability are core concerns of architecture.

Architecture is a blueprint for a family of applications. Probably one of the best ways to think about a new generation "systems architect" versus an "applications architect" is to think of them like you would a city planner versus a building architect. While the building architect (or individual application architect) can design unique structures with many idiosyncratic aspects to that particular application/model; the city architect must plan for the common support of many buildings and inhabitants of the city. The city planner does not know very much about the individual buildings size, shape and function; but the city planner will specify how a building will connect to city services and infrastructure (e.g., water and power mains) and will specify guidelines for the mutual benefit of all. So while each building may be unique, all must adapt to the same standards for connections to common services (e.g., water, power and communications). Each building architect will have to have their individual building materials and techniques approved by the city architect before construction and will usually be inspected during construction to ensure that the individual building does not jeopardize the mutual benefit. Similar specification is necessary for training systems architecture. Systems architecture often defines (Hayes-Roth, 1995):

a. Component behavior and/or characteristics
b. Topologies of connections of component assemblies
c. Specific "standards," for example:

 1. Information types
 2. Communications protocols
 3. User interface guidelines

d. Assumed "platform" characteristics, for example:

 1. Operating systems, libraries and middleware
 2. Resources and ways to access them
 3. Capabilities of hardware and other devices

LESSONS LEARNED (ADAPTED FROM HAYES-ROTH, 1995)

a. Beware of those professing to have the "right answer" and those who want to "dictate" standards. Architecture is an overused and under-understood term. At least in the United States, awareness and sophistication in practice in the Department of Defense is about 20 years from leading edge to trailing edge. Some new initiatives are based on old failed ideas.
b. Interoperability is hard. Reuse depends largely on prescient architecture.
c. Good architectures make possible high productivity development environments, they enable customers to "generate" applications themselves. Architectures are NOT cheap or easy. Architecture is neither a panacea nor necessarily a good idea. Sometimes an application is so unique, has such a limited life or is so low cost that architecture is not a worthy concern (e.g., one time stand alone applications). Architecture is most useful when the applications are likely to used by a number of users and may need to interact with other applications.
d. Architectures need human and automation support. No common infrastructure has emerged or matured. Few means yet exist for interrelating or translating between alternative architectures or views. The technology is emerging, rather than mature. We have insufficient tools to support architects. Good architectures are more dependent on good architects than on process or technology.
e. Rarely do we "get it right" the first time. Architectures must be evolved and the evolutionary process must be recognized need and planned for. Architecture-based development is a strategy that requires investment, commitment, follow-through, and continuing adaptation. The discovery of knowledge happens in its own time after an adequate number of trials, we are early in the development cycle and definitive answers are not likely to have long lives.
f. "Boxology" is insufficient, not powerful enough. Standards profiles are too weak. Weak constraints/standards are not very relevant, while strong constraints

are risky. Standards require careful specification. Architectures are domain-specific, hence numerous and varied. The desire to simplify architecture to more generic forms and looser commitments is strong and are politically appealing, but practically useless, frustrating and expensive to "fix." Overly particular solutions are not viable very long.

Those who attempt to force a standard before adequate intelligent discovery has occurred face the high probability that the accepted standards will soon be made obsolete from overwhelming consumer acceptance of a competing standard (e.g., VHS over Beta format video recorders) or will be overcome by breakthroughs in technology. Pre-competitive consortia of developers who are normally competitors and/or research collaborators have been useful in developing common understandings and practices and avoid the proliferation of proprietary or one-off standards. "Standards" are codified understandings, they are not "laws." No one country or company is likely to own the long term solution.

g. Architectures incorporate deep knowledge. The architects need to have extensive discussion with users and users must be involved in frequent validation and test of ideas. Architectural "test beds," like test ranges need to by used before specifications are agreed. Protocol compliance and claims of interoperablity DO NOT necessarily produce actual performance.

h. A product-line (domain specific. e.g., training models) focus can work. For example, lower fidelity standards may be perfectly usable for training versus those required for engineering design and test purposes.

i. Successful architectures are environmentally adapted. Cannot avoid real commitments. You have to "fit" the environment. One size DOES NOT fit all. Currently, the United States uses three types of simulations: Real (e.g., actual equipment instrumented to record battle actions, like laser devices and cameras), virtual (e.g., virtual reality and networked simulators, like flight simulators and SIMNET) and constructive (e.g., computer driven wargames using mathematical algorithms to determine certain battle events, like JANUS). We have found significant strengths and weaknesses in each. For example, in the "real" world, we can observe the effects of weather, fatigue, equipment failure and some crews are better shots than others and these all affect battle results and conclusions drawn. In the "virtual" world, we have been able to replicate fratricide incidents and "reset" conditions and try different approaches, and we have observed how actions of one or a few can affect the outcome or higher level decisions. In the "constructive" world we can engage large numbers an sizes of units quickly and cheaply and play them at unrealistic speeds to get the parts we are interested in. It appears that each form captures some unique aspects of battle and there is significant effort to try to make all three forms interact with each other to be able to have access and enhance their inherent strengths. To do so, involves many architectural issues.

j. They must be validated, verified and accepted (VV&A) and enforced. This is a many faceted issue, but the primary concerns are:

1. *Domain model standards*. Reliable databases of performance characteristics of "objects of interest" need to be established. Minimally, these databases need to contain a variety of valid operational characteristics of equipment of interest to the users. Simulation model designers can only represent what they know of what they are trying to model (the deep knowledge issue). In

order to conduct joint or combined training activities using networks or shared simulations, this database needs to contain the "official" reference operational characteristics of objects of common interest to the users. While this can pose concerns about security, without such repositories and their accurate maintenance, the models cannot be re-used and the results of their re-use by others cannot be relied upon. Objects to be contained in such a database would include terrain, weather, ocean currents and weapons systems. To achieve this means that there needs to be a common taxonomy of characteristics for various objects so that objects developed by different builders can be used with confidence..

2. *Consideration of intended use and re-use of simulation tools and models.* The intended use of models significantly influences how many and how accurate the characteristics required for reliable results. For example, we are finding that models needed for training purposes need to be only sufficiently accurate to cause humans to perceive what they need to decide and act and obtain a perceived realistic outcome. However, a model for determining design trade-offs for a weapons system may need to be accurate in areas invisible to the human and of no concern to trainees (e.g., metallurgy characteristics, actual flight times beyond human perception, sounds or light spectra beyond human perception). Some advocate specifying very high fidelity characteristics be included in a model to accommodate all possible users before the model can meet VV&A compliance, but this can unnecessarily drive developer and user costs.
3. *Networking and interoperablity.* There is a need to have architectural standards and/or protocols for models intended to interact with each other (e.g., I want to use my simulated tank on your simulated terrain). Models that work perfectly by themselves for their intended purpose may not behave accurately when networked with other models. Two models when VV&A'd for their respective uses do not maintain that validity or accuracy when networked together. For example, Simulation A may use a tank model that does not respond to rain. If these two are joined over a network they will appear the same and act for all apparent purposes as they should, until rain is introduced onto the simulated battlefield, at which time Simulation A's tank may gain superior advantage over Simulation B's tank and yield unrealistic results and which may remain invisible or undetectable to the users and cause them to draw the wrong conclusions from the battle.

k. Networks are great, but they DO NOT always work. Like all things mechanical, communications and networks break down and simulators and computers fail for a variety of reasons. Users need to plan for breakdowns and delays.

CONCLUSION

Significant improvements in military unit performance can be achieved through the use of advanced technologies for training. The training capabilities provided by advanced technology and their resulting benefits are expanding rapidly. Architecture is the most critical area for decreasing the costs and increasing the reliability of advanced technologies for shared training among member forces of the Alliance. Through some basic knowledge about the issues and state of the art of systems architecture, commanders and training officers who are responsible for the development and procurement of training systems and devices can play a key role in increasing the utility of their technology based training systems, increasing the useful life span of these systems and advance the overall state of the art, which will eventually drive down development costs. Architecture depends on user champions, commitments, and long time frames-all organizationally unnatural (particularly in military organizations). The key areas in which the utility of architecture can be advanced and increase training value are common agreements, documentation and new software tool products in the areas of:

a. Domain models
b. Reference architectures
c. Reference requirements
d. Application requirements
e. Application architectures
f. Component selections and design rationale (it is possible to have different architectures for different sub-areas/applications)

REFERENCES

Bessemer, D.W., *Transfer of SIMNET Training in the Armor Officer Basic Course*, ARI Technical Report 920, Alexandria, VA:U.S. Army Research Institute, 1991.

Defense Science Board, *Simulation, Readiness & Prototyping*, Alexandria VA: Institute for Defense Analyses, 1993.

Hayes-Roth, F., *Architecture-Based Development & Acquisition-Where are we and where are we going?*, Briefing for the Advanced Research Projects Agency Software and Intelligent Systems Technology Office, Westfields Conference Center, VA: Teknowledge Federal Systems, August 30, 1995.

Kelly, M., Anderson, T., English, N., Parkes, C. and Rees, D., *Combined Arms Tactical Trainer (SR(L) 4060) LSOR2 Trials: Overview Report on AGPT and SIMNET Phases. APRE Report 94R026*, Farnborough, Hampshire, United Kingdom: Army Personnel Research Establishment, 1994.

Kraemer, R.E. and Bessemer, D.W., *U.S. Tank Platoon Training for the 1987 Canadian Army Trophy (CAT) Using a Simulation Networking (SIMNET) System*. ARI Report 1457, Alexandria, VA:U.S. Army Research Institute, 1987.

COMPUTER BASED TRAINING LESSONS LEARNED FROM PROJECTS

Hilbert Kuiper

TNO Physics and Electronics Laboratory
PO Box 96864, 2509 JG The Hague, The Netherlands
Email: Kuiper@fel.tno.nl

1. INTRODUCTION

This document provides a number of guidelines for the design, implementation and evaluation of Computer Based Training (CBT). It is an approach from the designers and developers point of view. For this approach the experiences with a number of different projects on the field of CBT are described. These projects involve:

- The design of CBT material for a training simulator with an authoring system
- Design and implementation of multimedia CBT for helicopter maintenance
- Experience with ITS projects: Message Handling ITS and Design of an Intelligent Training System for training robotics procedures in space
- Experiences with an integrated instructional development system

2. AUTHORING CBT FOR A TRAINING SIMULATOR: EVALUATION

2.1 Introduction Authoring System

An instructional support system (ISS) has been developed for an anti-aircraft training simulator. The ISS uses automated instruction and is comparable to a CBT system. The system can be used for complex time-critical procedure training in general. The ISS includes an authoring system with which lesson scenarios including judgement criteria can be composed. The system runs on a SUN-SPARC workstation. This chapter describes the method of evaluation for the authoring system part and also the evaluation experiences.

2.2 Evaluation of the System

The authoring is running on a SUN-Sparc workstation under UNIX and is using the X-Window system. The user has available a WIMP (Windows, Icons, Mouse, Pointer) environment. The system has been evaluated on its functional completeness and its practical use by two methods:

- checklist method for functional completeness
- representative user evaluation to test the usability of the system

2.2.1 Checklist Evaluation. By means of a checklist the functionality of an authoring system can be checked on its completeness. In the case of an authoring system for example different checklists are available to evaluate the general functionality.

- Choose a proper checklist (if available) to evaluate the functionality of a system or to select the proper system.

A checklist is a good first indication if a system complies with the functions that should be present in general in a system, in this case an authoring system. Of course ultimately the functionality of a system depends upon the required instructional facilities, which, in turn, are a result of the educational goals. But, a checklist is helpful.

2.2.2 Representative User Evaluation.

- Perform an evaluation with users of different expertise levels in order to investigate whether the system can be used by a broad category of users.

The authoring system in this case has been evaluated with representative groups of future users:

- experts with the methodology
- novices with the methodology

How to do an authoring system evaluation with representative users

- Provide an introduction in which the ins and outs of the system and the purpose of the evaluation is explained. Also examples have to be presented.
- Let the users get sufficient time to play around with the system
  Especially when the system is complex the subject need sufficient time to play around.
- Make clear categories of subjects to gather information about
- Present realistic cases for exercises that have to be prepared with the authoring system. These cases should preferably be prepared by an expert in the field
- Increase the degree of difficulty with each subsequent exercise
- Use questionnaires, e.g. after each case to gather information about a certain topic and afterwards to get general information.
- Prompt the subjects to think aloud
- Let each subject be 'coached' by an evaluator
- Evaluator makes notes
- Record the operations of the subject

2.2.3 General Recommendations.

- Checklist is a good means to do a preliminary evaluation of the functionality of a system
- Involve future users in an early stage of the development to get feedback on the design of the system.

Involving future users creates a lot of goodwill; they get a feeling of being involved in the design of the system

- Be aware that users have a lot of wishes for modifications; how to deal with this
- Keep the user-interface simple and consistent
- Use of WIMP environment can be easy to learn
- Use of graphical representations is important

3. A MULTIMEDIA CBT PROJECT

3.1 Introduction

A project is being carried out for the Royal Netherlands Airforce to develop 10 hrs of multimedia courseware for helicopter maintenance training. The project is a pilot project to investigate the feasibility of multimedia training for the Royal Netherlands Airforce.

3.2 Experiences

After developing a number of hours of courseware the following experiences can be listed with respect to different phases of the training system development.

Analysis:

- Perform a thorough domain analysis
- Choose a learning domain for which (multimedia) CBT is a good solution to tackle a training problem

Development:

- Define a generic courseware structure to reduce development time
- Iterative development processes and partial delivery are required between developer and domain expert to
  - avoid miscommunication between developer and domain expert
  - keep better control of progress
- Keep interfaces simple to use, i.e. don't overdo (sober use of colors, sound, etc)
- Use one rich data type (video, animation) at a time
- Use multidisciplinary development teams with domain experts, courseware developers, video specialists, instructors, project managers
- making video fragments is complex and very time consuming
- make a good choice when to use video and when not

Evaluation:

- Make formative evaluations with instructors and future users
- Perform evaluations with users afterwards

Hardware/software

- Lack of hardware/software standards is still a problem

Other issues:

- Multimedia offers promising possibilities for better quality of CBT and improvement of CBT

- Integrate the multimedia CBT fully into the curriculum, i.e.
  - integrate it with lesson plans/curriculum
  - create the proper infrastructure
  - don't let it be instructor dependent whether the CBT is used or not
- Use of multimedia can save expensive use of operational equipment for training
- Involve users (instructors) in the design of CBT

4. USING INTELLIGENT TRAINING SYSTEMS

4.1 Introduction

Lessons learned from two projects on the field of Intelligent Training Systems (ITSs) are described in this section:

- A project called FELIX that concerns message handling involving procedural as well as factual knowledge; in this project about 10 hours of courseware has been developed
- A project called POINTER to investigate the feasibility of intelligent training for robotics procedures in a space environment.

4.2 Lessons Learned from ITS Projects

- Start an ITS project if there is a need to have an added training value as compared to conventional CBT developed by using an authoring system. In fact CBT and ITS should be compared for the same subject to make a fair comparison and to investigate the added value of an ITS.
- Perform a thorough domain analysis using knowledge based analysis techniques. Such an analysis will help storing the knowledge in a structured way.
- Decide what to store as domain knowledge and what to store as pedagogical knowledge; a clear separation should be made between domain knowledge and pedagogical knowledge. Too often it happens that domain knowledge is stored in the courseware, something that should not be the case.
- Evaluate an ITS extensively with respect to the following aspects:
  - *Student performance*...Is the student performance with ITS better than with conventional CBT?
  - *Cost effectiveness*...Data are difficult to obtain, but having at least some (correct) data available is better than nothing at all. The available data can give guidance to the decision maker when to choose CBT and what type of CBT
  - *Demonstration of intelligent features*...This is an aspect that continuously is asked when an ITS is demonstrated. However mostly it is difficult to demonstrate. Therefore much attention should be paid to this aspect.
- Choice of platform influences the potential audience
  It is important that the platform should join the platform in use with the target audience, otherwise the system will not become a success. Mostly ITSs are developed on a workstation whereas the target audience is using PCs as a platform.
- Knowledge acquisition tools and authoring tools are required. When no user-friendly tools are available to enter knowledge and to do the authoring of courseware it is likely that the ITS will stay in the laboratory stage.

5. LESSONS LEARNED WITH AN INSTRUCTIONAL DEVELOPMENT SYSTEM

5.1 Introduction

The integrated instructional development system (GOOS) is a system that supports the instructional developer in analysing, designing, realising, managing and maintaining training courses, with emphasis on training including advanced instructional aids. GOOS is specified by TNO for the Royal Netherlands Army and produced, introduced and maintained by the RNLA organisation itself.

5.2 Guidelines/Experiences

- Specify clearly the mission of the system that the person belongs to
- Formulate the training objectives carefully and in full detail by the three standard training objective description parts: activity, condition, norm
- Training objectives are important as descriptors of the training course, evaluation instrument of the training and students
- There is a need for a tool to formulate and maintain the training objectives efficiently
- Different types of training objectives lead to different kinds of training
- It is hard to find a good taxonomy of training objectives where each class of the taxonomy determines the learning environment and instructional method under certain conditions (time, money, resources, etc.)

6. REFERENCES

Kuiper, H. (1995). An Instructional Support System for Training Simulators. Dissertation, to be published.

Rikken, P.J. (1995). Richtlijnen voor de ontwikkeling van Multimediaal COO (Guidelines for the development of Multimedia CBT). TNO-FEL internal document.

ADVANCED TECHNOLOGIES APPLIED TO TRAINING DEVELOPMENT

Tony Mizen

Royal Navy

1. PREAMBLE

For the last ten years the British Armed Forces have been subjected to the increasing conflict between adoption of new and emerging technologies and the fiscal pressures of a diminishing procurement budget. No longer is the "sound military decision" acceptable as the prime mover In the acquisition of new training equipment or solutions to match a perceived training need. Military leaders are having to come to terms with mastery of fiscal strategies and tenets such as; value for money, just enough just in time, financial or investment appraisal, spend to save, etc. Little wonder that the "tried and tested" route for training development, design and media selection is far more commonplace. Some trainers have argued that we are experiencing a back to basics revival, albeit through the lack of purchasing power.

As a prime user and developer of techniques in the design and implementation of training, the Royal Naval School of Educational and Training Technology (RNSETT) also supports the more cautious approach towards the adoption of new and emerging technologies. Too often the uninformed Service customer has been attracted to the shiny gadget or software which, according to the pressure sales pitch by the company's, will solve the majority of their training problems. More likely they will end up buying a solution seeking a problem.

Consequently, the RNSETT is a strong advocate of the back to basics scenario through the tried and tested outcomes which bodies such as the NATO Research study Groups are capable of promoting to everyone's advantage. Using some of the headings adopted for the original presentations given at Venice, this short paper will address certain of those significant developments in the Royal navy since 1991 and which, it is suggested, might have a wider and useful impact on other NATO nations.

ADVANCED AUTHORING TOOLS

For CBT development in the UK, the packages attracting most attention are Authoware and IconAuthor. They are based at the high volume market and are both useful

Virtual Reality, Training's Future? edited by Seidel and Chatelier
Plenum Press, New York, 1997

and robust but relatively expensive at present. The former is pitched at the IBM PC and Apple Mac markets whilst the latter also includes the Unix environment. File sizes for these type of solution are very large and can only sensibly be distributed on CD-ROM or by network. Mandarin (GEC Marconi) for Windows is still in the market but since it is primarily a military-biased product, it has not had the development money spent on it that some of the others have enjoyed through their gaming connections. The Royal Navy has found Mandarin to be a useable environment that interfaces well with other Windows applications and protocols, but it has some inherent weaknesses and it certainly requires a high performance hardware platform. The most successful applications of Mandarin for the Royal Navy have been tailor-made drill and practise CBT packages for Passive Sonar Operators.

Although fairly dated now, there is still a market for Tencore. It was developed in the DOS environment but functions quite happily under Windows. Because of its low-end hardware requirement it is still offered by many of the large European CBT producers. However, for sophisticated, tailored solutions C++ and Visual Basic are gaining a lot of favour because they too are both cheap and versatile and seem to be favoured by contractors working in the Defence arena. Of particular note has been the application of these software packages to the sophisticated ADAWS, CACS and SSCS Ship Command System CBT installations at the Royal Navy's Warfare School.

In the area of CAI, Microsoft's PowerPoint seems to be gaining prominence but it lacks a real multimedia dimension. Toolbook appears to be the best, moderate-cost product that the RNSETT has come across for the development of multimedia solutions. Indeed, the progress being witnessed in multimedia authoring tools is seen as having the potential to make the in-house development of CIA materials much more cost effective. This is certainly a new venture for the Royal navy who has traditionally outsourced all CAI and CBT requirements. Of the three UK Arms only the RAF has developed the ability and set up a special unit for the in-house production of CBT material.

It is noticeable that with the growing demand for better computer-generated imagery in DIS, war-gaming and other large screen CBT presentations, the high programming costs of "high-end" systems such as Silicon Graphics is reducing as filters and compilers that use "low-end" development systems are coming on stream.

MODELS AND ANALYTICAL METHODS FOR TRAINING

Within the Royal Navy when there is a fundamental change in equipment, processes or people, it is now mandatory for the "sponsor" to carry out a Training Needs Analysis (TNA) which embraces the traditional Training Design process (= ISD) with an Investment Appraisal. It is by this means that the training developers present their case for investment in new training to the budgetary controllers. Many tools are available to the training designer for undertaking the familiar analysis and design work (eg EXVAL), but they have always lacked the means by which they could adequately define the "media" requirements. In other words, when defining the learning environment needed to enable the acquisition of knowledge, skills and attitudes, they lack a suitable model to identify the technology best suited to the task. This stage, when present in the model, has the jargon name "Fidelity Requirements Analysis" and is considered vital if the training developer is to meet the derived training objectives in the most efficient and effective way.

Fundamental to the issue of fidelity is the question of whether it is required for maximising the learning process or simply to achieve realism. The difference is that the fidelity levels required for enhancing the learning process are often lower than that for generating realism. How important is realism to the training task is therefore the question which must be asked during the analysis phase if the outcome is not to be biased, either purely to the learning process or to realism for realism's sake.

In conjunction with Marconi Simulation and Training the RNSETT has devised a fairly simple tool which applies number to decisions taken and, thereby, weight of argument to three key areas of fidelity; physical, functional and environmental. Each is defined as follows:

- *Physical Fidelity*—The degree to which the training replication of the man-machine/human-computer interface (MMI/HCI) with the operational equipment requires the exact physical representation of the spatial arrangements, the appearance and the direct tactile feel of the controls.
- *Functional Fidelity*—The degree to which the training replication of the interface with the operational equipment will need to represent and emphasise the informational aspects of the task including fidelity in data change rates, display responses and system performance.
- *Environmental Fidelity*—The degree to which the training replication of the system or systems host environment needs to be replicated to emphasise the constructive or interface effects of noise, motion and ambience

All these factors are recorded and through a simple matrix and series of flow charts generate a decision and justification for a training application that can be fully supported by the audit trail. Notwithstanding the idiosyncratic nature of each and every TNA project, early indications are that this tool can be adapted and universally applied where equipment changes are prevalent.

EMBEDDED TRAINING

There is considerable potential to incorporate training in operational equipment but lead/development times are long as provision really needs to be made in early design phases. Additionally Royal Navy job patterns and employment patterns at sea mitigate against widespread use of this facility. The RN uses trickle drafting and appointing for job changing its personnel, so team building is always in flux and rarely constant. Similarly, the demands on the ship-borne equipment by the maintainers for upkeep routines, calibration and proving trials means that time alongside and on long passage is generally given over to "housekeeping" not training. The same situation applies to federation (onboard linking of systems) and confederation (onboard land inter-ship linking of systems)—The technology exists but employment and operational usage patterns prevent cost effective utilisation of these training methodologies.

ADVANCES IN HARDWARE TECHNOLOGY

For training developers, the most noticeable advance has been the increases in processing power per $ which has made computationally demanding tasks, such as visually intensive applications in multimedia and simulation, more cost effective than, hitherto, has been the case. For Distance Learning requirements, the increases to information highway bandwidths offers the chance to use interactive "multiple media" more readily and effectively.

APPLICATIONS OF EXPERT SYSTEMS

The application of Expert Systems has much potential to offer training through the extension and development of job aids. In particular for the Royal Navy, new ship design and advances in operational equipment have demonstrated the value of Interactive Electronic Technical Manuals (IETMS) and "wearable" computer systems for on-site maintenance and repair. The Italian Navy are developing the latter for use in their new generation of Frigates being jointly built with France and UK.

USE OF VIRTUAL REALITY IN TRAINING

J. P. Papin and P. Gorzerino

Etablissment Technique d'Angers (ETAS)
Route de Laval, Montreuil Juigné, France

INTRODUCTION

Use of virtual reality techniques in military applications related to training began in the USA in the 1980s with the development of the first virtual battlefields. Today, advanced projects exist in such areas as the dismounted infantryman, armoured fighting vehicles and medicine.

Three years ago, an exploratory group was set up inside NATO Defence and Research Group to explore Human Factors and Virtual Reality. France has the lead among other participating nations (Italy, the Netherlands, United Kingdom, USA, Germany and Spain). On the same way, an active collaboration is in progress between France and the USA and common research are conducted. Other means of collaboration are going to be finalised, between France and UK, and France and Germany.

At the present time, France is:

- developing various applications, to be used shortly for training (Armoured Vehicles, Parachute and Medicine)
- conducting basic studies about memorisation and the use of cognitive resources

This paper identifies possible applications of virtual reality (VR) in military and discusses the use of VR techniques in training, examining the problems to be solved. The focus of this discussion is the location of the operator's position, interfaces (visual, auditory and haptic) and the psychological impact of VR immersion.

DEFINITION

The official NATO definition is: Virtual Reality is, for the individual, an experience of multidimensional environment which is totally or partly generated through computer, and which can be perceived as consistent by operators.

Before discussing the use of Virtual Reality techniques for training, we would like to present shortly other possible applications in military area.

Virtual Reality, Training's Future? edited by Seidel and Chatelier
Plenum Press, New York, 1997

Design Aid for Weapon Systems

As for the concept definition phase, faisability phase or system definition phase, it is now theoretically possible to simulate system architecture, tasks, or assess workload in a VR process. Such an approach seems to be a cultural revolution in which design is much more implicated than today, and consists of running trials before building a real object. However, nowadays, computerised simulation exist that solve most of the problems occurring during the conception phases. This raised up a question: shall we continue to use those simulations and use VR techniques only when the system definition is completed, particularly for the so called "Functional mockups".

Tests and Evaluation Aid

As previously said, it becomes possible to test and evaluate from an operational point of view, with a real operator, a system or vehicle which doesn't exist otherwise as a blueprint. It is also possible to perform tests upon a given system which does really exist but in some configurations which are difficult to reproduce in a standard test centre, or which may raise some risk for testers, given that these testers may not be professional ones. One of the objective of France is a response to that need. At a long term point of view, this kind of trial should be cost less, and must provide results more accurate than those we get today. This will be done quicker and much earlier in the material acquisition process.

Set Up and Mission Rehearsal Aid

In that particular case, the major interest is to build an environment, which correspond to the real mission. It is not necessary to remind that point, but during World War II some locations to be attacked have been entirely built as in the real world. As for training, we have to compare the entirely virtual situation with a mixed of simulators and virtual environments. Thus the weapon system (Human plus simulator) becomes the immersed subject.

Teleoperation or Remote Battle Aid

In fact, it seems to be the same situation as previously described. However, an added interaction is necessary, in order to include the subject in the real world, in real time.

SUGGESTIONS FOR APPLYING VIRTUAL REALITY TO TRAINING AND MISSION REHEARSAL

Using VR in this domain follow the wide spread using of combat training simulators. There is a lot of advantages including the availability of various environments, the possibility to use the same computers whatever the system is, and the infinite possibilities to vary the tested situation. However, we have to determine, in a cost/effectiveness way, which interfaces and environments issued from classical simulators have to be kept or not. The entirely virtual situation may not always be the best solution and it also remains some problems to be solved.

1. Location of the Immersed Operator's Position

In order to give the subject the illusion of being immersed in the world created through computers, we must provide the computer a series of real time data about instantaneous position of the body. This will provide the subject a virtual world, related to his own spatial and temporal references. This is all the more difficult as the subject is moving, even if these moves are including within short limits. However, it is easier when the subject is seated. We are going to deal with the most complex case, that is, the infantryman.

Actual positioning systems are more often based on magnetic sensors, but they have a huge sensibility to metallic environments. Others are based on ultra sonic waves. Current work is being done on tracking systems. For example, head tracking is assumed by a series of LED stuck on the ceiling of the room, and feet movements are picked up with the force sensors in the floor. For each mobile body segment, a particular system is needed. It might be of some interest to combine a spatial sensor and a stereographic three dimensional recorder system. This may be a first step of research. We must keep in mind that these positioning devices may be associated to the data related to the subject's actions upon the real world.

2. Interfaces

For each interface, various answers should be used in military area depending on the application. As mentioned earlier in this paper, the entirely virtual situation may not be the best solution. Importance should be given to the cost/quality and performance trade off to choose the best solution for each specific application.

Visual Interfaces. It is for this type of interface that VR technique is the most popular today. Infography progress permits to get very high quality numerical images. The remained difficulty concerns the way to present these images to the operator in order that he get the sense of immersion without physical, physiological and psychological constraint.

Physical constraints are related to the fact to carry a head-mounted display (weight, discomfort, difficulty of adjustment, moving limitation due to the physical link with computer). So the question of when using a headset should be asked. It may not be necessary when the operator works in a cockpit such a plane or a tank. In this case picture can be presented on displays in respect of usual opening on exterior world. This picture is related to vehicles' movements rather than head's movements. Stereoscopic vision cues can be reproduced with specific glasses. In the case of infantryman, the headset solution is preferred compared to the high cost of presenting a spherical image.

Physiological constraints are essentially related to the technical possibilities of providing a sufficient visual field and a stereoscopic illusion. Current experiments are showing that sense of immersion is directly related to the size of the visual field. Effort should therefore concentrate on getting displays with the biggest possible field. However, solution compressing the peripheral image should be analysed while the need of high resolution image concerns only 40 degrees around the eye axis.

Stereoscopic vision is important for tasks taking place in a space smaller than ten meters. Canadians obtain very good results by using flat (2 dimensional) images to train Navy officers for navigation. We are actually experimenting a mixing of stereo images on flat background to simulate parachutists' environment. We also try the pasting of video or photographic images by texture. Choice is related to the task involved.

Psychological constraints are involved at various levels including realism issues. Is it necessary to provide an image strictly identical to the usual environment or is it possible to provide the operator with only a realistic image? (i.e. giving him the illusion of real environment). This mental aspect is very important and it has been recognised as a priority of research in the last NATO meeting on virtual reality in training. We must focus on providing information in terms of virtual space of activity rather than in terms of picture realism with the reality. From this perspective, techniques of image enrichment have a lot to offer. "Enhanced reality" is one important point to look at for applications regarding training, teleoperation or remote battle.

Auditory Interfaces. Actually there are two possibilities: stereo sound and 3D sound. In terms of practical application, 3D sound is interesting only when we want to improve the presentation by giving more information. Studies on this area for the Air Force should continue. For other military applications, providing sound through speakers seems sufficient in most cases.

Haptic Interfaces. It is an area where experience and technical progress are opening a wide field of research that has to be focused on real needs. The development of whole body data suits is very difficult and is probably more aesthetic appealing than of practical utility. However, providing the operator with information on physical aspects of environment other than visual and auditory is an absolute necessity. The problem is then relating to how: by stimulating the relevant organic sensor without simulating real surroundings or by simulating real surroundings without any specific interface (e.g. electrical excitation of thermal sensor or acclimatisation of the room). For workstation surroundings, the second solution is the easiest one but may be not the less expensive. On the other way, when the operator has to operate objects in virtual environment, VR techniques are recommended but with some limits. Are we going to use a wheel on which we bring efforts, vibrations, texture or are we going to use a virtual wheel with a glove on which this information is provided? This question remains an opened one. Such a data glove able to give some information on the haptic nature of virtual object should present a real interest. Compromise between approaches should be also considerate, for example bringing the information to only one part of the body while the whole body is involved in the real world. In a driving context, we are thinking of providing the information regarding all the physical characteristics of the ground/vehicle/operator's interface only through one hand control device.

In this way, it is possible to consider the "immersed system" concept and not only the "immersed operator". System refers here to the operator and his individual equipment or the operator and his workstation or combat role (that is his "tool"). The tool is perceived as the extension of the body. The idea is to immerse the operator and this extension. Tool is restricted here to its control devices. This way of thinking should simplify significantly VR interfaces. It becomes possible to place sensors or actuators not directly in contact with the skin but with a mechanical device. Real button, real wheel, real keyboard, real pedal, etc. This is justified by the fact that in most cases and whatever the complexity of the system is, the communication is performed through control devices as well as the feedback of sensation.

A second advantage concerns the simplification that it would bring to create pictures of operator in the virtual world. Rather than modelling the operator from its dynamic picked up at the level of his skeleton or muscles, it becomes possible to realise this modelling with information picked up on the tool, and to represent for example position of the fingers, hand or wrist by applying predefined algorithms. Such computer tools, able to represent the individual and to move him through his tool's movement, exist today. The considered object is really part of the user and the movement of the object implies automatically the realistic movement of the body. It is important to emphasise this concept of *realism* which is different from the concept of *reality*. In the area of virtual, the main thing is that the VR experience gives to the immersed subject the illusion of reality.

Regarding taste and smell, it is not technically possible yet to generate these cues. Very few studies are leaded in this area. In Italy, for example, trials to modelling the mechanisms involved are beginning. Others study concern the development of artificial noses for identifying combat gas. However, it will probably take a long time to see some implication in military area, particularly in virtual environments.

3. Psychological Issues

Virtual reality impact on operator's mind has to be considered seriously. As with each new technology, virtual reality will probably change our way of life. Some effects will be positive, teleworking will probably reduce the traffic as well as the stress. But there is also some risk of negative effects. Research has to tell us in detail what the impact of full immersion VR will have cognitively and emotionally. As with a drug, the side effects of VR experiences will need to be monitored closely. Possible concerns are individual differences in perception of the boundary between reality and VR fantasy, and the post VR follow-on effects on behaviour.

LESSONS LEARNED CONCERNING DISTANCE LEARNING

G. A. Redding

Institute for Defense Analyses
Alexandria, Virginia

As reported to the NATO Defense Research Group Panel 8 in the Fall of 1993, multiple technical issues coupled with political and administrative constraints often hamper a comprehensive implementation of Distance Learning (DL) programs. While many of the issues reported in 1993 have abated, several still linger, and new issues have emerged.

Recent Department of Defense (DoD) downsizing, continuing budget reductions, an evolving strategy to implement new education and training technologies, and past tendencies to focus on isolated technology solutions constitute major challenges to meeting DoD's readiness training responsibilities. The sheer magnitude of education and training needs and requirements requires a new look at when, where, and how emerging multimedia technologies can be effectively integrated into formal education and training programs. Training is the key to readiness, and accessibility to top notch instruction is the DoD's top priority.

All Military Departments have policies that address education and training programs, encompassing a wide variety of types: 1) functional skills such as staff planning, 2) general military subjects, 3) professional military development such as leadership training, 4) reclassification training into new skill areas, 5) skill progression for complex jobs, and 6) special skills such as hazardous materials handling. Each training type can, to some degree, leverage existing resident instruction resources and convert them to DL courseware using a variety of multimedia technologies.

This paper addresses the impact of certain multimedia technologies on the military education and training environment is a variety of settings, specifically multimedia and video teletraining (VTT) technologies as they apply to DL. In embracing DL technologies the military training community must ensure that high student achievement is preserved, capital investments in computing and telecommunications provide real economies, access to learning resources is equitable for students and instructors, and management policies address academic and organizational strategies.

As the multimedia industry agrees to more open architectures, thereby enhancing system interoperability and courseware portability, military trainers must look beyond the technology push and address the full spectrum of training systems management. Technologies are only as good as their applications, and systems should not be acquired until tangible benefits can be identified. These benefits normally relate to fiscal issues, however, both students and educators need to rethink their respective roles and responsibilities. As training moves outside the traditional classroom experience, the educator and the learner will need to adjust their styles. Unfortunately, DL data furnished to the Assistant Secretary of Defense for Reserve Affairs does not indicate the military services are embracing a comprehensive and responsive training/learning system (ref 1). Based on data from the US Army Training Support Center for FY93, funding for interactive courseware (ICW) was $322,700, as opposed to $527,000 for multimedia contracts, and a disproportionate $7,698,000 to lease VTT sites (ref. 2). In a recent report, the US Army stated that only seven of 532 resident courses (1.3%) were scheduled for 100% conversion to DL (IDA draft paper, Sep 1995). Overall, this indicates a continued technology push, with minimal courseware development.

In addition to developing and maintaining opportunities for resident and on-site training, military educators need to seize the opportunity to structure an education superhighway by assessing emerging technologies, adjusting courseware to complement proven technologies, validating training effectiveness, and ensuring equitable access to quality resources. Research has identified economies, and training policies are being ratified to ensure successful implementation.

POLICY ISSUES (ADMINISTRATIVE/MANAGERIAL/REGULATORY)

Electronic Superhighway. The Clinton-Gore administration is committed to the networking of business, industry, and education. The exploitation of the Superhighway is cited in continuing programs such as the National Performance Review (NPR), and Business Process Re-engineering. The Superhighway's potential for education and training is being tested in multiple interactive environments, but at significant costs. Military trainers are using both bottom-up and top down infrastructures by providing Internet connectivity to individual users and VTT systems in more formal group settings.

Internet Access. Accessing for the superhighway is essential. Online resources provide opportunities for educators to expand distance learning experiences, and are not restricted by political or geographical boundaries. Holding an account on the Internet, or similar data exchange network is becoming more commonplace. Growth of the Internet is phenomenal, an affordable. Numerous private Internet providers in the US offer local dial-up services to their clients for as little at $15.00/month, with unlimited access time. Establishing individual accounts within most education and government Internet domains is inconsistent. While commercially available, many DL providers in the US Military still do not have Internet access sponsored by their commands. But then there are successes. The US Army Management Staff College (AMSC) recently entered into a contract with America On-Line (AOL) and established the Military Community On-Line (MCO) to deliver non-resident instruction in Management and Leadership Development. This contract filled a need for asynchronous/collaborative telecommunication to meet a specific DL objective.

Intellectual Property Rights. The ownership of intellectual property rights continues to inhibit the distribution of multimedia titles, to include academic resource materials. Intellectual property rights cover the conversion of ideas into physical objects (film, discs, graphics, text, etc.). These media have direct impact on distributing DL materials.

Copyright. The US Department of Commerce just released (Sep 1995) a report affirming copyright law applied to the National Information Infrastructure (NII): 1) rights to electronically distribute remain with the copyright holder, 2) the definition of "transmit" includes "reproduction" of works, 3) no difference in international transmission electronically or via air mail, 4) libraries and archives are limited to three digital copies, 5) products and devices designed to circumvent "rights" under the law are banned, and 6) disseminating false information and removing copyright management information is prohibited. For technical and academic libraries maintained by military trainers there is no exemption. For instructors, distributing copyright materials electronically in support of classroom instruction is not considered "fair use". It now appears that permission to distribute needs to be obtained, and releases granted along the lines of more traditional audiovisual materials. The widespread publication of books and articles on the Internet without compensation to the author undermined incentives to share information. The effect on education and training is obvious.

World Wide Web. The growth of "Home Pages" is phenomenal, especially those published by educational institutions. It is now possible to engage multiple home pages providing catalogs of courseware never before available. Within the US, each Federal organization has been left to its own devices on how to identify education and training offerings, however, a consolidated home page for all formal Federal course offerings is under development. This Virtual Training Mall Home Page, maintained by FEDWORLD, will provide links among all Federal education and training facilities, bulletin boards, courses offered, course materials, schedules, and student registration (National Technical Information Service/National Audiovisual Center) (ref. 3). Many of these databases already exist, but heretofore there has been no formal linkage. Given the fact that home pages are internationally accessible, non-US students and training organizations will have access to dozens of catalogs for both resident and DL opportunities.

Privacy. Both personal and organizational privacy is a concern in DL applications. For the purpose of matriculation, students need to be afforded privacy with respect to both their personal data and their academic achievement. Organizations need to be able to protect instructional resources. These objectives are extremely difficult to balance against a remote learner's need to access instructional resources for legitimate reasons and a DL provider's desire to preclude unauthorized access to data. Home pages developed by educators are essentially public documents, however, the underlying data files may be targets for contamination or exploitation.

Dual Use. Military education and training programs have long been considered a rich resource, and have generally been available to the public. In the current economic environment educators have been pressing military training communities for increased access to courseware. This serves to meet military goals, especially for the justification of new training programs and courseware. But this need not be a one way street. Military trainers need to take reassess adopting courses offered through the public school system, secondary schools, colleges, and universities. As the military downsizes, training facilities need to right size . Several colleges and universities have been directly approaching DoD schoolhouses to offer degree producing studies. Many have previously offered courses through the Defense Activity for Non-Traditional Education Services (DANTES).

Residency Requirements. The impact of residency on accreditation is non-trivial. In the military, being in "the class of __" carries credential over course completion by distance learning, though official records provide the same level of credit. Outside the military, accrediting bodies are wrestling with DL courses since remote learners are presumed to enjoy limited access to rich on campus library, faculty, and student resources. For military students (regardless of nationality) geographically located all over the globe, overcoming residency requirements provides a seamless environment in obtaining formal college credit. To meet this need the New York Institute of Technology (NYIT), for example, offers several degree programs through the Master's level without a residency requirement, accessible through the World Wide Web. Based on a perceived need for student-student-instructor interaction, however, military trainers often refuse to consider certain courses for full or partial DL conversion. They argue that collaborative work in the classroom is essential to the development of leadership. As public education moves to embrace accessibility, military educators need to follow.

TECHNICAL ISSUES

Multimedia equipment. This collective term still plays an important role in DL applications. With the increased digitization of instructional resources, analog media holdings are suffering from neglect. Multimedia workstations within the DoD are almost exclusively digital, with little consideration to continue analog media courseware development. The increased availability of 2X- and 4X-speed CD-ROM drives have made the display of digital video more attractive, especially when coupled with Pentium processors operating at 100 MHz speeds.

Compact Discs. The military services are producing hundreds of hours of instruction, and thousands of pages of course material into CD media. As of this writing significant issues still need to be resolved for CD use. As a publishing media compact discs require application software to retrieve the data files. Universal access tools are needed. Adoption of industry recommended practices will be useful in achieving portability of courseware developed by the military.

Parallax Project. The Interactive Multimedia Association's (IMA) Parallax Project may provide a path to CD-based courseware management (ref 4). The project goal is to identify and recommend industry practices to increase the success rate of installing CD-ROM titles. A uniform label would identify the configuration requirements of the multimedia platform to run a certain title, a free-ware configuration program CD MatchMaker (available in DOS, Macintosh, OS/2, Windows, and Windows95) is available to users to analyze their system, and a series of recommended practices urge developers: to provide an un-install icon, to provide a pre-install program to ensure system resources are available, not to modify files on a consumer's system, and not to all software products of technologies into a user's system.

Compression Software-PC Applications. Compression software continues to enhance the marketability and affordability of video products to educators. There is no single solution to compression since different algorithms were developed to handle different media, i.e. digital compression is different from analog compression. The common denominator is the increased use of software to accomplish both the compression and the decompression function. Software developed by the Joint Picture Experts Group (JPEG) and the Moving Pictures Expert Group (MPEG). Compression algorithms based on MPEG standards are currently offered as options to proprietary vendor algorithms.

Compression Software-Broadcast Applications. Compressed digital video (CDV) is affording scales of economy in broadcast television that make video teletraining (VTT) an attractive option for live interactive instruction. Under contract to the Defense Department, AT&T offers a satellite transmission capability using a 3.3 MHz bandwidth, as opposed to 45 MHz for full analog broadcast. The savings are attractive, from a market price of roughly $1,000/hour to $150/hour.

Video Teletraining (VTT). In the US, the military operates six (6) video teletraining networks, using a combination of terrestrial and satellite circuits, offering both one-way and two-way video transmission. The budgeting, management, and use of VTT systems to educate and train service members has been taken "out of hide" by the training communities with each military Service left to apply VTT to meet its specific training requirements. Components are commercially available, and telecommunications services are provided by government contracts. The networks are "closed" to organizations that cannot use military or government telecommunications services, and the "reach" of these VTT networks is confined to the US. An exception is the Navy's Electronic Schoolhouse Network (CESN) which augments government telephony with commercial circuitry, thereby extending its DL reach to Japan. There are approximately 130 VTT sites using two-way video (teleconferencing) technologies and over 250 VTT downlinks using one-way (broadcast) technologies. By establishing base line thresholds for image and audio quality, these networks are able to share courseware. Federal Agencies have also joint in and by the end of 1997 there should be over 1,500 downlinks able to accept over 25 channels of educational and training programs. At this time, each network is independent of the other in: levels of funding, sponsorship, classroom design, mode of interaction, course scheduling, course design, student throughput, network management, and cost effectiveness. Independent studies have confirmed that the quality of instruction is as good as resident instruction, and the "conversion" of course materials into a VTT format results in other efficiencies, specifically the reduction in time required to present the instruction. The diverse choice of VTT technologies support other findings that organizations acquire and use DL systems to satisfy organizational cultures as well as for academic applications (ref 1, Bagnara). The Defense Department is developing policy to better manage these resources.

Interoperability Standards. DoD distributed training communities use two standards to achieve interoperability: 1) MIL-STD 1379D, Appendix D, issued by the DoD, and 2) Federal Information Processing Standard (FIPS) 178 issued by the National Institute for Standards and Technology (NIST). Interoperability of systems and the portability of courseware using commercially available technologies is critical to providing access to military learners.

- MIL-STD 1379D, Appendix D, incorporates the "Recommended Practices for Multimedia Portability (RPMP)" developed by the Interactive Multimedia Association (IMA), an industry trade association of over 260 members involved in all facets of multimedia. Designed to ensure ICW portability across operating systems, the RPMP specifically addresses issues associated with developing and using interactive videodiscs (IVD) conforming to the commercial LaserVision standard and controlled by computer-based instruction.
- MIL-STD 1379D compliance is required by DoD Instruction 1322.20 "Development and Management of Interactive Courseware (ICW) for Military Training" for the development of ICW developed or purchased by the Defense Department. In brief, 1322.20 requires ICW developed for DoD use to be portable. It defines portability as "the capability to run courseware and associated application programs without modification on a delivery system other than the one for which they were originally designed." The emergence of CD-ROM as a media capable of handling motion video at acceptable levels of resolution for training is overtaking the analog production of instructional materials. This has effectively set aside MIL-STD 1379D, however all other provisions for courseware portability apply.

New criteria have been established and are being introduced into equipment profiles for multimedia workstations.

- FIPS 178, addresses covers digital data transmission protocols for teleconferencing systems operating at 56 to 1,920 Kbps using compression/decompression (codec) algorithms. Not all International Telecommunications Union - Technical Standardization Sector (ITU-TSS), formerly CCITT, recommendations have been incorporated in the FIPS (Federal Information Processing Standard), but they have been accounted for and will be included later. Effectively, FIPS 178 establishes an interoperable baseline for world-wide VTT connectivity.
- Use of FIPS 178 is mandatory for all US Federal Agencies, and became effective June 1, 1993. Its use will ensure interoperability among two-way video systems teleconferencing networks across all agencies. The migration of existing VTT systems to comply with the FIPS will pose networking problems, but new contracts for technologies will incorporate the FIPS requirement. An important specification in the FIPS is the identification of Class 1 and Class 2 terminals. Class 1 refers to low-end video applications such as videophones and some desktop video workstations. Draft DoD VTT implementation guidance states that the military requires a Class 2 terminal for distributed training interoperability allowing near full motion (broadcast) quality.

Strategy for Success. Educators and trainers view distributed training as a mixed opportunity. There is the personal threat to the educator's job security, and there are competing issues; maintaining schoolhouses with their inherent physical limitations, or redirecting capital investments to secure technologies that expand the reach of the schoolhouse. For either course of action retaining a community of competent educators is critical. The following issues arise:

1. Distributed education will not eliminate the need for qualified instructors. Remote site instructors, especially in VTT will be required to administer to the students and support materials provided by (often scarce) subject matter experts.
2. Educators can be compensated for handling larger student loads by offering accelerated tenure path for designing, producing, and presenting VTT and ICW courses.
3. Military schoolhouses based on current staffing guidance, are often reluctant to give up counting Instructor Contact Hours (ICH) as the criteria for authorizing instructor positions and schoolhouse budgets. New "reward" structure need to be developed for schoolhouses as they integrate DL technologies into established courses of instruction.
4. Traditionally, costs saved by not sending a student to resident training are not returned to the schoolhouse providing the distributed training resources. DL beneficiaries are students who are not being required to be away from their homestations as much, and their organizations that do not pay for sending them.
5. Distributed education policy needs to ensure equal access for all students. Current applications of distributed education are unique to each military department, and there is little consensus on a comprehensive equitable training strategy, for VTT or for ICW.

Overall, DL seems to be "in vogue" and has recently been "discovered" by the DoD's senior leadership. Implementation is still left to the Military Services, and that carries certain cultural anomalies. Some Services simply do a better job of managing their resources than others. Data still is being reported on the effectiveness of VTT, citing "as good as, or better" student performance, coupled with cost per course savings of 10–30%. While the technologies are becoming more affordable, the costs of converting courses into DL media still represents a significant funding challenge. Draft DoD Instructions have been prepared for the "Development and Management of Distance Learning Teletraining Systems" establishing procedures for the entire DoD training community. Publication is scheduled for late 1995.

REFERENCES

1. "Learning Without Boundaries: Technology to Support Distance/Distributed Learning", R.J Seidel & P.R. Chatelier (eds), Defense Research Series - Volume 5, 1994 Plenum Press, New York
2. US Army Training Support Center, FY93 Annual Report
3. Human Resources Development Council, Committee on Cross-Servicing/Franchising On-Line Systems Workgroup, "Virtual Training Mall" discussion draft, May 1995.
4. "Keeping the Customer Happy - A Call to Action" Multimedia Monitor, Augiust 1995.
5. "Distance Learning and the Reserve Components", DRAFT IDA Paper, Aug 1995.

GUIDELINES FOR SELECTING AN AUTHORING SYSTEM

Robert J. Seidel

Advanced Training Methods Research Unit
U.S. Army Research Institute

For the last several years, the computer has been developed as a multi-media device and its applicability to education and training is greater than ever before. Thus, increasingly more training in industry and the military will be implemented through computer-based training (CBT). However, software technology to use the hardware capability is significantly behind the hardware development, and skilled software programmers are still scarce and expensive.

Authoring systems, tools developed to assist the design of training by training developers without programming skills, have become indispensable for the efficient development of training and educational programs in the military, other government agencies, schools, and industry. Currently, a few hundred authoring systems are estimated to be available in the market. In addition to the large number of systems, the rapidly changing technology, particularly hardware capability, makes it difficult for NATO training developers to select the best system for their current and future needs. For the last ten years, a number of guidelines for selecting an authoring system were developed. However, some criteria in the guidelines need to be modified because of the rapid change of hardware capability and lessons learned from the last decades of use. For example, Park and Seidel (1989) included the capability for allowing computer to interface with other hardware systems (e.g., interactive video player) in the selection criteria. However, this criterion should be changed because the interactive video capability is now an integral part of most personal computers.

Thus, selection of an authoring system requires not only examining it with a comprehensive set of evaluation criteria*, but also considering recent and future technological changes, including hardware and software, feedback from experience with authoring tools, and other supporting factors. In the following sections, we describe updated procedures and resources for selecting an authoring system.

1. *The first step necessitates having an updated set of evaluation criteria to permit the training developer to make systematic judgments about the type(s) of authoring tools needed for his or her specific applications.*

---

* The specific details of these evaluation criteria are provided as an Appendix on Page 4.

2. *The next step for selecting an authoring system is to obtain a general survey type of information about currently available authoring systems.*

Because of the large number of systems available, selecting a system without the general information about the available systems increases the chance to choose a sub-optimal system. However, surveying all available systems is very difficult because identifying the systems and obtaining relevant information about them will be a very time consuming task. To provide this survey type of information on authoring systems, the U.S. National Library of Medicine (NLM) and the U.S. Army Research Institute (ARI) have assembled a data base of authoring systems available on the Internet. Currently, the data base, called **AuthorBase**. contains about 80 systems with active support from the vendors and 30 additional systems that may still be in use but do not have active support. AuthorBase is being updated on n annual basis. Once the data base is accessed through the World-Wide Web (WWW), the user can browse the list of systems to selectively examine them or can select specific systems using the search name (e.g., Authorware Professional) or different features (e.g., window and/or interactive video and/or record keeping). If the user provides specific input features, the list of systems that satisfy the input features is listed; the user can selectively examine the listed systems. AuthorBase allows up to 4 inputs in 'and/or' form. To assist the search including the selection of input features, "Help Index" and "Glossary of Terms" buttons are presented in the home page.

Each authoring system in AuthorBase has the following information: (a) Title of the system, including the version number; (b) Source, including the vender's name, address and phone numbers; (c) Packaging, including manuals and deliverable forms (diskettes, CD, etc.); (d) Hardware Requirements, including platform and memory sizes, (e) System Options, including monitor, sound card, video board, input devices, audio devices, CD-ROM, etc.; (f) Utilities, including text, graphics, animation and sound editors, lesson organizer, etc.; (g) Record Keeping; (h) General description; (i) Cost/Terms; (j) other miscellaneous notes, including the information source.

AuthorBase is the only data base of authoring systems currently available on the Internet. The Internet address is: *http://wwwetb.nim.nih.gov/authorb/irx*

3. *As the third step, it is recommended that the user select 3–5 potentially useful systems from the examination of the information in AuthorBase.*

From these candidate systems, many factors needs to be considered in selecting the final one. For example, the compatibility with existing hardware systems and cost/affordability are particularly important because these factors are usually uncompromisable by the user.

4. *The fourth step is to evaluate the candidate systems selected from AuthorBase with a comprehesive set of criteria.*

In addition, the final evaluation should be determined on the basis of unique needs for the given situation. For example, a complex graphic-based simulation would require powerful animation editor. However, a task that calls for mostly a text-based approach would be more beneficial to have an efficient text editor than a powerful animation editor. There are essential requirements that an authoring system should have and the training developer needs to look for in the evaluation process. They include: (1) built-in instructional design aids: (2) built-in development (programming) aids; (3) expandability of the system capability; (4) user friendliness. In addition, (5) cost/affordability is an important factor for the evaluation.

Park and Seidel (1989) have proposed to use the above main criteria in the development of an evaluation checklist.

The other noted important variables to be considered include the training and experience of the system users (i.e., training developers), general characteristics of the subject domains, instructional goals and objectives to be achieved with the courseware, general types and formats of courseware to be developed, and the expected period and frequency for using the system. Since computer technology is rapidly changing, the vendor's commitment to the system and periodical upgrades is an important factor to consider.

PROCEDURES FOR EVALUATING AUTHORING SYSTEMS

The general guidelines for developing an evaluation procedure using the above crite ria are proposed as follows:

1. Determine two primary pre-existing conditions for selecting an authoring system: (a) existing or intended hardware systems to use for the development and delivery of courseware; (b) budget affordability.
2. Select and review all the authoring systems in AuthorBase, that are relevant to the pre-existing conditions. If the pre-existing conditions (e.g., hardware types) are provided as the input parameter for the search, AuthorBase will provide the list of systems that can be browsed selectively or sequentially.
3. List all the important situational variables for using an authoring system and describe the current status of the variables (e.g., intended users' ability in instructional design, experience in the use of authoring systems, programming skills, frequency and expected period of the use, etc.).
4. Select 3–5 authoring systems on the basis of the consideration of the important situation variables (Steo 3 noted earlier) and the information review of the selected authoring system in AuthorBase (Step 2 noted earlier).
5. Develop an evaluation check list by listing all the evaluation criteria and criteria and subcriteria (see Appendix on page 6) and assigning a weight to each of the evaluation subcriteria based on the analysis of the situational variables (for example, "Provision of development templates" - *very important because the intended user does not have programming skills).*
6. Check whether the given authoring system has each of the features or functions listed in the evaluation criteria (for example, "Aids for laying out courseware structure" - No).
7. Assess the functional capability for performing each of the sub-criteria from the analyses of user manuals and/or user surveys (for example, "Aid for developing animation" - very limited).
8. Analyze the evaluation results obtained in the above procedure, and select one or two systems.
9. Empirically validate the evaluation results, if it is necessary and feasible. This procedure requires careful selection of the characteristics of lessons to be developed, and training 2–3 persons to use the systems (for details, see Seidel & Park, 1993).
10. After checking the consistency between the checklist and empirical evaluation results, select the final system.

HYPERTEXT MARKUP LANGUAGE (HTML) EDITORS RECENTLY ADDED AS AUTHORING TOOLS

Information accessible through the WWW must be coded in the HTML, and HTML Editors are simple programming tools for developing home pages or other documents in the WWW without programming skills of HTML.

A database of HTML Editors will be available on the WWW as a part of AuthorBase before the end of October, 1995. Currently, ARI has compiled about 30 HTML editors in a data base. The data base structure and procedure to access to HTML Editors in the data base will have basically the same type of information as in AuthorBase.

Since programs on the Internet can be directly accessed using its the WWW links or can be downloaded to store in a personal computer, the Internet has provided a new opportunity to deliver training programs. Many technical issues, such as the system's response time, instant interactions between the user and program, data collection, record keeping, etc., need to be resolved before the Internet is successfully used as a training delivery system. As these issues are resolved, however, the use of the Internet as a training delivery mechanism will be rapidly increased; the HTML Editors will be used as an authoring tool for the development and delivery of training programs on the Internet.

REFERENCES

Park, O. & Seidel, J. R. (1989). Evaluation criteria for selecting CBI authoring system. *T.H.E. Journal, 17,* 16–68.

Seidel, J.R. & Park, O. (1993). Evaluation of CBT authoring systems: Need a data base. In R.J. Seidel & P.R. Chatelier (Eds.), *Advanced Technologies Applied to Training Design,* Plenum Press, New York.

APPENDIX: CRITERIA AND SUBCRITERIA FOR EVALUATING AUTHORING SYSTEMS

I. Instructional Design Aids

1. Aids for laying out the various forms of courseware structures
2. Aids for selecting instructional strategies
3. Provision of templates for developing specific lesson components
4. Aids for selecting specific data collection options

II. Development (Programming) Aids

1. Aids for developing presentation displays
   - A text editor
   - A graphic editor
   - A sound generator/editor
   - A video production aid
2. Aids for developing interaction procedures
   - Aids for selecting questions types and required response modes
   - Aids for specifying the number of questions to present

- Aids for specifying the presentation order of questions
- Aids for specifying the replacement of question items
- Aids for specifying number of trials allowed for the student to answer to the given question
- Aids for limiting the student's response time
- Aids for specifying types of feedback
- Aids for specifying the time to give the feedback
- Aids for specifying branching control options (learner control versus program control)
- Aids for selecting student input devices

3. Aids for developing data collection procedures

- Aids for collecting student input data
- Aids for collecting student on-task time data on various levels of instruction
- Aids for generating new data

III. System Expandability and Flexibility

1. Interface with other software development tools
2. Interface with programming languages
3. Interface with built-in utilities in the operating system
4. Interface with utility software programs
5. Interface with training management system (e.g., CMI)
6. Interface with hardware peripherals (e.g., interactive video disc) 7. Interoperability among independent hardware systems
8. On-line communication and network capability
9. Use of variety of input devices

IV. User Friendliness

1. Flexible design and development process
2. Easy development and revision
3. Provision of built-in development templates
4. Easy integration of the developed materials: Overlays and lesson integration
5. Adaptation to author skill levels
6. Development in the student mode
7. Help features built into the system
8. An adequate manual

V. Cost

1. Hardware requirements (main system and configuration requirements)
2. Price
3. Contract terms
4. Training expenses

For more detailed description about the evaluation criteria see Park & Seidel (1989); for the evaluation procedures, see Seidel & Park (1993).

INDEX